Path to Enlightened Turkey Hunting:

A Naturalist's Observations, Memorable Hunts, and Camaraderie

James E. "Jim" Miller

Library of Congress Control Number: 2021915551

ISBN: 9781735289212

Manufactured in the United States of America

Crane Publishing Group, LLC
P.O. Box 811
Starkville, Mississippi 39760
662-268-7776

Distributed to the book trade by:
James E. Miller
1436 Pinecrest Rd.
Starkville, Mississippi 39760
662-418-8638

First Edition

FOREWORD

Before I focus on the book itself, I think a look at the author will give the reader perspective and is thus warranted. Jim Miller is a rare individual in this day and time from several perspectives. First, being a good biologist AND a good hunter/naturalist is not that uncommon. But excelling, and I'm talking about the top 1 or 2 percent, is very rare. Second, finding a modern individual who grew up in a rural environment where hard work of all types was taken seriously, and community service was important is becoming rarer all the time. And, when you combine all that with solid Christian values that focus on integrity, hard work, and treating folks with respect and fairness—well, that's a person tough to find. When you top all that off with his desire to educate others by sharing his knowledge and experiences, you have fodder for a good book. Jim conveyed his experiences learned while hunting, angling, and trapping as a youth to his formal education and later professional life. His significant contributions to the science and art of natural resource conservation were strengthened by his practical experiences and direct ties to the land, which continue to this day.

As a biologist, Jim has won many awards, including the Clarence W. Watson Award (the highest wildlife and fisheries award in the Southeast) and the Aldo Leopold Award (the highest in the nation). He also served as national president of The Wildlife Society, the premier professional organization of wildlife biologists.

This book focuses on turkey hunting, so what are Jim's unique credentials for that? There have been, and currently are, many good turkey hunters—some of whom have written outstanding books about turkey hunting. What's different about Jim Miller? First, Jim has been hunting turkeys for six decades and has harvested hundreds of turkey gobblers. But more than that, he has hunted extensively all over the wild turkey's range from Vermont to Mexico and Virginia to California. And he didn't just go a few times to those far-reaching places; he went to many of them year after year. He's hunted mosquito-slapping hot weather, deep snow mountain weather, and from prairie ridgetop to river bottom. His typical season started mid-March in Florida and ended late May in the Northeast, year after year.

Jim's excellence as a biologist, turkey hunter, and educator didn't just happen by accumulating years. It's all due to the passion he has for the things he believes in. His love is gut-level, and it drives him to go all out at everything he does. I've known Jim for somewhere close to 50 years. We were both Extension wildlife specialists—he in Arkansas and me in Tennessee—when we met at a Colorado professional meeting. Our personalities meshed, and we quickly became friends. We soon became frequent hunting friends, and in those first few years, much of what I knew about turkeys, I learned from him. Even though there weren't many turkeys anywhere back then, Jim grew up around turkeys, and I hadn't.

Now, about this book. First, I'll admit that I'm a sucker for a good hunting story. I subscribe to several sporting magazines—not to learn about the latest gizmo, nor the how-to's, but to read hunters' stories. In my opinion, that's the strength of this book. But Jim doesn't just tell unrelated stories, one after another. He uses stories to illustrate the hows, whys, and whens of turkey behavior and their responses to hunters. He uses the stories—all real and factual—to teach the reader how to hunt this unique and mysterious bird. And the details and imagery he uses make each story come to life for the reader. I was present when several of these stories took place, and I'm amazed at the accuracy of Jim's recollections—even though he didn't keep a journal.

I've had the pleasure of hunting with some terrific friends over the years. The ones I've continued to hunt with have had at least three things in common: they've had integrity, followed hunting regulations, and have been generous in sharing opportunities at game. I don't know anyone more unselfish than Jim Miller. For that reason, among others, Jim has many excellent hunting friends all over the country. This has allowed him to hunt diverse habitats and circumstances, and that wealth of knowledge about turkey hunting is passed on to readers of this book.

Jim could have, no doubt, accumulated several records, but that's not what he is about. So, he's never kept count of the number of birds killed, nor how they would score as trophies. Jim is an excellent turkey biologist, but that's not the focus of this book either. The focus is to share with the reader six-plus decades of his adventures, excitement, and passion while observing and chasing the magnificent wild turkey. I, for one, have enjoyed this book, and I believe you will, too.

James L. Byford, PhD.
Dean Emeritus,
College of Agriculture and Applied Sciences
University of Tennessee Martin

PREFACE

Any quotations noted in this book identify the author or are explained within the context of what the discussion is about. Some can no longer be fact-checked as the originator is deceased. They are, however, factual, based on the author's memory, and published documents that remain available for verification.

The information contained in this book is both as true and historically accurate as possible. Although, many details surrounding these events and activities have been reduced to brief descriptions. The hope is readers can grasp the significance of what is being shared without becoming bored or bogged down with additional details.

Those of us in my age bracket recognize and acknowledge that individual personal perceptions about hunting, angling and trapping have changed significantly during our lifetimes. Earlier in our history, most people had either some rural background, rural relatives, or direct or indirect ties to the land.

It is no secret that urban/suburban human populations have significantly increased in the past four decades, as concurrently, the number of farm families has decreased precipitously. Growing up in rural north Alabama, it seemed that most people saw hunting, angling, and trapping in our community as a natural part of life.

Today, our predominantly urban population across this nation has few, if any, ties to the land. Currently, children who in previous decades had the freedom to explore their outdoor surroundings are contained and restrained by their urban environments and their parent's apparent fear of nature. As Richard Louv so eloquently described in his 2006 book Last Child in the Woods, most of our children are suffering from "nature-deficit disorder."

The social and survival issues have changed dramatically from the 1950s and 1960s, when the nation began its recovery from World War II. Back then, most boys went to school every day carrying a pocket knife, and there was no worry by the teachers or administration about violence, aside from an occasional fistfight.

Unfortunately, over the last two to three decades, virtually anything that could potentially be considered offensive or a threat to anyone is prohibited. Because of this loss of ties to the land, sadly, it appears that not only do most people not have any idea of the management, harvest, or processing of food, or how it gets to their table, they do not care.

Further, most people today have no concept of why managing our natural resources, including wildlife and their habitats, is essential for sustaining these resources that belong to us all. Yet those of us who are directly or indirectly involved with sustaining these public trust resources for future generations to use and enjoy understand why their wise use and sustainability are critical. What is sad about this dilemma is that if we fail to sustain these treasured resources, future generations will be the losers, even if they and their parents fail to recognize their loss until it is too late.

Having long ago been convinced that the thrill of the chase and responsible stewardship are essential, one of my passions has been outdoor education for both youth and adults. Working with others smarter than me throughout a long career, I have tried diligently through educational programs to help others understand the need. Unfortunately, it seems that more and more Americans have progressively ignored these responsibility and sustainability needs. This has resulted in less and less support for hunting, angling and trapping today, yet the nature-deficit disorder continues to grow.

What many today would describe as primitive instincts for the thrill of the chase, are to those of us who participate in them absolutely essential to our existence. I truly believe that such instincts help instill in us respect for God's awesome creation, for nature, a proper reverence for life, and our responsibility to be good stewards. In addition, such participation in the decisive life and death experiences helps us attain respect for our quarry, respect for ourselves, self-sufficiency, and self-confidence.

As humans, we should have sincere gratitude and appreciation for our rich inheritance, made possible by some early conservationists. Although this listing of early conservationists and those following them could be enormous, a few that most historians might recognize include President Teddy Roosevelt, George Bird Grinnell, Charles Sheldon and other devotees who followed them in our earlier history.

These were great American patriots who took action because they were passionate, dedicated, insightful, and persistent. Those of us who have followed them recognize and appreciate many other dedicated individuals and professionals whose contributions to the sustainability of our public trust resources and the thrill of the chase have been critical. We owe them great respect and gratitude and feel compelled to take up the mantle of responsibility for educating those who follow us, regardless of their lack of appreciation.

Aside from the hunts describing the thrills of the chase for spring turkey gobbler, it is my earnest desire that readers will somehow absorb some of the other treasures I have obtained from these experiences and observations. Hopefully, these benefits are understood, but the unique observations, anticipation, sharing, and the deep and abiding respect and appreciation expressed for others mentioned are critical to my memory bank. If you fail to recognize at least some of these things, then I have been unable in my intentions to share them with others as heartfelt treasures in my memories.

When we approach the long of tooth years of our lives, what will be some important memories? I cannot speak for others; however, for me, it will not be the number of scientific reports or body of work in my chosen profession, although treasured. I strongly suspect it will be some of the enjoyable hunts or angling trips with family, friends and respected colleagues, and the continuing appreciation for God's marvellous creation.

INTRODUCTION

With roots in rural north Alabama from childhood until leaving for college at 17, I progressively realized what an education my exposure to the outdoors had provided. This book offers memories of a small portion of activities and events that took place growing up on a small farm on "Sand Mountain."

After some difficulty defined by working and going to college over the next eight years, my education and persistence ultimately enabled me to become a wildlife professional. Over the next 56 years, with counsel from some great mentors and learning from mistakes, this career helped me become a naturalist and ecologist.

From an early age, however, it seemed inevitable that I would become a hunter. The following information and stories of observations are not captured and shared from journal notes, although I genuinely wish I had maintained one. In addition, they are not identified nor cataloged chronologically. The following randomly captured observations and historical references are simply part of my memory collection. Hopefully, they might be of interest to readers, family members, friends, colleagues, and others who care about wild places and wild things.

I have been convinced that the thrill of the chase and responsible stewardship are two fundamental passions of humankind for most of my life. I am convinced that hunting blood courses in all our veins. Those of us who do not suppress our inborn instinct for the chase and the desire to be responsible stewards feel compelled to pursue these activities. In addition, we obtain great pleasure and satisfaction from the pursuit of these efforts.

The thrill of the chase and the desire to be a good steward

is both primitive and natural. Aside from feeling genetically and instinctively predisposed to hunt, I have grown to love everything about it. This includes planning, preparation, sights, smells, sounds, scouting, observing animal behavior, physical and mental challenges, utilizing learned skills, personal discipline, responsibility, and ethics to guide my actions.

In addition, the memories of hunts with family, colleagues, friends, and especially youngsters, include respect for the quarry, the meticulous handling and cleaning of game harvested, the gourmet meals of organic protein that my family and friends will enjoy, recharge my batteries, improve my perspective and attitude and enable great pleasure from continued honing of skills as a naturalist. Although I didn't learn from sitting at the feet of an expert/master naturalist or turkey hunter, I benefitted from association with knowledgeable professionals and colleagues and experiences in wild places.

Admittedly, there are significant costs associated with these pursuits. Aside from the time away from family, the monetary costs of licenses, permits, stamps, firearms, ammunition, archery equipment, angling equipment, traps, and related articles needed all add up. Although not consistently recognized, we should appreciate that some of these associated monetary costs of hunting, fishing, and trapping have a very positive return for all Americans. They provide the essential support to the North American Model of Wildlife Conservation that benefits all wildlife species.

Rarely recognized, however, is that they benefit all people who want to enjoy wildlife, whether by hunting, observing, or just knowing that wild places and wild things exist. My passion for these has grown and matured with age and professional experience. The great majority of my professional career has been devoted to conserving and managing public trust wildlife resources and educating others of the need to sustain these resources for present and future generations.

CONTENTS

ACKNOWLEDGMENTS

CHAPTER 1

Influence and Motivations

With that synopsis of my naturalist perspective, perhaps a brief history of what motivated me from my earliest days of memory would be beneficial. I was born in 1941 while my dad served our nation in WW II, and my mom worked in Bessemer, Alabama. When I was about three years old, my mom took me to the country to live with my grandmother in a very rural area of north Alabama.

Grandmother Miller lived alone, and three of her four sons were serving in WW II. She was about as self-sufficient as anyone can be who doesn't have access to a regular paycheck. She lived on a dirt road, had no automobile or other transportation, and no electricity or running water. She did have a barn, smokehouse for hanging and curing meat and canning storage, a small chicken house, a big garden, some fruit trees, a hand-dug well, a good milk cow, and a couple of hogs. Her wood stove had a warming oven and cooked some of the finest meals anyone could imagine.

Grandmother taught me from my earliest memories what types of behavior were acceptable or not and how to make the best use of the resources available. If we went anywhere, we walked on the dirt roads, except occasionally on a Saturday afternoon. Her cousin Hess, on those particular Saturday's would load all the community kids, including teenagers, on the back of his ton and a half flatbed truck and take us to Albertville about fifteen miles away. We would all go to the Saturday matinee for 10 cents and usually saw Tom Mix, Gene Autrey, or Lash Larue westerns with WW II trailers/snippets between the movies.

Grandmother took me on my first fishing trip after first showing me how to "fiddle up" some nightcrawlers. For those who may not have heard of "fiddling up" worms for fishing, she located about a three-foot-long piece of wooden board scrap (usually sawmill slabs) from the woodpile. Next, she sharpened one end of it with an ax, then walked down into the woods behind the barn. She located some mature white oak trees, picked a spot, and with a flat sand rock drove the pointed end of that slab into the ground about twelve to eighteen inches. Before doing the "fiddling," the two of us swept the leaves back in a circle around that board for about 30 feet.

She then took that flat sand rock and started scrubbing it across the top of that wooden stake. Usually, you would see shiny nightcrawler worms emerging after starting the fiddling within a couple of minutes or less. Within five minutes or so, you could easily pick up fifty or more big nightcrawlers on top of the ground. We would always add some moist soil to the can with the worms to keep them cool and fresh until we could go fishing. This probably sounds absurd for those who have never done this, but the vibration of the wooden stake caused by fiddling or scrubbing the flat rock across it somehow makes the night crawlers come to the surface.

On my first fishing trip, she fixed me a pole out of dried switch cane, using some heavy sewing thread for a line, a straight pin bent to form a hook and a small cork float. We walked to her cousin Hess's spring-fed branch, and she helped me catch some spot-tail minnows, bluegills, and green sunfish.

Later, because she had a critter getting into her chicken house and killing chickens, she taught me how and where to set a leg-hold trap. Other observations included watching her dispatch a copperhead snake in the yard, a rabid dog, and scaring off a chicken hawk as she called them, with her 20- gauge single-barrel shotgun. She demonstrated what is necessary when you are sustaining yourself without ready access to a grocery store. She churned the milk to make butter, dried fruit, and canned both meat and vegetables for use later on.

The peddler came by every two to three weeks, and Grandmother always had eggs, butter, canned vegetables, or a live chicken or two to trade. Usually, her needs were for coffee, sewing thread, salt, black pepper, sugar, snuff, some Doan's liniment, and whatever else she needed but could not make herself. She later took me to Big Mud Creek and showed me with her cane pole and tiny fish hooks how to catch white suckers. We brought those home and scaled, gutted, and removed the heads. She cut them into chunks and pressure-cooked the pieces in quart-sized Mason jars to eat later.

By her example, we did not waste much, and we enjoyed many good times in the evenings churning butter by the fireplace. We often listened to her radio, hearing the Lone Ranger, Creaking Door, the Phantom, and other stories. Although I didn't learn a lot about hunting from her, she taught me many tremendous and valuable skills. Examples included when and how to harvest poke-salad greens, sassafras roots for making tea, making toothbrushes from black gum tree stems, identification of different trees and vegetation, and which snakes were poisonous.

She taught me by example that hard work, whether in the garden, splitting and hauling wood for the stove, or drawing water from the well for washing clothes and bodies, was necessary. She also helped me understand that pulling sweet potato slips for planting, pulling corn, picking cotton, and other farm duties were necessary and wouldn't hurt you. She demonstrated that regardless of how bad you cut yourself or otherwise injured an arm, hand, leg, or foot, some coal oil (kerosene) on a clean rag covering the wound for a few days would enable it to heal.

My interest in hunting was growing; I understood that hunting was not just a tradition. It provided welcomed protein.

After all, we genuinely enjoyed the wild meat occasionally supplied by relatives or neighbors. In those days, wild game mainly consisted of rabbits, squirrels, and quail that were a part of our diet, and Grandmother knew how to prepare it.

Following hunting seasons, we depended on fish, chickens, pork from the smokehouse, canned meat she had prepared, and an occasional guinea. When others would bring by the game they had harvested to share with us, my dreams included me hunting one day. A few years later, when rural electric lines were extended to the area, I remember her two greatest prizes were getting electric lights and a refrigerator.

CHAPTER 2

Learning for a Neophyte

My first true hunting skills were learned from my dad after he returned from the service in Europe in 1945. I moved back from my grandmother's place to be with Mom and Dad when he returned. We lived in Bessemer, Alabama, until 1949, when my folks bought a small farm and country store within a few miles of my grandmother's place. The little community was called "Highmound," and it was about 15 miles out in the country between two small towns, Albertville and Oneonta.

Dad had a good bird dog named "Rip" and let me drag along behind him occasionally when he went quail hunting. Dad was an avid slingshot maker. We commonly referred to it as a "flip." If he ran across a well-formed slingshot stock on a dogwood tree, he would cut it and bring it home with him. He always cut the arms and butt longer than needed and pulled the arms together, tied them, and hung them in his shop so they would be appropriately shaped as they dried.

When well-dried, Dad cut everything down to the appropriate size and peeled the bark away. Then he cut a notch around the top of each arm so the rubber slings could be securely attached. He made a pocket out of an old shoe tongue or some scrap leather he had available. He made me a slingshot with rubber slings from an old innertube and taught me how to use it. With practice, I became pretty capable of hitting anything in range with the rocks that fit in the flip pocket.

Rip would often point a rabbit in its bed, but he would not chase them. When that happened after I was strong enough to shoot the slingshot accurately, Dad would carefully bring me up behind Rip while he was pointed, identify the rabbit to me, get Rip by the collar and lead him off quite a distance.

When he felt it was clear for me to shoot, he would whistle. With practice, I got pretty good at hitting them in the head with that flip and would bring the rabbits home, dress them, and we would have them fried with biscuits and gravy. Dad taught me early how to clean game correctly, whether quail or doves he killed or the rabbits and squirrels I killed. After a couple of lessons, it became my responsibility to clean all the game and fish after getting home from a hunting or fishing trip.

After receiving a Red Ryder BB Gun from one of Dad's uncles, my hunting skills grew. My dad, however, strongly admonished me that you do not shoot at everything you see. My parents and grandmother identified those species not to be shot, including eastern bluebirds and mockingbirds.

When I was about ten years old, my Uncle Wilmer helped me start trapping on both Little and Big Mud Creeks, where my catch was primarily muskrats, an occasional mink, and raccoons. I used long spring traps set so that drowning would usually occur, occasionally an animal did not drown and would have to be dispatched other ways. Over time, I saved up $7.00 from the pelts after cleaning, stretching, and drying the fur and selling it to Sears and Roebuck. Dad took that $7.00 and bought me a used single-shot .22 rimfire Harrington and Richardson "Pal," bolt action rifle from a pawn shop. Although chambered for shorts, long, and long rifle ammunition, we always bought shorts because you could buy a box of 50 rounds for $ 0.25 per box, and they were sufficient for my needs.

With this rifle, rabbits, squirrels, and raccoons were harvested, and it was used to dispatch any animal that had not drowned when my sets were checked. It was pretty easy to kill a limit of six gray squirrels while wading the creeks to check my traps most mornings. I always tried to shoot them in the head for a lethal kill. Often, I would go by a disabled great uncle's house and leave him a mess of squirrels from which his wife made wonderful squirrel dumplings. He always responded the same way on examining the squirrels, "Son, I shore appreciate these squirrels, but dagummit, I wish you wouldn't shoot them in the best part." He liked to eat the jaw muscles and the brains after Aunt Minnie fried them up.

It may sound boastful, but no conscious exaggeration is intended or needed in sharing these hunting stories. With many opportunities of shooting practice, my skills improved enough to occasionally take running rabbits and squirrels with that little single shot.

We acquired two beagles when I was about 11 years old, and rabbit hunted a good bit. Dad later gave me a Winchester Model 42 pump-action shotgun in .410 gauge and a cylinder bore choke. After that, my quarry included quail and doves, along with rabbits and squirrels. Clearly, by this time, although still young, I had become an inveterate hunter, angler, and trapper.

Almost every spare minute not taking care of our farm animals, working in the crop fields, or going to school would find me in the woods or on the creeks or rivers around home. Fortunately, almost everyone in walking or bicycling distance from our place would allow me to hunt, trap or fish on their property or farm pond. Thankfully, Mom was mostly supportive of my outdoor activities as long as school work and the daily chores were completed. I was required to be respectful to everyone in our community, especially our elders, and fortunately, most of them tolerated me.

CHAPTER 3

A Naturalist for Consideration

Dictionary definitions summarized say that a person is a naturalist who studies nature, especially by observing animals and plants. As a person who was intrigued by and loved studying wild things and wild places since early youth, it seemed apparent that my calling had something to do with the study of nature. The experiences described in these pages are part of the outdoor education that ultimately led me to become a professional wildlife biologist and naturalist while continuing to be a hunter.

Although not fully recognizing it at the time, these responsibilities and other work that my folks expected of me helped me become more and more a budding naturalist. They also helped me better understand why we conducted certain activities at specific times of the year. Most of these things were based on knowledge learned from their elders' experiences and passed on down to us while we were growing up.

Although there are hundreds of examples of lessons learned, the point here is that learning why these things happened was essential and contributed to my curious interest in nature. They helped me better understand the rhythmic patterns associated with changing seasons and the impact of our actions on wild things and wild places. It also whetted my appetite throughout my life to learn more about the natural world. Bible studies later revealed some insight, i.e., reading King Solomon's account in Ecclesiastes Chapter 3: 1-8, it became clear to me that Solomon understood God's plan, suggesting an appropriate time for everything.

On entering high school and participating in football, basketball, and other sports, my hunting, fishing, and trapping time became more restricted but not eliminated. I can remember as a senior driving our old 1953 Chevy flatbed truck to school with my beagles in the dog box tied down to the truck bed. There was always a rifle or shotgun stowed behind the seat so that other friends could join me for an after-school hunt. In those days, we all carried pocket knives, which were of no concern to our teachers or principal. Fortunately, when the bluegills were bedding, usually the first full moons in April and May, I used my fly rod and homemade poppers to catch limits of big eating-sized sunfish (mostly bluegills) and some bass.

Although most people scaled fish while cleaning, I learned that when skinned properly and fried whole, you could eat the meat right off the skeleton, and the taste was much better. My girlfriend's dad (the girlfriend later became my wife) loved to eat bluegills, so a limit of fifty would be taken over to him occasionally and skinned. When preparing these for him, he always wanted me to leave the tails on them so that he could eat those as well when fried up crisp.

The information above helps describe some of my instincts for the thrill of the chase and the observations it enabled me to make. Those recollections also remind me of many other great memories and the knowledge gained through active involvement with hunting, fishing, and trapping in my early years.

Before it appears that I am classifying myself as a know-it-all, or expert in hunting, fishing, and trapping, perhaps the following will help explain. First, most of what was learned about these thrills of the chase came from either being taught or observing others with more skill and experience than I possessed. I did, however, learn from my mistakes, like accidentally cutting into the musk glands on a boar mink. Once I started trapping, my observational skills increased significantly. However, being a slow learner sometimes, these mistakes had to be made multiple times until finally, the light bulb came on.

Having been raised by frugal parents and a grandmother who had lived through the Great Depression of the 1930s, these hardy souls learned to survive tough times. They soldiered on, regardless of how difficult times were for most Americans during those years and until WW II was over. These and other lessons learned from elders helped me appreciate what we were blessed to have, how to survive the tough times we would face, and to keep our heads up. Remembering that most of my shirts were made out of former feed, flour, or fertilizer sacks while in school, and our simple farm lifestyle helped keep me humble. It also encouraged me to retain a sincere interest in learning from my observations of natural things, lessons taught by others, and the multiple benefits of good stewardship.

I became an early riser not necessarily by choice but by need. Even today, I still wake up around 5:00 a.m., make coffee, then begin undertaking whatever is planned for the day. It was my responsibility as the only boy, and oldest child in the family to feed and milk the cows, feed the hogs, water and feed our chickens and hunting dogs, then get my two younger sisters up so they could get ready, eat some breakfast and catch the school bus. Except for having to wake my sisters up, those same chores had to be repeated every evening before dinner.

That habit of rising early in the morning stuck with me through college, graduate school, and 56 years of working as a professional wildlife biologist, administrator, and educator. Even since retiring twice, I still enjoy rising early, getting outside, and listening to the world wake up.

CHAPTER 4

Looking Back Observations

Turkey hunting as it developed during my adult life, and why it is so important to me, cannot be easily explained to anyone who has not become an active participant in this thrill of the chase. Like most who have become addicted to the thrill of the chase, regardless of our quarry, it wills us to activity in the spring, fall, and winter. It continues to be necessary, at least for me, to maintain my stability and my passion for wild places and wild things.

Unlike some people who may have become immediately addicted, it is easy to remember distinctly the first gobbler that ever came to my call. It was an immense joy, yet it took me a while to realize I was irretrievably hooked. Looking back and trying to determine why, it is obvious for many reasons. However, one of those is listening to the world wake up.

One morning after climbing to the top of a mountain in the Ouachita's in west-central Arkansas well before daylight I stopped to rest and listen. I listened intently as the sun began its ascent in the east. While watching those first pink rays of light appear, I realized that listening to the world wake up had become an anticipated blessing. First, the whippoorwills began to quieten from their nightly serenade. Next, I heard a barred owl, then an ovenbird, a wood thrush, a mourning dove, a cardinal, some coyotes, and I began to listen as a variety of other creatures awoke and began moving around. Primarily, while listening and hoping to hear a gobbler sound off, it occurred to me how much this scenario of listening to and watching the world wake up had become an integral part of my being.

That is a pleasure still enjoyed as a special time whether in Florida, Oregon, South Africa, New Zealand, Mexico, Hungary, Pakistan, Canada, or Alaska. In addition, after the darkness progressively fades to light, it is gratifying in the spring, observing and smelling the spring flowers and watching the trees recover from a drab winter appearance. That renewal of redbuds, dogwoods, red buckeye, serviceberry, and a myriad of other shrubs and flowers beginning to leaf out and bloom provides hope eternal. It also revives my appreciation for the awesome creation that God has provided for us. These pleasures may seem somewhat esoteric to some, but to me, they are a part of why spring gobbler hunting became more and more like "turkey fever." They certainly complement my quest to observe and enjoy wild things and wild places.

When you hear that first raucous gobble in the spring, whether scouting or hunting, it stimulates your pulse rate and excites you for what may or may not lie ahead. Regardless, what stimulates that gobble is appreciated. Whether because of your owl hooting, crow cawing, a red-tailed hawk screaming, sandhill cranes leaving their roosting area, or some other noise that you can't identify, it is anticipated excitement. When provoked, if a gobbler responds, it usually makes you do your best to determine its source and focus in that direction.

Although the spring season can offer some challenges, like rain, snow, wind, cold, or sweltering weather, one fact learned very early on is that you can't kill a gobbler unless you are in his territory. The die-hard turkey hunter going back to bed because of inclement weather or being tired is not an option. Once you take up the thrill of the chase with wild turkeys, it becomes an annual challenge that commits many actions and outcomes to memories.

Anyone taking up turkey hunting expecting to kill a turkey every time they go hunting is in for a major disappointment. Those who are persistent and willing to admit defeat most days soon realize that it is a vast and likely never-ending learning experience. Even the so-called experts don't kill a gobbler in a fair chase hunt every day. However, on those days when things go according to the plan, and a gobbler does come to the call, the exhilarating thrill is gratifying. Regardless, whether a kill is made or not, you have experienced the joy of being in wild places, hearing and likely observing wild things that many people never see or hear.

The combination of all the sights, sounds, surroundings, and mystical appearance of that majestic gobble makes spring gobbler hunting so special to me. If my heart does not race at some point, and my mind does not anticipate what will happen next with a gobbler that just responded to my call, then I will surrender. It will be time for me to quit hunting and take up knitting or crocheting.

CHAPTER 5

What's the Attraction?

After attempting many times to explain to other hunters and non-hunters what makes me so passionate about spring gobbler hunting, it is evident most just don't get it. And, admittedly, it isn't easy to understand unless you have participated. Serious turkey hunters are plagued by an obsession that is difficult, if not impossible, to explain or define to others. In my opinion, it is inextricably linked to the wildness and ties to the natural world we feel where we hunt them.

Once infected by "turkey fever," as some would describe it, that urge becomes incurable to many of us. It is likely, at least partially, triggered by the vocal interaction between the hunter/caller and the gobbler that responds. Clearly, that raucous, belligerent, ancient, territorial, and uniquely wild, almost hostile sound is a significant part of it. It creates an anticipation that is rarely comparable to any other stimulus or endeavor I can imagine. Regardless of the outcome, that vocal interaction, and possibly watching the gobbler display, even if the trigger is not pulled is a thrill of the chase not soon forgotten.

Others who have attempted to define what makes turkey hunting so special have struggled as well to explain it to others so they can understand and appreciate the fascination. A few of these include my good friend, Kit Schaffer from Lynchburg, Virginia, who wrote in the Third National Wild Turkey Symposium (1975): "The esthetic appeal of wild turkey hunting stems from its ability to satisfy our needs for the total experience—companionship, challenge, anticipation, tests of skills, anxiety, success, and rewards all in an environment that produces the right stimulus to all the senses." Well-known author Tom Kelly in his book The Season

(1996) stated: "Turkey hunting is not a game that needs a score or a score keeper and does not require the production of a dead turkey to qualify as a success. Done properly and unscored, it is about as close to even as anything can be when one of the participants has a loaded shotgun, and the other one has not."

Even Aldo Leopold in describing a turkey hunt in the Datil National Forest area of New Mexico in 1919, had difficulty articulating his thrill of hunting wild turkeys. He stated, "Rounding the point of a little bench, I suddenly felt a shock that seemed to freeze my feet to the ground (I'm sure I felt that turkey in my knees as soon as I saw him). There he was right over the point of the bench, a big hump-backed gobbler, clipping the seeds off a stalk of wild oats— But I couldn't make my knees behave! I freely confess it, they were wobbling—wobbling like a reed shaken in the wind. I can look the biggest blacktail buck in the face without a tremor, but turkey? Never!"

As previously noted, I have been blessed to hunt many different game species in many different places from my earliest hunting adventures in rural north Alabama. Although I continue to enjoy the thrill of the chase for other species, my greatest hunting passion and pleasure grew into spring gobbler hunting. Because of my many years of experience chasing spring gobblers, some people who know me have suggested that I am an expert. That is a mistake.

I have never considered myself an expert in anything, and especially not as a turkey hunter. At best, my skills as a turkey hunter and caller could be considered "fair to middling," as the old-timers used to say. Any beneficial attributes that have helped me call up gobblers for myself and others over the years include practice, honing my limited skills, and a continuum of learning experiences.

In addition to those gained learning from numerous mistakes, these efforts have contributed to hopefully enabling me to become a pretty good woodsman and naturalist. Mistakes made over the years have helped me learn from observation quickly where and how to make a good setup from which to call a turkey. In my opinion, one's ethics about hunting are critical. In striving to be a responsible naturalist and steward, we must adhere to ethics we believe strongly about, and those indeed encompass hunting. Developing a passion for the quarry we love to pursue in a fair chase hunt is strengthened by a naturalist's continual learning efforts. These include trying to understand more about these amazing renewable natural resources while behaving responsibly.

CHAPTER 6

Pre-Hunt Scouting

The first and most important thing to learn about turkey hunting is hunting where there are turkeys. Scouting, if you can find the time and discipline to do it, can provide a great dividend. If you can scout before the season, and listen a few mornings to see if you can locate a bird or birds gobbling on the roost, you enhance your chances. If you can determine which direction they head after leaving the roost, that is even more information you can store away for future reference.

My preference while scouting is not to turkey call to a gobbler before the season. I prefer to use owl calling and crow-cawing in the mornings, and then again in the afternoon just before dark to stimulate a gobble. If successful, you have some idea of his roosting area for the next morning's hunt. While scouting, you should be looking for tracks, dusts, strutting areas, scratching, droppings and feathers. Any scouting you can do before the season opens will likely be worth it if you have located some gobblers, their territories, or where you have seen a lot of sign.

On the negative side, having hunted many states, it has always been a priority to avoid being charged with a hunting violation. Aside from reading and abiding by the respected agency regulations, it pays to do what scouting you have time for before hunting. Pre-scouting before hunting, if time permits, is both wise and beneficial. On several occasions, while scouting, I have located bait where someone either had hunted or planned to hunt, and baiting for turkey hunting in most states is illegal.

Here are a few examples for consideration. My Dad joined a deer hunting club in a county in south Alabama one year, solely for turkey hunting there. He asked me to hunt with him the following spring. I flew down to hunt with Dad, and we headed to the area. We stopped to meet and visit with the landowner to be sure it was permissible to look around that afternoon before hunting the following day. He said that only a couple of gobblers had been killed so far, so we located a place to camp and started driving and walking out areas that looked promising to hunt the next morning.

After locating turkey sign in a few places, I walked out a ridge for a couple of hundred yards. Observing quickly that the top of the ridge was scratched up more than usual, I got down on my hands and knees to look. I soon located cracked corn, wheat, oats, and other grains. Then, I found the blind overlooking the bait a little further out the ridge. Immediately, I headed back to the truck, met Dad, and told him why we could not hunt in that area. We left to inform the landowner. The landowner indicated that he likely knew who was doing the baiting and would call the local enforcement officer and inform him. He told us that he was sorry but suggested we hunt another area. This area was where a recent timber sale had been made on a ridge above a creek. The owner had seen a gobbler a couple of times in the creek bottom and mentioned that no one in the club ever hunted that area.

Although it was getting late, I wanted to look the area over. I left Dad in the truck, quickly walked down to the creek bottom, and found where a gobbler had been strutting on a sand bar near the creek. The following morning, we went there and had a great hunt, and Dad was able to kill that gobbler after we called him across the creek into the bottom. We went to camp, packed up, and left, going by the landowner's house to thank him for the privilege and the suggestion of where to go. He told us the enforcement officer had caught two guys sitting on that bait earlier that morning and arrested them.

While living in Virginia, a professional colleague and friend in Kentucky, Tom Barnes, had invited me a couple of times to come over there and take him hunting as he had never killed a gobbler. We planned the dates. I shared them with another friend, Wayne Bell, and told him that I would be hunting in Kentucky that spring to try to call a gobbler in for Tom.

Wayne knew a landowner in southern Illinois, so we planned a hunt in both states, applying for and obtaining an Illinois permit. Tom had a County Extension Agent friend in Kentucky who got permission for us to hunt a friend's farm. He knew both farms had turkeys using them, and we would supposedly be the only people hunting.

We met Tom at the appointed time and location near a little community named Rabbit Hash, Kentucky, and set up camp on the County Agent's farm. We decided to make a quick scouting trip on both farms before dark, if possible. We scouted the friend's farm first, then got back to our campsite and walked up to a couple of wooded ridges behind the old barn.

I spotted scratching that looked like someone had been there with a garden rake on the second ridge. Looking closely with the help of my flashlight, I found cracked corn and other grains. Then, looking further, I located a blind. We immediately went back to our campsite. Tom informed the County Agent, who then called the local enforcement officer and told them where we were camped.

We were abruptly awakened at 3:30 a.m. the next morning by two enforcement officers who asked me to take them and show them where the bait was, which I did. Wayne had made coffee when I returned, so we stayed up and got ready. We met Tom at the agreed-upon time and hunted the friend's property. We had a good hunt after moving a couple of times and finally getting some birds to gobble. Tom and I got set up where we were able to work several gobblers for almost an hour before they left their gobbling zone and moved our way. We knew there was more than one, but when they came into view there were five adult long beards. These birds were coming straight toward us following a deer trail. Tom waited until one separated himself from the others and fired, connecting on his first gobbler ever. It was a huge, 24-pound bird with a great beard and long spurs.

Before he headed home, he came by our camp, and I caped the gobbler out for him, filleted the breast meat and thighs, and placed them in zip-lock plastic bags. He informed us that the enforcement officers had caught a local man and his young son in the blind that morning hunting over the bait. Tom had to work the next day so Wayne and I hunted the friend's property, and both killed nice gobblers. We hunted one more morning before heading to southern Illinois, and I got lucky, killing my second gobbler there about 10:30 that morning.

On a Wildlife Management Area (WMA), Kinterbish in southwest Alabama where I had hunted for several years, another pre-scouting effort paid off. I had come to know the area biologist/manager quite well over the years named Larry Rush. I talked with Larry about hunting a new area. He suggested an area between Kinterbish Creek and a nearby county highway. He said he knew it held turkeys and that not many people ever hunted it, so I planned to go there the following morning.

I covered a good bit of territory that morning early, calling with owl and crow calls and listening, but no birds gobbled. Continuing to explore, I stopped and called occasionally. Finally, a response, and I was pretty sure it was a jake (juvenile gobbler). I moved to the head of a little gully that dropped off to the creek, and found a place to set up and call. Once seated, I called again, and the bird answered right back. Having been fooled before, however, I decided to wait and see if a mature gobbler might accompany him. Sitting there watching and listening for that gobbler, I glanced to the right of the gully, and it was completely scratched up. Then, looking on up the side of the ridge, I spotted the blind.

At that point, I quickly got up, unloaded my shotgun, went to the scratched-up area, and found gobbler breast feathers scattered about as well as various kinds of grain.

I headed directly to the WMA headquarters, found Larry, and told him what I had seen. He asked me to take him to the baited area, which I did. Larry and the local enforcement officer caught two men in the blind the next morning.

A wildlife biologist never wants to violate the game laws for obvious reasons. I once called up a Merriam's gobbler for a client on a massive ranch in New Mexico that was loaded with turkeys. We had walked several hundred yards up the side of a mountain before getting a gobbler to respond. After calling the bird from another ridge about a half-mile away, he came into range, and the client killed him. While dressing the bird later, we found that he had yellow corn in his crop. We had seen no evidence of bait before we set up and called to that gobbler. There wasn't a cornfield within a hundred miles of that ranch, nor did the ranch have any cattle near the area. That corn had been placed there by someone.

While living in Arkansas, a County Extension agent friend of mine and a retired company forester suggested that the three of us go to Alabama for a hunt. We were going to hunt on some paper company land that a forester friend of his managed. We drove over to the area, found his friend's office, and dropped by to find out where the property was located. The property had an old vacant house that we would stay in. He gave us a key and showed us on a map the property boundaries. After getting our gear unloaded at the house, we decided to scout the property and see if we could locate a gobbling turkey.

Not far from where we parked, we found an old sawmill site and a place where a gobbler had strutted nearby, so the other two guys decided they would scout that area. Leaving them, I decided to cover as much territory as possible by looking elsewhere. My scouting resulted in bumping one hen, but I did not observe a great deal of sign. After walking some 300 yards due west, I found a property line with some scratching and fresh droppings nearby. One of those was a large gobbler dropping.

Heading back toward the truck late that evening, I heard a bird gobble twice, apparently as it was going to roost near where the other guys had scouted. It was almost dark. When we got back to the old house, they indicated they wanted to go to that bird they had roosted. We split from the truck the next morning, with them going to the bird they had roosted, and me prospecting on the remainder of the property. About an hour after daylight, I heard one of them shoot, so I assumed they had gotten that gobbler. I continued to walk, stop and occasionally call, trolling to try and locate a gobbler.

After some time, I had worked my way back near the property line to the west. I decided to try to locate a place with good visibility, sit down and do a little calling. Most of the morning, a bunch of crows had been raising a ruckus about something on the neighboring property. I could hear several of them cawing across the posted line to the west. Calling a few times, I received one muted gobbler response. Shortly, however, the crows began cawing more frantically and moving toward me. I could see over the property line for quite some distance across the flat open bottom. As the crows got closer, I could see them swerving through the trees and diving toward the ground.

Having experienced crows harassing a gobbler before, I got my shotgun up on my knee and soon saw a big gobbler coming my way. I watched as the crows continued diving at him as he moved on toward me. Waiting until he ducked under the barbed wire fence onto the property we were hunting, I shot him at about 35 yards. My friends were at the truck and had killed the other gobbler. We headed back to the old house and went in to fix some breakfast.

Before long, we heard a pickup drive up. It was the

company forester who had allowed us to hunt the area. He seemed almost surprised that we had killed two mature gobblers on that property and suggested another area for us to hunt the next couple of days. As we started to dress those gobblers, the one I killed had yellow corn in it, and the one they killed did as well. Had I not given some attention to the crows harassing that gobbler, I would have never killed him. That is the closest I can remember to ever killing a gobbler over bait.

CHAPTER 7

Basic Gear Innovation and Evolution

Essential turkey hunting clothing, calls, guns, and ammunition effectively used in my early turkey hunting years reminds me of the simplicity then versus today. My pants were olive green Army surplus. My shirt and jacket were green and black plaid flannel, the cap was brown, and gloves were brown cotton. Footwear was either tennis shoes or LL Bean's, rubber bottomed boots.

The author with his 1960 version of "camouflage."

My turkey call was a piece of blackboard slate sanded down to fit in my palm, and my striker was a cedar stick with an empty 30 caliber Winchester brass hull driven down over the top end. My shotgun was a pump-action Model 12 Winchester 12 gauge with a full choked barrel, and my ammunition was 12-gauge two-and-three-quarter inch heavy loads of number six lead shot. No turkey vest, face mask, nor proper camouflage were even available then, and most hunters had never even thought about decoys. Yet somehow, I managed to kill gobblers with some consistency.

The keys to success were having learned where and how to set up, staying still, when to call, when to shut up, and what to look and listen for, as well as learning from numerous mistakes. My gobble stimulator was either owl-calling or crow-cawing with my voice. Having previously purchased a box call and a wooden scraper call, even with practice, I could not become as consistent with either, as with that homemade slate and striker. Therefore, I stuck with the calls I felt confident using.

Everything needed could be carried in the cargo pockets of my pants and in my shirt pocket, which usually consisted of gloves, my slate and striker, a sharp pocketknife, and about four or five shotgun shells. Three of these shells were loaded in the gun when I was in the woods and hunting. I had no shotgun sling but did have one backup call. It was a wing bone call that research biologist Lovett Williams, with the Florida Game and Freshwater Fish Commission, had given me when I worked briefly with him as a technician.

Later someone told me about a man named Jack Anderson who lived in Mobile, Alabama, and made diaphragm turkey calls. I called him, and he informed me he would sell me eighteen calls. I don't remember the price, but you had to buy them eighteen at a time. Placing an order, I sent him a check and a week or so later received a package that contained a large snuff-can-like container with eighteen calls in it. Each was simply a lead washer clamped over a piece of prophylactic stretched between each side of the horseshoe.

After some practice, I eventually learned how to make a yelp, cluck, and whine and used these calls for several years. Fortunately, other call manufacturers later came on the scene with improved diaphragm material and tape-covered mouth calls.

After finishing my Masters of Science with a Forestry and Wildlife major, my wife and I moved to Arkansas in 1967. I became an Extension Wildlife Specialist with the University of Arkansas Cooperative Extension Service. By that time, I had been hunting turkeys for several years, although my hunting equipment had not changed significantly. With a new hunting buddy, Thurman Booth, we began to examine how to locate and record where we heard turkey gobblers while scouting before and during the season. We found that county-by-county topo maps better enabled us to determine the steepness and elevation of the rough Ouachita Mountain public lands we hunted. They also showed old roads, trails, and other landmarks. My clothing, firearm, ammunition, and calls described previously continued to be used. We periodically tried some new call or equipment like a camouflage hunting vest to carry stuff.

By the early 1970s, the turkey population had increased significantly in parts of the state, and I had become quite involved with the National Wild Turkey Federation (NWTF) in its infancy. Working cooperatively with turkey biologists for the state wildlife agency, Gene Rush, followed by Bob McAnally, we made a successful effort to get a turkey tag added to the annual hunting license.

I developed a survey that was sent out to all hunting

license buyers in Arkansas to see how many of them hunted turkeys. This effort proved beneficial and later resulted in the sale of turkey tags. Part of the need was to decide whether they would support a tag so the agency could get some idea of how many people were hunting turkeys. Obviously, with the checking of turkeys then required, it also helped determine some idea of the number of turkeys killed every spring.

This and other work led to significantly more voluntary involvement, and I helped initiate a state chapter of the NWTF about 1974. Further participation with the NWTF and support for additional management efforts enabled me to contact and invite guest speakers to our Annual Meeting. Some of the folks contacted, Ben Rogers Lee from Alabama and Harold Knight and Dave Hale from Kentucky, brought their calls over with them and stayed at our house overnight. Then, at our state meeting, they demonstrated how to use their calls by conducting calling exhibitions and took orders for calls. Beginning to explore new equipment options, like the tube call, improved diaphragm calls, and locator calls, helped me find some that worked.

When entrepreneurs began marketing effective camo clothing, I purchased some and found it increased my confidence. Later, as more call manufacturers began making diaphragm calls, I bought some new Perfection diaphragm mouth calls that Jim Clay and Tommy Duval, from Winchester, Virginia, were selling. Both these guys later became great friends, and we often conducted seminars together. By the mid-1970s, turkey hunting interest grew exponentially as more and more states began to stock quality habitat with wild-trapped turkeys, and populations increased. The turkey hunting gear manufacturers, big and small, recognized the market potential and exploited it. Some, including me, failed to recognize the potential market for specialized turkey hunting gear. As a consequence of my ignorance, some innovative ideas were given away.

Some innovative ideas were stimulated after a morning hunt of a big gobbler in a North Florida swamp in the early 1960s. There were no effective insect repellents available at that time, and the mosquitos had feasted royally on blood from my face and any other exposed flesh. On the way back to Gainesville, thinking about the need for some relief, I stopped by the Army surplus store and bought some olive-drab mosquito netting.

After getting home and looking around, I saw a pair of old sunglasses, knocked the lenses out of them, and asked my wife to sew those frames into that netting. It could then be pulled down over my head. With the sunglass frames sewn in, it remained in a position where I could see without the mosquitos biting my face. It never occurred to me that there might be a market for a head net.

Later, in the early-1970s, I decided that a turkey gun needed a short, tightly choked barrel that would shoot small shot in dense patterns. Taking action on that idea, I had the barrels on an old over/under 12-gauge shotgun cut back to 23 inches, and an excellent gunsmith sleeved both barrels. These sleeves were made with a long taper and tight constriction so that each barrel would shoot dense patterns. The following spring, I was asked to guide some hunters from Remington Arms on a turkey hunt in Arkansas.

I tried diligently on this hunt, but unconvincingly, to get them interested in having Remington make a camouflaged turkey gun with a short barrel, very tightly choked (I had previously painted my shotgun with dull-colored spray paint). They insisted, however, that there was not a viable market for such a shotgun. In retrospect, I should have teamed up with that gunsmith to start buying, modifying, and marketing shotguns for turkey hunting, and we would both have been well ahead of the curve.

Other examples of missed innovation and entrepreneurial opportunities included the request from a good friend, Richard Teague, in California. Sometime in 1972, knowing of my turkey hunting addiction, he called me and asked if I knew of an audiotape of how to call turkeys. Not aware of any available at that time, I agreed to try and make one for him. My good friend and Extension colleague, John Philpot had a small recording studio in our building, and he decided to give it a try.

Another good friend and avid turkey hunter, Gene Denton, and I sat down and discussed when and how to make multiple turkey call sounds and make the different calls depending on how the gobbler responded. John recorded nearly 20 minutes of our discussion and demonstration of calls. John made a few copies, and I sent one to Richard. He made additional copies and shared them with other people in California as the turkey population increased. Somehow a friend of mine in Tennessee found out about this tape, asked

This audiotape was made in 1972 and given to friends.

for a copy, and I sent one to him as well. He also made copies and shared them with interested people he claimed learned how to call, as he did, by listening to the tape.

Duh! It never occurred to me that there might be a growing market for such how-to audiotapes. Over the next few years, as turkey populations grew across many states, the markets for such tapes and related turkey hunting gear grew progressively. Any guesses of how many thousands of how-to call turkeys audiotapes were developed, marketed, and sold across the nation?

Admittedly, not having an entrepreneurial drive and never wanting to try every new or different hunting gadget or widget that was developed, I missed out on some great opportunities. However, after trying some of these, I did find a few that proved both practical and beneficial.

One item I experimented with after seeing it marketed was some underwear-like knitwear called "Bug Skinz." The two-piece outfit was made from thin, elasticized material with very tight cuffs around the neck, ankles, and wrists. Having previously been hospitalized with Rocky Mountain spotted fever, I purchased a set of these, hoping that wearing them would prevent ticks from getting on my body. Admittedly, any friends who spotted me wearing these before getting my shirt and pants on had a great laugh at my skinny legs, but it was worth a try. My first real test of their effectiveness came in Kentucky while hunting with my good friend Wayne Flowers.

Wayne and I had chased a big gobbler, accompanied by some hens, around several steep hills and hollows that morning. We decided to make a big circle and try to outflank him by coming into the woods on the backside of a knoll slightly below where we had last heard him. With Wayne in front as we entered the woods adjacent to a small gully, I looked up the hill and spotted the gobbler in full strut, and he had some hens with him. I whispered for Wayne to stop where he was, with Wayne a little uphill from me toward the turkeys which had not seen us. The only place for me to sit was against a small red cedar tree, and I was afraid to try to put my face mask and gloves on without being spotted.

Within a minute, I could see and feel a swarm of seed ticks on both hands. I felt sure they would get all over me but couldn't move without spooking the turkeys. I called softly on a mouth call, and surprisingly the hens started moving down toward us. They stayed across a bit of a gully, but the gobbler kept strutting and followed them toward us. As they came into range with the hens getting closer, Wayne shot that gobbler at about 40 yards.

We were both delighted, and I could not have been prouder to start scraping those seed ticks off my hands and clothing. Undressing that evening, I examined myself looking for ticks. I found one dug in on my left wrist below the cuff of the Bug Skinz that actually worked, keeping ticks from gaining access to the rest of my body.

Another helpful item I procrastinated about purchasing was the Thermacell mosquito-repelling device. I borrowed one in Florida one spring when the mosquitos were horrific and found that it worked. Since then, I have purchased a couple more. In fact, in much of the south, when mosquitoes are bad, these devices, if kept functional with batteries, wicks, and cartridges, are a lifesaver and become an integral part of my hunting gear.

Other items I have found to be very functional include a carrying strap that someone gave me back in the early 1970s. It is simply a blaze orange, three-inch-wide, tightly woven strap with a sliding rubber pad that can be placed on your

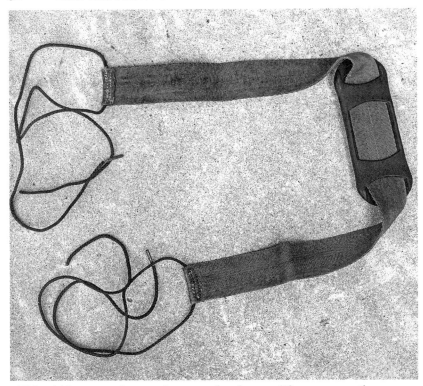

This old homemade carrying strap has been a lifesaver over the years.

shoulder to carry out a turkey. Both ends have heavy cord strings about 18 inches long on each side of the end of the strap. These are used to tie around the neck and legs (above the knees) and make carrying one long-distance much easier. I used that strap so long that the strings in the ends wore out. I had to have a shoe shop owner replace them with a heavier cord some fifteen years ago. There is no telling how many miles I have carried that strap, nor how many turkeys it has helped haul out of the woods.

For many years, I couldn't find a factory load of shotshells to provide the pattern density and effectiveness in any shotguns that I wanted to use to shoot a turkey. After quite a bit of experimentation loading and patterning with different handloads, I found one that provided improved pattern densities. Previously, my 12-gauge handloads had been two-and-three-quarter inch shotshells with a mixed load of one and three-eighth ounces of number four and number six shot. Later I started loading number 7 1/2 copper-plated shot. These proved in the appropriate choked barrel to be effective as long as the shots taken were not more than forty yards. With the advancement of the three-inch magnum load and shotguns chambered to shoot these loads, further experimentation became necessary.

With other handloading trial and error experiments, a friend and I found that we could stuff about two ounces or seven hundred number 7 1/2 copper-plated shot into the three-inch magnum hulls. Then, with a shotgun barrel that patterned such small shot densely, we could come up with an even more lethal load out to forty yards or more.

At that time, some misunderstood research based on shooting turkeys in the body to kill them had been widely published. That researcher had recommended that number five lead shot (or larger) was necessary to kill a gobbler at ranges out to 40 yards. Therefore, most state wildlife agencies that published shot sizes in their regulations decided to limit shot size to number fours, fives, or sixes.

Often, I conducted turkey hunting seminars and workshops in states where shot size was not restricted to those three sizes. Once I determined the effectiveness of the copper-plated 7 1/2 shot, I began suggesting that hunters try them. However, unless they handloaded, they would likely have to locate some custom shops to develop and test such loads. Almost invariably, the comment or question from hunters afterward was that they just didn't believe the smaller shot had enough energy and penetration capability to kill a gobbler effectively.

During these seminars or workshops, I attempted to drive home that you should never try to shoot a turkey in the body unless it is already crippled and trying to escape. Instead, the aim should focus on that gray squirrel-sized head and neck. With that in mind, what is needed is a very dense pattern of hard, high-antimony, copper-plated shot that penetrates better than a standard lead shot. These smaller, harder shot, when properly loaded, significantly increase penetration and retained energy.

A good friend of mine, Bill Stevens, with whom I had worked on conservation education and 4-H youth projects over the years, was employed by Federal Cartridge Company. I had told Bill about the effectiveness of those handloads in the hope of finding a manufacturer who would load and sell them. Bill was not a turkey hunter, but he recognized the growing interest in turkey hunting. He also realized my passion as I tried, on several occasions, to see if he could convince his Federal colleagues to manufacture such a load. He planned to come by my office one Monday morning, so I spent a good bit of time shooting patterns with turkey loads on the previous Saturday, primarily using the handloaded 12-gauge, 3-inch magnum number 7 1/2 copper-plated shot. These had been identified on paper targets at various ranges with different shotguns and choke tubes. When he dropped by, I laid out several of these targets to show him the dense patterns achieved.

Bill was impressed and asked me how lethal they were in killing turkeys. I assured him of their lethality out to at least forty yards. With those patterns and my assurance based on experience, he asked if I could send him the handloading data, i.e., primer, powder, wad, and amount of shot. He also wanted to know the crimping pressure which was unknown to me, and I had no way of determining. Regardless, I wrote all of this down and sent it to him along with some patterns. I also listed the type of shotguns, their choke constrictions, and range distances. He had agreed in our earlier conversations to discuss it with Federal's ballistic experts.

In about a month, Bill called and said he was sending some three-inch magnum shotshells that their Federal folks had developed using the small 7 1/2 copper-plated shot. He wanted me to pattern them and get back to him. As soon as possible, I took these loads and my shotguns and patterned these loads extensively. They were definitely superior to the handloads in pattern density. I responded quickly to let him know how effective these loads were and sent along some of the patterns to show his colleagues.

Shortly after these interactions, Bill told me Federal would have these on the market before the next spring turkey season and that he would send me some to use hunting. Some hunters were reluctant to try such small shot, having been convinced by previous marketing information that the larger shot sizes were necessary. Other friends and colleagues whom I shared some of these loads with were very impressed and began diligently trying to find these shotshells. Sporting goods store buyers were apparently skeptical about these small shot size loads and did not stock them the first year they were available. Some state wildlife agency regulations failed to list shot size smaller than the number six shot as being legal for turkey hunting. Therefore, after two years, Federal ceased marketing and manufacturing that load.

Federal Premium 7 1/2 copper-plated shells.

Fortunately, I still have some of these loads and use them sparingly. Later, Federal realized how deadly such small shot could be in the right load and began experimenting with bismuth shot. They soon realized that a number seven-sized bismuth shot load could be developed for use by turkey hunters. It quickly became the most effective load for turkey hunters with the right combination of shotgun and choke tube.

Further experimentation by Federal and other shotshell manufacturers proved that even smaller bismuth shot sizes like number nine and number ten shot have both superior penetration and energy to be effective. However, it is essential to have a shotgun capable of shooting a dense load of these small shot. This is dependent on shooting a gobbler in the head and neck rather than in the body. Currently, virtually every shotshell manufacturer, both here and abroad, offers bismuth shotshell turkey loads with small shot and in smaller gauges. However, there are a couple of downsides. Because bismuth shot is considerably more expensive than lead or copper-plated shot, the price of turkey loads now has risen to as much as $8.00 to $10.00 per shell or more. Thus, the price of a five-shell box generally costs from $40 to $50 or more. This cost will likely discourage some people from shooting them on paper to determine how well they pattern.

Regardless, if they plan to shoot them at turkeys, they need to pattern them on paper before hunting. Not all shotguns or choke tubes will pattern the same or shoot to the point of aim with different loads. The other downside is that some of the marketing advertisements for these loads claim killing shots on gobblers out to 60 yards or more. I don't doubt that a bird might be killed that far occasionally. Such marketing, however, ignores how many birds shot at such extreme ranges may only be crippled and escape when shot at such distances.

My choice of shotguns is either a 12-gauge or 20-gauge over/under that is chambered for three-inch magnum loads. Other preferences for my turkey gun include a selective single trigger, with interchangeable choke tubes. Even then, with special choke tube capability, that load and shotgun should be patterned on paper. Proof of providing the dense, lethal patterns must be determined at ranges I consider acceptable. Some advantages of the two-shot over/under rather than a pump or semi-auto is that I can use different patterning choke tubes in each barrel and select the one needed depending on the range and situation. In addition, for left eye dominant or left shoulder shooters, the over/under can easily be adapted.

Further, one shot should be all needed if you know your gun, load, pattern capability, how to judge effective range, and it shoots to point of aim. Because most turkey loads generate significant recoil, for many youth hunters or others who don't like the recoil, a 20-gauge shotgun may be a better choice. Several manufacturers currently market "low-recoil" turkey loads.

Some hunters choose to hunt turkeys with their bow and, and in states where legal, with rifles. Earlier in my quest to try new ways to kill a gobbler, I shot three gobblers with a compound bow. The first two were cleanly killed. Sadly, on the third one, my aim was slightly off. I had aimed for the wing butt but hit slightly low with the arrow passing completely through the breast. The arrow hit almost caused him to drop, but he recovered and flew off the ridge toward the valley. I searched diligently for the rest of the day and only found a few breast feathers and small amount of blood. That was enough to convince me to put the bow away and concentrate on using a shotgun for gobbler hunting.

My friend, Wayne Bell, an avid and very skilled bowhunter, came out to Vermejo Park Ranch one spring while I was still doing seminars and guiding there. He brought his compound bow and, as insurance, a shotgun. After my clients and I had limited out, Wayne's guide asked if I would go with them to try to help Wayne get a gobbler with his bow. He had taken one already with his shotgun, but they were having difficulty getting a gobbler where he could shoot it with his bow. I agreed to go with them the following day. Although we worked a couple of gobblers and got one close, we could not get Wayne a good bow shot.

We had hunted a couple of good places, but the howling wind made it difficult. About 10:00, we drove up a ridge that had a gap in it with a long straight roadway that had been cleared for a future timber harvest. Stepping out to the side of the truck, I called as loudly as possible on a mouth call, but all we could hear was the wind. After standing there a few minutes drinking a cup of coffee, a big gobbler came out from one side of that opening about 400 yards below

Merriam's gobbler shot by Wayne Bell (center) at Vermejo Park Ranch.

us. Apparently, the gobbler did not spot the truck and spook, and walked across the open area into the woods.

Wayne grabbed his bow quickly, and we started sprinting down that slope. When we got about 75 yards above where the gobbler had crossed, we entered the woods. We didn't go more than 50 yards into the woods, a mixture of mostly aspen and a few fir trees. Finding a small opening, we sat down at the upper edge in a little depression with me directly behind Wayne. Then calling as loud as I could in that howling wind, we both thought we heard a faint gobble. Within a couple of minutes, a gobbler came strutting out into that opening about sixty yards away. About that time, Wayne saw him as well, so I just ducked down behind Wayne and called again. Wayne said he was coming, and shortly, I heard Wayne release the arrow. I heard a thump, and looking up, saw the gobbler running down to our right. At about thirty yards, he tumbled over, and I could see part of the arrow sticking out of him. The arrow had gone through with part of it sticking out front and back. Elated, we picked the turkey up, walked back out to the roadway, and motioned for the guide to bring the truck down and pick us up.

Several Western states and a few others across the U.S. allow rifle hunting for spring gobblers. I have no interest in shooting a gobbler with a rifle. There are likely some ethical rifle hunters who try to call the bird in reasonably close, shooting them only in the head or neck with a rifle. Others, however, often use a rifle to shoot gobblers at long ranges when they can see them, killing some and likely wounding others. Calling the bird into close range is not part of the hunt for them, and to me, that becomes shooting instead of fair-chase hunting. A few years back, one of my friends in Virginia found two gobbler carcasses in pastures on different days that had been shot with rifles, and the only thing the shooters took were the beards.

While living in Virginia for 23 years, I and others tried diligently to get the Virginia Commission of Game and Inland Fisheries to eliminate rifle hunting for spring gobblers. Sadly, although we came close, political forces prevailed at the last minute, and they failed to take action. One spring, after finishing the Comprehensive State (CSRS) Review of the Virginia Tech Wildlife and Fisheries Department on a Friday afternoon, I had hoped to get in a one-day hunt. A friend who worked in the area suggested a place to hunt one morning on the Jefferson National Forest. Driving there in the dark, I was able to find the right spot, parked, grabbed my gear, and headed southwest into the mountains. After getting to the top of a ridge and walking out several hundred yards, it appeared that there was a nice saddle between two ridges that would be an excellent place to listen. Stopping there as the world began to wake up and the sun began to appear in the east, I owl-called, and two gobblers answered. Both were about the same distance away, one to the south and one to the north in good calling distance. I located a spot, made a quick little blind from a dead tree limb, settled in, and listened to those birds gobble from their roost.

After several minutes of their roost gobbling, the one to the north flew down and, when he next gobbled, was on the ground. After calling, both gobblers answered, and it sounded like the one to the north was getting closer by the next call. Not having heard any hens or anyone else calling, I turned and focused my attention on calling to the closer of the two. He gobbled several times on his own, and after about ten minutes, I called to him, again getting an immediate response. He was definitely on his way to me. Watching intently for him, I soon spotted his neon white skull cap as he came down toward the saddle. When he was about 40 yards away, he did something I had never seen before. He jumped up on a boulder about three feet high and popped into a strut. Previously, I had seen gobblers jump up on a dead log and strut, but never on a rock. Enjoying that rare scene, I knew I could kill him there but wanted to get him in a little closer, so I hesitated to shoot.

Suddenly, a rifle shot rang out, and that gobbler just seemed to explode with feathers flying. He was blown off that rock. Afraid to move as I did not know where the shooter had fired from, I sat frozen. About five minutes later, I saw this guy coming down the ridge carrying a scoped rifle. At this point, I stood and shouted to him to let him know of my presence. He acknowledged me and, when we got closer, he asked if I was working that gobbler. I answered him yes, but that I was certainly surprised to hear that rifle shot. He said he had always hunted turkeys with a rifle. I inquired if he had called to the gobbler, and he said he had not. Upon further questioning, he revealed he was using a .244 Remington, often called a .6mm Remington, and that he was shooting handloads.

We walked over to the gobbler, seeing his feathers scattered around for some distance. When he picked the gobbler up by the legs, you could see that a large portion of the breast had been blown away by the energy and explosiveness of the rifle bullet. He mumbled sort of a halfway apology and said he hadn't heard me calling to the bird, but saw him jump up on that rock, had a good shot, and took it. Then he walked away. What I failed to share with him was at the crack of that rifle shot, my butt cheeks had likely scooped up a handful of gravel from where I had been sitting. In fact, I was not sure that I had not dampened my knickers. This experience confirmed my decision not to hunt turkeys with a rifle and avoid places where rifle hunting is popular.

CHAPTER 8

Turkey Vocalizations

I do not pretend to know all of the vocalizations and sounds that wild turkeys make. I have, however, listened to wild turkeys of the five distinct subspecies and can discern no significant difference among them. I have done this in many different situations, except for the Gould's subspecies, which I only hunted for a few days. However, many other turkey vocalizations have been heard while scouting, hunting, or guiding for others. Some of these are mimicked as best possible by turkey hunters in attempts to call in turkeys.

Most hunters determine what works for them and develop a pretty standard repertoire of calls they use. Some, however, are willing to try some unusual calls or series of calls. Occasionally, this change of sounds or calls sometimes stimulates a gobbler to respond, and he might come to a different sounding call. No call or other potential stimuli in my experience works every time. But, when it does, hunters feel confident it might work again. This new call then potentially gets added to the repertoire.

In my opinion, the senses considered to be the two greatest capabilities wild turkeys utilize to stay alive and to communicate with other wild turkeys are their eyesight and hearing. Their vision provides them with the unbelievable capability to spot movement and distinguish color. Their auditory ability is phenomenal, not only in hearing a call but in coursing its location. Some examples of different calls that turkeys make may seem unusual. Most of these I have never even tried to mimic in calling to a gobbler. My commonly preferred repertoire of calls will explain what sometimes works for me from much trial and error.

My two favorite locator calls, the barred owl scream/squall/hoot, and the crow-caw, are my go-to calls. Many other sounds stimulate a turkey to gobble from the roost, and occasionally I try some of them. I have heard turkeys gobble to numerous sounds that may appear unusual. These include a train whistle; a tug boat horn; a vehicle door slammed; a donkey braying; a motorcycle starting; thunder; coyotes howling; hawks screaming; an early gunshot off in the distance; bull gators bellowing; geese honking; sandhill cranes leaving a roost; and of course, other turkeys gobbling. I have also heard birds gobbling at other bird and animal sounds.

Some common and unusual turkey calls I have heard may be difficult for some people to believe. Yet, having listened to and witnessed them myself, there is no reason to lie about it. Many people may not think a mature turkey gobbler can call and yelp, sounding exactly like a hen yelping. I have watched gobblers do this on at least three occasions.

While in the mountains of southwest Virginia, on the backside of a WMA, on property that a friend owns, I decided one spring morning to sneak in well before daylight to a little cove. In past years, I had often heard gobblers answer from that general area. It was a very steep area, and I carefully slipped down into that cove. Before stopping, as the leaves made for pretty noisy walking, I looked up the side and could see the silhouette of a gobbler in a tree. So, I froze in place, then slowly slid down beside a tree. After getting seated, I started hearing some muffled grousing, grumbling, and abbreviated gobbling from several gobblers. These birds seemed to be virtually all around me. As the sky lightened up, the hiccupping, grumbling, and grousing continued occasionally. Soon I saw some of the gobblers begin to stretch their wings as they stood on the limb.

The grousing, grumbling, and hiccupping sounds continued. Finally, one gobbled, and the rest gobbled almost simultaneously. Somehow I had worked my way right down into the middle of a group of seven mature gobblers on the roost. Four of these birds were less than 40 yards from me. Surprisingly, I had not spooked them while I was getting settled. It was a fantastic show as some began strutting back and forth on the limb. One continued to stay hunkered down on the limb but gobbled just as loudly as the others. This displaying and gobbling went on for probably ten more minutes.

Then, downslope about 70 yards away, I heard several hens start yelping and cackling as they flew down. One big gobbler soon sailed down toward them, and all but one followed. He sat there for five minutes before he too sailed down toward the others. Once they got on the ground, not a single one of them gobbled nor would answer my call. Some people would ask, "Why didn't you pick one out and shoot him off the tree?" My ethics, however, just do not permit me to kill a gobbler from the tree.

Following that experience in the cove, I decided to make a huge swing up the mountain. I could only stimulate one other bird that shock-gobbled to my loud cutting. That gobbler never answered again. I had walked in a large circle over and around the mountainside. About 10:00 a.m. I came to a slightly open hillside where some red cedar trees had been cut and piled. This ridge top was only a few hundred yards from the cove described earlier. I sat down, called, and immediately two gobblers responded that were very close. After a couple of minutes, I gave a soft cluck that was answered by both gobblers. Shortly afterward, they walked up over the top of the ridge into that opening, and I killed one of them. I have no idea if these two gobblers were part of the earlier group or not.

Sounds of gobblers fighting are difficult to describe to anyone who has never heard them. They mainly consist of loud wing-flapping and bodies and wings clashing together, accompanied by raucous, loud purring, clucking, and gobbling occasionally. I have heard and witnessed this very serious fighting several times while hunting or scouting. I have also, on occasion, used that distraction to enable me to move closer, set up, and be prepared to call. If you can do this without spooking them, you may call one or the other in when the fighting is over. Although it hasn't worked, every time I wouldn't hesitate to try it again. Generally, there is a lot of pushing back and forth with their necks intertwined and some pecking of the wattles, skin, or snood. When they fly up together with a loud beating of wings, the legs and spurs are thrust toward the other bird, often causing deep wounds if they are mature gobblers. These wounds are most often seen on the breast, thighs, and back. If this happens fairly close, whether it is just two birds or a gang, you will be amazed at how much noise they make.

A couple of springs ago, on a rainy morning, my good friend, Jim Byford, watched two gobblers fight for over thirty minutes just out of range. He was so pinned down that he couldn't move. He said it became evident that one of the gobblers was getting the best of the fight over time. Finally, the other gobbler just gave up and squatted down on the ground, completely exhausted. He said the other gobbler pecked him a few times and then walked off. Even though Jim called to them, neither gobbler responded. He said that the exhausted bird laid there for quite some time, flat out on the ground, before finally getting up and staggering away.

There are indeed many other sounds turkeys make that I am likely not aware of. Those noises produced by some old hens when they are with a gobbler remind me of a cuss fight. They seemed to have cursed me out with cuts, loud yelps, and cackles when they thought their gobbler might get pulled away from them. Some of these sounds are impossible for me to mimic. Therefore, I stick to what works for me, using three calls: a diaphragm/mouth call, a slate, glass, or aluminum pot and striker, and a tube call.

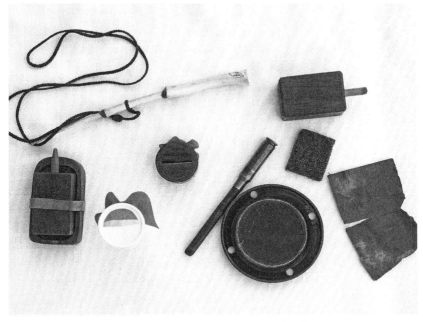

Some of he author's arsenal of calls.

With these three calls, I can make the calls needed to mimic, as best possible, what wild turkeys sound like. Most hen calls can be simulated, and if need be, so can a gobbler. Also, these calls don't take up a lot of room in my vest. Important turkey sounds to mimic include: the cluck, yelp, purr or whine, cackle, cut, putt and gobble. Admittedly, there are variations of these calls, and it is essential to know when to use what call and how loud to call. It is equally important to know when not to call. Because hens, like gobblers, may sound different, it is not so much the perfect sound needed as the cadence or rhythm. Different rhythms are necessary for some calls like the tree yelp versus the regular hen yelp, the "kee-kee run," or the lost hen call. After listening to many turkeys, I feel pretty confident in saying the right rhythm to simulate the call needed is as critical or more so than the exact sound of the call.

If a bird is not gobbling much, you may want to change calls from a mouth call to a slate or glass and see how he reacts. When calling a gobbler and he responds every time, you may want to stay silent for a while. Regardless of what he does for some time, unless he has hens that come to him, he is still interested. It is fun and exciting to hear them gobble but not always productive if you call too often. My silent time limit without calling depends on how the gobbler has responded, and the maximum is 20 to 30 minutes unless I can see him. However, you need to stay very alert and watch during this time because he may well come slipping in silently. When working a gobbler, and it becomes apparent that he is committed and coming closer, I stop calling. That is the time to be on high alert for any movement and listening carefully for drumming or other sounds.

In previous discussions of observations, tree-yelping has often been mentioned. The tree yelp is a very soft cluck or two, followed by a series of four or five soft yelps done a little slower than you do after the birds are on the ground. A cackle is a call that hens often make when flying up to roost at night and sometimes when flying down in the morning.

The cackle is usually a series of eight to twelve high-pitched yelps, followed shortly by a soft yelp or two. Although not a call used very often, I have often heard and watched an occasional single hen fly down while a gobbler is still on the roost and yelp constantly as she runs to the tree where he is sitting. One can only assume she is looking for love and wants to get to that gobbler before any other hen does. The cut is a series of sharp, high-pitched sounds, similar to an alarm putt, but done sharply, with a little more coarse or raspy sound and a slightly different rhythm.

It can be just a couple of cuts or as many as a dozen, which are most often heard from what most hunters call a "boss hen." The boss hen is frequently encountered when a gobbler has a harem of hens with him. Every time you call, the gobbler responds, but she excitedly attempts to cut you off with her angry cutting and yelping response. If this discussion between you and her continues for some time, she will usually lead the gobbler and other hens away from the area. Or, she will get so fired up that she decides she will come over and lay a butt-whipping on you. Sometimes, when this occurs, the whole group follows her until the gobbler is in range for a shot. Regardless, it is an exciting encounter that will test your endurance and patience.

Hunting in Mississippi years ago, I got close to two gobblers on the roost in a big flat, partially-flooded, hardwood bottom. I knew there were hens nearby, so I stopped about 130 yards or so away and found a big tree to sit by. Two gobblers began gobbling and continued back and forth for about ten minutes. Then, some of the hens started to tree yelp and cluck, and they started flying down once it was light enough for them to see. They flew off to my right, about 80 yards away.

Occasionally, I could see about a dozen or so milling around across the open bottom. Those two gobblers, one behind the other, then flew out and landed among the hens, as did a jake or two, from another direction. It was a fantastic display by those gobblers as they strutted around trying to interest the hens. However, the hens seemed uninterested in the courtship displays.

Now and then, one or more of the jakes would get too close to the hens. They were met by a rushed charge by one of the gobblers. Later, after calling, I could see both gobblers turn and gobble toward me. At that time, a boss hen started cutting and yelping, to which they also gobbled. We continued this discourse for about ten minutes or so. Suddenly, the two gobblers squared off and began fighting, with necks intertwined and wings flapping. They occasionally jumped into the air, flailing with legs and spurs at each other. They fought a good ten minutes or more, with the hens and jakes watching. After the fight was over and they separated, I called again. The gobblers both answered, and the boss hen started raising a ruckus again and headed my way.

I then watched as 18 hens and two jakes followed the boss hen almost in single-file toward me. They walked past through the shallow standing water to within 15 yards of me. The two gobblers brought up the rear some 20 yards behind. As they passed, I could hear the hens and jakes calling or purring softly as they went behind me. One of the gobblers strutted out in front of the other, stopped, and raised his head and neck at about 35 yards, so I shot him.

This was not an occurrence that happens often. Most of the time, when finding myself in battles with a boss hen, she usually drags the group away from where I'm calling rather than toward me. But, you have to try, and sometimes it works.

Once I set up on a gobbler, with him on the ground, my calling is usually confined to clucks and yelps as long as the gobbler seems interested and willing to respond. However, a gobbler by himself will often come almost into range, then go the other direction and gobble, trying to get the hen to go to him. Having had this happen many times, he might be tempted to come on in by changing calls. If that doesn't work after several of these "come then, go away" encounters, I will wait until he goes away and gobble at him if hunting on private land. I start by using my tube call and cutting two or three times very loudly, followed immediately by a gobble. Over the years, this has been one of my "go-to" call sequences in that situation, and it has occasionally been successful. Some gobblers may be intimidated if they have recently been whipped by another gobbler and quit responding. However, a dominant gobbler may come in with blood in his eyes to fight a suspected rival for a hen. Another technique that sometimes will break loose a hung-up gobbler is to move away, if possible, then call with two calls simultaneously, like with a mouth call and a slate.

We hope to learn from our mistakes, and in my earlier days, my tactics probably scared off a lot of gobblers, like calling too much, too loud, trying to get too close, or setting up where a gobbler does not want to go. Aside from the calls mentioned, my favorite technique, once I'm set up in a good place and the gobbler has been responding, is to stop calling for a few minutes. Then I begin by clucking softly and maybe purring. If he responds to that call, I call very sparingly. Once a gobbler seems committed to coming in, I quit calling altogether. I have likely called in as many gobblers with the slate and peg as all the other calls combined. I do, however, always keep a mouth call in my mouth when working a gobbler. Sometimes, with a bird in sight but not yet in range, I will cluck or purr softly with it.

The distance a gobbler can hear and determine where the call is coming from is challenging. But being able to observe gobblers come in from long distances has thoroughly convinced me that their hearing is phenomenal. My friend, Jim Brooks, whom I hunted with almost every spring for over 20 years, would often contact me for counsel. Jim, and his friend, Keith Jennings, were usually asking questions about some aspect of turkey hunting. One spring season, they had grown frustrated by a gobbler near the cabin. Jim left a message for me to call him. They had seen this bird, knew he was a large gobbler, and had him pretty well-patterned but could not seem to close the deal.

Having just returned home from a hunt in New York, with the Tennessee season about to close. I called him. He told me about this gobbler and asked if I could come up and assist them. I drove up the night before. On arriving, Jim said to me that Keith was not going with us, but he had roosted the gobbler the previous evening. We walked in off the top of a mountain, down toward a steep cove and hollow. We were easing along when I looked up and saw a jake gobbler in a tree about 30 yards away. I whispered to Jim to stop and sit down, or we would likely spook that jake and, ultimately, the gobbler. We both found a tree to sit in front of without spooking the jake.

The gobbler gobbled shortly afterward, below us, and we heard several hens clucking and yelping close to him. He gobbled several times, and hens started flying uphill toward us. The gobbler then flew down, in sight, about 65 yards downhill. I called to him. He immediately gobbled, and the hens started moving up toward us with him behind. Then, to my right and directly behind me, I heard deer hooves stamping and a snort. That triggered the jake to fly down over the other turkeys. They all turned, walked over the lip of that hollow, and went silent. Jim and I looked at each other and watched that deer run off snorting. This certainly was not the first time we had experienced deer spooking a gobbler.

We discussed where Jim had heard the gobbler later in the mornings. He said that usually, the bird would gobble later somewhere around a large bowl-shaped field surrounded by mountains on three sides. We moved in that direction, coming in over the top of the nearest of those mountains. I called loudly, and the turkey gobbled below us. The next hour we followed his movements around the bowl on the side of the mountain, above a creek. By about 9:30, the turkey had pretty much quit gobbling, at least that we could hear. Jim said he had heard this bird gobble a few times on previous days around 10:00 to 10:30 on the side of a mountain beyond that bowl. We gathered our gear, walked back to the main road and down toward the bowl about a quarter-mile away. The bowl had a couple of pine plantations and old fields that were circled by the creek.

About 10:15, I called loudly on a mouth call. I did not

hear the turkey, but Jim said he heard a gobble up on the side of the mountain. It appeared to be above the old road and one of the pine plantations. We decided that Jim should move down around the side of the ridge toward the gobbler but set up within range of that old road. I felt that my best bet was to stay put at the top of the bowl in some small Virginia pines and red cedars and call from there and see what happened. I allowed Jim sufficient time to get set up and then gave a softer call on the diaphragm call and heard a gobble across the road behind me. It was a different gobbler; I also thought I might have heard a faint gobble on the side of the mountain. My elevated position allowed me to see down that old road going into the bowl before it went out of sight around a pine plantation.

I estimated that it was at least 450 yards to the curve in the old road. Although not expecting the bird to come to the road there, I soon saw a black object move into the road at the edge of that curve. With my binoculars, I could see him pop into a strut, and I watched him to see how he responded to my next call. I was pretty sure he couldn't hear me by clucking on my little hand-held slate but thought it worth a try. I clucked and could see him run his neck out and gobble, but I could not hear him. It was incredulous that he could hear me that far away.

I watched as he strutted up the old road about 20 yards, then stopped. I clucked again, and his neck immediately jutted out as he gobbled. The bird behind me gobbled once more, then went mute as the gobbler down the road got closer. This sequence went on for another 35 to 40 minutes. When I clucked softer, and he moved closer, I could both hear and see him gobble.

Unsure just how far around that ridge above the road Jim had gone, I waited a little bit after each call sequence. I was getting ready to cluck again when Jim shot, and the gobbler flopped over. Jim got down to him well before I did, and the gobbler was indeed a fine old monarch. He had a beard over 12" long and 1 ½" curved spurs. We weighed him when we got back to the cabin, and he weighed 24 ½ pounds. That observation and watching Merriam's gobblers out west respond from a long distance to a call was a great lesson. I have toned down the volume of my calls ever since. Even though a turkey has no external ears and only a small flap or pinna over the ear hole on the side of their heads, their hearing and ability to course where the call is coming from still amazes me.

Examples of a turkey's long-distance hearing capability usually are best observed while pursuing either the Rio Grande, Merriam's, or the Gould subspecies. These subspecies are most commonly found in more open habitat types than are the Eastern and Osceola subspecies.

One spring, three of us colleagues, all with the first name of Jim, planned a hunt in southeastern Montana. Two of us, Jim Byford and I, flew to Rapid City, South Dakota, rented a car, and drove to Montana. We had to buy both a spring and fall license to be able to take two gobblers potentially. It was snowing, and we had a heck of a time getting to the ranch, which was 12 miles off the highway on a slick, greasy, curvy dirt road, but we made it with very tight pucker strings. Jim Knight was already there. He showed us where to stow our gear in the little cabin, then took us out to the barn. We all worked diligently for about an hour to get three 4-wheelers gassed up and running for the next morning's hunt. It had snowed about five inches by the next morning. We got directions from Jim Knight and headed out through some beautiful mountain country, each going to a different area.

The terrain was a mix of bare mountain outcroppings, shortgrass prairie, and ponderosa pine canyons. Once getting into what looked like suitable turkey habitat, I stopped the 4-wheeler and started walking. After daylight, I heard a couple of gobblers, so I moved toward them, found a place on the side of a ridge, and started calling when the turkeys were on the ground. Both gobblers responded. They continued coming closer to my calls, and within 20 minutes, they worked their way up through some scrubby oak brush to where I had set up. Both were nice gobblers and, with the weather uncertain, I decided to kill them both. Limiting out the first morning with unknown weather conditions would enable me to have time to explore this unique country.

I placed my carrying strap around both gobblers' legs, tied them to the front deck of the 4-wheeler, and headed back to camp. Once there, I cleaned both gobblers and packaged the meat for the freezer. When the other two came in, I found out they both had heard and worked turkeys but had not killed one.

After exchanging stories of our morning's activity, they cleaned up. I told them to come on in and let's have some turkey leg stew I had prepared. With some soda crackers and raw veggies, it became a delicious meal. Neither of them at that time had ever eaten it before.

I planned to scout for them that afternoon. By then, much of the snow had melted. Although it was slick, the 4-wheelers enabled us to get around without too much trouble. I located a big gobbler with some hens not too far from the area where I had killed my birds. When we got back to the cabin that night, both of them had heard birds as well. They each wanted to go back to gobblers they had listened to the afternoon before. I decided to continue scouting some areas not previously examined to try to locate other gobblers.

We met back at camp at noon, and although they had not killed a gobbler, they felt it was simply a matter of time. Jim Knight had to go to Billings that afternoon but said he would be back in a couple of days. I suggested to Jim Byford that we try to locate the big gobbler I had spotted the first afternoon. He was agreeable, and we left together.

We stopped short of the area and walked on in, spotting a big gobbler with three hens out in the middle of a large remote fenced pasture. We backed up into some scrub pines and scattered brush. Jim found a place about 50 yards from the edge of the fence. I sat about another 15 yards behind Jim. As soon as we were both set, I called on a mouth call. The turkeys were at least 350 yards or more out in that pasture. The gobbler was strutting. We saw him turn and gobble toward us, even though we couldn't hear him, partly because of the wind. They stayed in the same area out in that huge pasture with the gobbler displaying for some time. I got my little slate and peg out, just to see if he could hear it, and called fairly softly, to which he turned and gobbled back toward us again. But we still could not hear him.

We stayed there for almost three hours. Although they had moved our way about 100 yards, they were still a long way out of range. I kept calling softly and purring occasionally. The gobbler kept gobbling until we could finally hear him as well as see him. Two of the hens by this time had moved away. The gobbler now had only one hen with him. I continued to call, and occasionally the gobbler would move closer.

Finally, he ignored the lone hen and began to increase his pace toward us, occasionally stopping to strut. I whispered to Jim that the gobbler was committed. We watched as the gobbler came up to the barbed wire fence, ducked his head, and came under the bottom strand of wire. He walked right straight toward us. Jim killed him at about 30 yards. It was a beautiful gobbler and an excellent occasion to see just how acute their hearing is, as well as their ability to locate precisely where a call originated.

Another sound that gobblers occasionally make can be confusing and is what I call "muffled gobbling." I have

Jim Byford proudly displays a Merriam's gobbler taken in
southeastern Montana.

observed gobblers do this several times, usually when they
have a group of hens with them, but often by themselves
as well. It is difficult enough, especially for those of us with
hearing problems, to determine how far away a gobbler is
when we hear them. But to watch them muffle gobble helps
explain how we sometimes think a gobbler is a long distance
off yet stumble into and spook them trying to get closer.

I first witnessed this in Mississippi many years ago when
blindly in the dark, I got very near a gobbler and a bunch
of hens. They were roosted closely together, and I didn't
realize how close to them I had gotten. After the gobbler

had gobbled several times, I could see him in the tree about 60 yards away when it got light. I could also see several hens even closer.

It was a real show watching those birds stretch and move around on the roost. Then they started flying down into a little open area. The gobbler soon joined them, immediately popping into a strut when he got on the ground. Fortunately, I had a diaphragm call in my mouth. When it did not appear that any of the turkeys were looking my way, I called softly.

Each time the gobbler stretched his neck out and gobbled. Even that close, it was obvious you could not have heard the gobble if the bird had been more than 75 yards away. It was that muffled. I have, however, noticed that when I see them do it, each time their head and neck are directed downward toward the ground. I watched that gobbler strut and muffle gobble a dozen or more times before the hens finally moved away. He followed the hens still in a strut. I tried diligently to follow them, but the gobbler never responded again.

I witnessed muffled gobbling in Tennessee late one morning. I started across a gas line right-of-way about 10:00, that was grown up in tall broom sedge along the top of a ridge. I stopped and called. A loud gobble cut off my call in a hollow to the south. Looking around quickly, I saw a large red cedar tree fairly close to the gas line, and I sort of dove beneath it. It sounded like the gobbler was close. Once set up, I called softly, and he thundered back just over the top of the ridge not 60 yards away.

Getting my gun up on my knee, I watched and soon could hear him drumming on the far side of that gas line. But, I could not see him because of waist-high broom sedge. He moved directly across the gas line from me, not more than 50 feet away, then muffle gobbled twice. I could not see him. He went on over the top of the ridge, still on the gas line, and gobbled again loudly when he was down the hill about 80 yards. Later that morning, I called him back and watched him muffle gobble twice more just out of range but never got a shot at him.

I have observed muffle gobbling by other gobblers and am still not sure how to explain it. I speculate that a gobbler is just trying to get that hen to show herself, especially when he knows he is near where he heard the call. Gobblers toll hens in with either drumming or muffle gobbling, or both. They obviously can regulate the volume when they gobble.

CHAPTER 9

It's More Than the Shooting

Having been observing wildlife since childhood, once I was old enough to appreciate such observations, it became a habit. Mainly, this has been the case regarding turkey hunting. Some of these hunts are remembered better than others, although observations made on other hunts are appreciated as well. A few examples of special turkey hunts that stand out in my memory for various reasons are described below.

One such hunt occurred in about 1980. I flew into Little Rock, Arkansas, rented a car, and drove to our Ouachita Mountains camp. The plan was to hunt with my great friend, Thurman Booth, my dad, and at that time, my brother-in-law, Dan Russell, who had driven over with Dad from Alabama. They arrived the day before and had been scouting to locate gobblers before my arrival late that night. I was glad to be there just after the opening morning of turkey season with my good friend and family. This was to be Dan's first gobbler hunt. Honored to take him, I was delighted when Thurman told me Dan had roosted a gobbler that evening just before dark.

The following day, Dan and I headed to the area, which I knew pretty well, having hunted gobblers there in past years. We stopped the vehicle and walked about a quarter-mile up to a ridge overlooking a deep branch bottom. I asked Dan if he could describe where he thought he heard the bird gobble. He did, and it sounded like the gobbler had roosted about 200 yards from where we were. I suggested to Dan that we wait and see if we could get the turkey to gobble before we went too far and possibly spooked him. We waited anxiously, and after owl-calling, the bird gobbled across the steep branch bottom, about 150 yards up the ridge from where we were. There was no way we were going to be able to get across the steep gully without the gobbler or other birds nearby spooking.

We carefully moved up the side of the ridge and heard a hen yelp behind us, so we sat down. Shortly, I heard three or four hens fly down behind us and start yelping, to which the gobbler answered. I suspected the hens would likely go straight to him—flying or running across the steep gully was no problem for them. As they got closer behind us, continuing to yelp loudly, I got up and walked toward them. Two of them flushed, flew right by me and across to where the gobbler had been gobbling.

We decided the thing to do was get above the gobbler, if at all possible. We then headed up the slope staying on our side of the creek. We stopped, and I occasionally called on a mouth call, and for some time, he answered every call. By the time we got high enough where we were hopefully above him, he had just about quit gobbling.

We circled the mountain. The gobbler answered about every 20 minutes or so when I cut coarsely and yelped loudly. We followed the gobbler across several ridges and hollows for almost two hours. Amazingly, when he gobbled, it appeared he was headed back toward where he had roosted.

Dan was an electrical engineer for the National Aeronautics and Space Administration (NASA) in Huntsville, Alabama. He sure was not used to hiking up and down those mountain ridges, so I knew he was getting tired. When we last heard that gobbler, I told Dan the bird was across a steep gully and branch on a little mound of a ridge, only 200 yards away. If we could get across that gully, I thought we might be able to get close enough to call him in.

We worked our way around the gully until we found a

place we could cross. Then we walked up the rocky branch trying to be quiet until we had gotten below that ridge with the mound above us. By now, it was after 10:00, and I told Dan the gobbler might respond to a call since I had not called for some 30 minutes. Leading, with Dan following closely behind, we started slipping up the point of the ridge.

Almost halfway to the top, I found a great place for Dan to hide. I told him to sit down in front of a big pine tree with some downed brush in front, looking up the slope. I was close enough to whisper to him with me directly behind him on my knees, leaning over his shoulder. Once set, I called fairly softly, and the gobbler responded not more than 80 yards away over the crest. I urged Dan to get his shotgun on his knee and watch up toward the slope's crest.

The gobbler thundered out a gobble, and we could tell he was getting closer. Leaning over Dan's shoulder, I spotted a hen coming toward us. I whispered to Dan not to shoot that it was a hen. Then another hen came down behind the first one. I reminded him not to shoot because they were hens. He whispered back that he didn't see them. What? Could he not see them? It was unbelievable; as looking right over his shoulder, I could see them.

Then, another hen came over and started down, and behind her came the gobbler. He was not in strut, so I whispered to Dan that the gobbler had come over the top and was walking down toward us. He responded that he didn't see him. It was incredible that he could not see them. They were as obvious as a diamond in a billy goat's butt.

The hens came down to about 30 yards above us, turned to our left, and walked down out of sight, one by one, with the gobbler behind. When the gobbler got to where the hens had walked, he paused, and I urged Dan to shoot him. He did not fire, and the gobbler walked over the hill to our left out of sight as well. I called very softly on my mouth call. The gobbler did not answer but walked back up to where he had paused before.

I pleaded with Dan to shoot him, and his response was, "I can't see him." So, at that point, I leaned over as far to my right as possible, and I shot the gobbler. We both jumped up, and as we did, the gobbler's fan raised from where he lay. Dan then said, "Now I see him." To this day, it is still a puzzle to me why he could not see those turkeys. I felt terrible that he didn't get to kill that gobbler, but we had a great hunt.

Fortunately, that afternoon while scouting, I was able to roost five gobblers right at dark in a different area. I knew where we needed to be set up before daylight. Although thunderstorms were predicted, we felt obligated to try to get on these birds, if possible. Sneaking into place well before daylight, we fixed Dan a quick blind. I sat down behind him while thunder rumbled off in the distance. Pretty soon, the gobblers began to sound off. We were well-positioned above them, and I felt they would work uphill after flying down, so we sat and waited.

The gobblers serenaded us as they gobbled while the storm moved closer. They flew down in a little bit, so I started calling. They answered every call, as well as the occasional thunder, for some time. Then, they started working their way up toward us. I instructed Dan to get his gun on his knee and watch to the left. Soon, I saw those cotton-topped skull caps and red wattles coming up over the side of the ridge. Dan saw them as well, and when one of them gave him a good shot, he killed it.

By then, the thunderstorm was almost on top of us. I quickly put my carrying strap on Dan's gobbler, and we started toward his truck. We loaded up and headed to camp, wet but happy that he had killed his first-ever gobbler. Thurman

The Author, John Miller (author's father), and Dan Russell
(author's brother-in-law) with Dan's first turkey.
The Ouachita Mountains in Arkansas, April 1987.

and I had killed gobblers the first morning and Dan on the second. After that storm moved on, Dad and I went back to the general area where those five gobblers were earlier that morning, and we called up one for him. Sadly, Dad passed in 1989, Dan passed in early 2000, and my long-time buddy, Thurman, passed away in December 2019. These memories, and many more, are treasures and a part of my life.

Another special hunt took place late in the season at Quantico when one cool, rainy, and windy morning I came to guide a VIP who had not shown up. Bill Windsor suggested that if I still had a tag, I should hunt and tag out.

A Marine officer named Colonel Wells, who hunted almost every day, was in the place drinking coffee. He had hunted an old gobbler down behind the FBI headquarters quite a bit. After learning he was not hunting that morning due to the nasty weather, I asked if he minded me going after that gobbler. He said emphatically, "No!" and then added, "I sure hope you kill him."

The Colonel suggested starting down behind the headquarters where a branch between two ridges tapered off to a steep gully. I found the head of the gully in the dark and waited for first light. It was still raining or drizzling; the temperature was in the low 40s and very windy. When it finally started getting light, I tried owl-calling, then later crow-cawing, but got no response. I worked my way around and down the southern ridge adjacent to the gully, set up, and called several times. Still no response.

About 9:00, the wind had picked up, was gusting, and so far, I hadn't heard a gobble. By this time, being a little wet and danged cold, I worked my way back toward the head of the ridges on the south side of the gully. Stopping occasionally, I tried several calls, then started crow-cawing like a mob of crows chasing a hawk or owl. As I was finishing up the crow calling, I questioned myself, Was that a gobble at the end of that crow-cawing? Not sure, I called again, stopping abruptly, and I faintly heard a gobble, way down in the gully where it narrowed with steep ridges on both sides.

Quickly, I dropped down toward the little branch, where it flattened out a bit. I found a place to hide and called. Getting an immediate gobble from down the branch boosted my confidence significantly. It was so windy I felt it was necessary to call pretty loud. The third time I called, the turkey gobbled much closer. I stopped calling and waited. In a couple of minutes, I caught a glimpse of a big gobbler working his way up the branch. When he got into good range, I had a clear shot, and I nailed him.

He was a huge bird. At the check station, the gobbler weighed over 24 pounds and sported an 11 ½", hefty beard and 1 ½" spurs. He was an old gobbler. Going over to the natural resource office and meeting place, I found Colonel Wells still there. With some trepidation, I informed him his gobbler was dead. He responded, "I am sure glad you got that bird. He has about worn me out this spring." He added, "I just have one request. Could I step on his head one time for all the frustration he has caused me?" In a way, I hated killing the Colonel's gobbler, but I honestly think he was glad the bird was dead.

Although I have hunted spring gobblers in many states, with varying degrees of success, I have never focused on bag limits as a gauge. I do, however, make sure I never exceed them. However, a hunt shared with Jim Byford in Tennessee in 2016 was exceptional. We first hunted near Kentucky Lake on some property Jim owns there. He went to a nearby property while I stayed there and hunted behind the cabin. I had heard three different gobblers going to roost the evening before.

I wanted to start above them, so I stayed on the peak of the ridgetop. I was very confident of hearing gobblers while setting up to listen and call from that location. As it got light that beautiful morning, nothing gobbled on its own, even though there were barred owls hooting and songbirds singing like crazy.

I waited until well after daylight to make a sound. At first, I crow-cawed, then hen called softly, then loudly, but heard no response. I sat there for almost 45 minutes before deciding those gobblers I'd listened to the evening before must be with hens.

Moving down toward the creek and some gas line right-of-ways to the east, I eased down those steep slopes and stopped after locating a little saddle not too far above the creek with the gas lines still to the east. I called several times and stayed there for 30 minutes or more. I then moved to a couple of other locations and called; however, no gobbler responded.

Since my truck was not far from the top of the ridge, I headed back, but on the way, I decided to go back to my initial setup spot. My makeshift blind was in front of a couple of twin chestnut oak trees and had initially appeared to be sufficient. It was pretty open on the second look, so I took a few minutes and spruced it up. I was determined just to sit there another hour and do some calling. Instead of calling with a mouth call, I got out a glass slate-type pot call and clucked loudly on it. Surprisingly, it was answered immediately by at least two gobblers together from behind me over a ridge.

It was so open on the ridgetop there was no chance of turning around. I waited a minute or two and called again. This time I heard several gobblers. They had moved around that knob to the west and were still over the hill but close. I had my shotgun ready and was expecting to see them coming from my left. Then, I heard them gobble down the ridge below me. There was a thicket of waist-high blueberry bushes between me and those gobblers. They gobbled again closer, and I occasionally could glimpse movement. At about 30 yards, a big white skull cap and red wattles stuck up out of the blueberry bushes, so I shot. He disappeared, but another gobbler's head and neck stuck up and made me wonder if I had missed. The daily limit in Tennessee is one gobbler per day. I was unsure but cautiously stood up and saw three other gobblers run, putt loudly, and fly away. Then the last of the five took off. Walking to where one had stuck his head up, I could see my dead gobbler. I was glad not to have mistakenly shot another one.

Jim had killed a gobbler where he went that morning, so we had some turkey processing to do when we got back to the cabin and traded stories. Jim had to go back home to Martin, Tennessee that night, so I planned to hunt one more day there at the cabin. I listened attentively but didn't hear any gobblers go to roost that evening.

I felt confident that with another beautiful day predicted, they would gobble their heads off the next morning. I hunted until noon that day and never heard nor saw a turkey. After cleaning up the cabin, I loaded my gear and drove to Martin. Jim took me to a place the following day that we had hunted in previous years that always seemed to have gobblers. Dropping me off, he said that he would be hunting several miles away but would pick me up at around 10:30.

As it was getting light, I walked a quarter-mile and stopped at the edge of an opening with huge mature hardwoods that dropped down into a big hollow. I backed into the edge of the woods and cut a few branches to improve my vision of the opening. Before it even got light, I thought I heard a couple of gobblers grumbling, along with a hen cluck or two, almost directly behind me. Two turkeys gobbled behind me in about five minutes and one in the distance to my left.

The next time they started gobbling, it sounded like five different gobblers. As it got lighter, they periodically continued gobbling. I waited for a break in their rhythm and called softly. Only two birds continued to gobble, one just behind me and the one in the distance to my left. Shortly, I heard hens start yelping and moving around in the trees. Then, they started flying out into the opening, directly in front of me.

After several hens had flown down and started milling around, the gobbler flew down to my left. He was far enough over the crest of the opening that I could not see him. I called very softly and heard the gobbler start drumming. He drummed right up over the crest into range. When he got on top of the crest of the opening, I clucked to him, and as he raised his head and neck, I shot him.

Turkeys flew in every direction. Another gobbler flew out of one of the trees behind me. Waiting until they were all out of sight, I then walked out and picked up a beautiful mature gobbler. Placing my carrying strap on him, I walked out to where Jim had dropped me off. I gutted the gobbler, removed the empty crop, and hung him in a red cedar tree where he would be in the shade. I found a comfortable place and took a nap before Jim arrived at about 10:00. He had worked and missed a big gobbler that morning.

The next morning, we went back to the same area. I decided to hunt the distant gobbler I heard the morning before that sounded like a dominant gobbler. Jim dropped me off at the same place. This time I went down and around a 35-year-old pine plantation to a point on that big hardwood ridge near where it sounded like the gobbler had been the previous morning. Looking around, I located a good hiding place from which to see and call. As it got lighter in the east, I heard an old gobbler thunder. He seemed to be less than 200 yards away. Having a good setup, I was reluctant to try to get any closer. That bird gobbled at least 20 times on the roost, and the other bird I had heard some distance away quit gobbling.

Thinking that this was indeed the dominant bird, I called to him one time. It sounded like he turned and gobbled right back at me. Within a minute, he gobbled again and was definitely on the ground. When I yelped softly on my slate call, he cut me off, gobbling almost behind me, definitely to my right. So, shifting slowly to see better in that direction, I soon saw two hens making their way toward me with him behind them in a full strut. I sat there and watched as the hens walked about 25 yards in front of me. Fortunately, they never spotted me.

The gobbler followed about ten yards directly behind the hens. When the turkey got about 25 yards away, I clucked on my mouth call with my shotgun aimed in his direction. When he straightened up, I shot him. It was still very early in the morning, so I placed my carrying strap on him and walked back to the same spot as the day before, stopping at a small pond to gut him. I hung him on the same limb, in the same red cedar I'd used the previous day.

Again, I found a good spot to lie down and take a nap. About 10:00, Jim came driving up. He had killed a nice gobbler too. We then headed back to his place in Martin to process our birds.

That evening, Jim informed me that he had a meeting in Martin the next morning and suggested I go try out a small piece of property he owned. We had deer hunted on it before. He had never heard any birds gobbling there but knew there were some around.

I parked at the gate with some memory of the property line boundaries, not wanting to get on either of the neighboring properties. Gathering my gear, I walked about 350 yards to one of the highest spots on the property, stopped, and sat down on a log until it got light. As it got lighter from the east, I owl-called but did not get a response. I sat there until I heard a crow calling in the distance and started my attempt to sound like crows mobbing something. With this ruckus, I heard some gobbling. I waited a bit before calling again and soon heard four or five different gobblers answer.

None were very close, and I felt pretty sure one was on a neighbor's property, so I headed toward one that seemed to be down in a deep hollow to my right. There was an old dim road that snaked around the top of that ridge. Coming to a small grown-up field, I could see a curve in the road. Beyond the curve, it appeared to open up into another small grown-up field. On either side of that curve, however, the slope dropped off into mature hardwoods. Looking around, I located a good place to see from before calling.

By the time my setup had been completed, three of the birds had continued gobbling. The two I thought were on my left, however, had quit. Calling on a mouth call, I thought I was at least 200 yards from the closest of those gobblers. This time, when they all three gobbled back, it was easy to course their locations. One was definitely to my right, down in the hollow, and one was almost straight in front of me but still some distance away. The other was definitely on the neighbor's property. I felt like all three were on the ground. The one in the hollow to my right was the most vocal. The one in front of me quit gobbling, as did the one on the neighbor's property. I focused my calling toward the bird below and to my right that had gobbled at every call I made.

Fixated on watching to my right, I occasionally glanced back toward the curve in the road. Although the bird to my right was still some distance away, I soon saw a fan coming around the bend in that road. He never gobbled but strutted up and back in that road, once coming close enough for a shot. With my shotgun pointed at him, I considered it, but his head and neck stayed behind some large blackberry canes.

Confident he would come closer, I did not risk the shot.

Now and then, he would go out of sight, but I could faintly hear him drumming, so I stayed put and decided to wait him out. The gobbler to my right had been working his way up the hollow and gobbled. That prompted the gobbler in the road to fold up and walk back the way he came.

I called again, thinking he might return, but the gobbler to my right gobbled very close. It walked out of the woods to the edge of the field, stopped, raised his head, and looked my way, so I shot him. I found that he was at least a four-year-old gobbler with a good beard and spurs. I had not thought about it until walking out with the gobbler and the carrying strap on my shoulder. But that was the fourth mature gobbler I had called up and killed in five days of hunting. The bag limit in Tennessee was four gobblers per spring.

I drove back toward Martin and was in the process of cleaning the gobbler when Jim drove up. I reiterated the morning's hunt, and he seemed very surprised that five gobblers were heard on that property. Later, he told me that he went back a couple of times but never heard a gobble.

CHAPTER 10

Biological Observations

Wild turkeys are native to the North American continent. They also are our largest gallinaceous bird. The various subspecies exist in multiple habitats throughout their range and were abundant before colonization by European settlers. The wealth of wild turkeys for food was first referenced by early Native Americans and later by colonists.

Over time, however, historical records reveal that the elimination of habitat by expanding settlements and over-utilization began to diminish populations. Wild turkey populations, although once abundant, declined, with likely their lowest population level occurring around 1900. A few remnant populations survived in several states, primarily because of the inaccessible wild habitats in which they existed. Those remnant populations served as seed stock when successful restoration efforts were initiated in the late 1950s and early 1960s.

Some brief discussion of just a few of the physical capabilities of the bird, which most turkey hunters likely know, might be insightful at this point. Although weights vary depending on the subspecies and where the bird lives, most adult gobblers weigh 15-22 pounds. Some, however, exceed this by several pounds.

A gobbler can run like a racehorse and, unless flight is necessary, prefers to walk or run. They can, however, fly across rivers or over mountains if required. Their eyesight for distinguishing movement and coloration is legendary and well-deserved. However, to me, their most extraordinary capability is their hearing and ability to determine the precise location where noise or sounds originate. Even though they have no external ears, their ability to distinguish the location of a call is amazing. Many other significant characteristics and capabilities are associated with wild turkey gobblers, like a diversity of vocalizations that others have identified and described.

Turkey hens usually weigh 8-14 pounds and are equally adept at flying and running, and are, of course, vitally essential to the sustainability of the species. Listening to and learning about their habits and vocalizations are critical to a spring gobbler hunter. Some of the capabilities and diverse vocalizations of gobblers and hens may be difficult to understand until you have witnessed and heard them yourself.

As a wildlife biologist and inveterate hunter interested in wild places and wild things since my teenaged years, the more I learn about turkeys, the more I desire to learn. I have always been interested in determining what game species eat and why, and the physiology of their systems to effectively utilize these forage items. Obviously, with any species like the wild turkey, an omnivorous opportunist like many other species, it depends on seasonal availability and production of the food or prey they seek.

Learning through study and observations has certainly aided me in gaining a better understanding of wild turkeys. These efforts include examination techniques I have found helpful and vital in locating the type of habitats they desire during various seasons of the year and understanding why.

One of these observations that I have long been interested in when gobbler hunting is the timing and content of what they have been eating. This is easily done through visual examination of crop and gizzard contents. Turkeys eat an amazing variety of both plant and animal materials, depending on season and availability. With occasional exceptions, based on my examinations, most dominant gobblers in the spring do not usually have a full crop if killed in the morning before about 11:00. Conversely, a gobbler killed afterward, particularly late in the afternoon (unless he is staying with a group of hens), will usually reveal a nearly full to an extended crop of plant and/or animal foods. There are exceptions, of course, and I have killed quite a few gobblers early in the morning whose crops were full. Their digestive system had not operated very efficiently overnight, or they had fed extensively, filling their crop, just before going to roost.

Some examples of unusual crop and or gizzard contents will hopefully explain a part of my naturalist curiosity and how it has helped me better understand some of what I have learned. Many published research and management food habit studies elaborate on the diversity of what has been confirmed by examining turkey crops and gizzards. The variety of materials found is truly amazing.

The following items and examples are just a few of the unusual things I have observed by examining birds harvested. One of the first that comes to mind is a gobbler killed in the Land Between the Lakes (LBL) area in Tennessee back in the early 1970s. A good friend and professional colleague and I were camped in the back of his pickup truck. We only had a couple of days to hunt before I had to make a presentation at the University of Tennessee at Knoxville.

The first morning he went to an area he had previously scouted and heard a gobbler. I went to a different place about a mile away. This was one of those springs when insects and insect larvae were plentiful. There was an overabundance of leaf-eating A Looper (Phigalia titea) larvae (sometimes called linden loopers) throughout the area we were hunting. These pale yellow and green larvae hang down on silken-like threads from oak trees as they are first leafing out and are very abundant for a short time. The area we hunted was infested with these larvae. They were crawling all over anything sitting or standing very long in one place.

Once I got into the area Jim had suggested, I waited until it started getting light. The whip-poor-wills began to quieten down as it got nearer to daylight, and after owl calling a couple of times, a gobbler responded. Moving closer, I realized that he was roosted below the ridge I was on, about 150 yards away near a small stream.

In this area of predominantly mature hardwoods, the understory was quite open. So, I found a large oak tree where I had a good view down the slope. Not wanting to spook the gobbler or any other turkeys that might be nearby, I did not move around much trying to fashion a blind. He gobbled several more times from the roost, and I heard some hens relatively near him, so I expected it might be a long morning.

Once the gobbler flew down and gobbled on the ground, I waited about a minute and called to him by clucking and yelping very softly. When he virtually cut me off gobbling, it was time to get quiet and listen for a bit. Occasionally, hearing a hen call, I would cluck back, and he would gobble, but he and those hens stayed near that little stream for quite some time. Whether I called or not, he would periodically gobble. This went on for some time, so I quit calling for about ten minutes to see what the gobbler did. After that wait, I called softly, purred on a slate call, and he gobbled closer. He had crossed that little stream yet was still down the ridge. Expecting to see him work his way up the ridge, I turned slightly in that direction.

The next sound I heard was someone else calling to him on the other side of where he had earlier roosted, but he did not gobble. Not being sure if it was another hunter or just a weird-sounding hen, I sat quietly and soon heard that call again. The turkey did not gobble at that call either. After about ten minutes of silence, I clucked softly, and he gobbled closer than where he had been the last time. Almost immediately afterward, I heard a turkey take flight and watched as the gobbler flew right across in front of me about 20 yards away. Although tempted to shoot but not wanting to cripple him possibly, I just sat and watched him as he flew by and over the ridge.

Those looper larvae almost entirely covered me by this time, so I stood up and started brushing them off my clothing. Shortly, another hunter came walking up the ridge. He apologized for trying to get too close and spooking the gobbler when he knew someone else was calling to him. I asked him if he would be hunting that afternoon, and he responded, "no," that he had to work. Walking back to camp, I considered going somewhere else that afternoon. However, knowing there was a gobbler where I had just been, I decided to go back there.

Jim and I arrived back at camp about 11:30, ate lunch, and Jim mentioned the abundance of those larvae and wondered if turkeys ate them. I responded that I was not sure but did not see why they wouldn't. Admittedly, to that time, I had never found them in a turkey crop. About 2:30 that afternoon, Jim headed back where he had worked a gobbler that morning, and I went back to the area I had previously hunted.

I slipped back into the area cautiously, moving around on top of the ridge, and calling sparingly in hopes of getting a bird to gobble. I purposely stayed above the little stream at the bottom. Hearing no gobbles and with the suspicion that he might roost along that stream somewhere, I decided to play a hunch and set up on one of the ridges above the creek.

Assembling a small natural blind, I sat down about 4:30 with the crest of the ridge to my right, hoping maybe to hear the gobbler fly up or gobble before going to roost. Calling softly twice, in the next ten minutes or so, I heard a muffled ffst-vroom sound to my right. Looking out my mask, I saw a gobbler about 25 yards away, drumming down toward the stream on the crest of the ridge. When he went behind a fallen oak limb, I moved around a little to the right and got my shotgun pointed in front of the oak limb. When he strutted on out from behind that limb, I clucked to him; when he raised his head and neck, I shot.

As usual, when I kill a gobbler in hot weather, and there is water nearby, I try to remove the intestines and crop before carrying the bird out. Among items I always carry in my vest are a few large plastic zip-lock bags for carrying the heart, liver, gizzard, and testes.

Picking the gobbler up, I could see and feel the swollen crop. Upon getting to the stream, I quickly slit through the breast sponge and removed the crop intact. It was bulging with those A Loopers. I placed the crop and its contents in one plastic bag, the heart, liver, gizzard, and testes in another, and removed the rest of the intestines and lungs.

Because we had to go to the University of Tennessee at Knoxville the next day, I placed the crop on ice until we got there. I hoped that we might locate someone from the

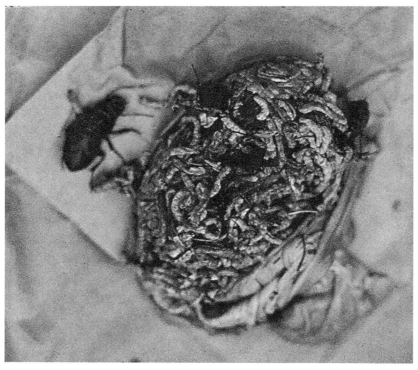

Linden Loopers larvae in gobbler's crop.

entomology department who would count the number of larvae and other contents in that crop. When I got back to the camp, Jim had killed a gobbler as well, so we processed both birds and got the meat, crop, organs, and bulging crop on ice.

The next day, we drove to Knoxville, and on arriving at the University, we carried the bag with the crop into the entomology department. After explaining to the professor what it was and where it came from, I asked if he could have someone count and send me a note telling me how many larvae were jammed into the crop. He consented and about a week later sent me a note stating that there were 910 A Loopers, two spiders, three katydids, and four crickets in the crop. Like most opportunistic predators, that gobbler had easily picked up these readily available larvae and insects earlier that day in his travels.

Years later, I took my dad to an area in southwest Arkansas for a few days of turkey hunting, where my friend Thurman and I had a camp. We were lucky, and each killed a bird early the first morning. On examining the crops of those birds, they only had a few acorns, a small amount of green grass, and some objects that looked like acorns but were not. There were two unknown objects in one bird and six in the other, so I put them into a small container for later study to see if I could determine what they were.

I speculated that the turkeys were picking these up, thinking they were acorns similar in size and color to southern red oak acorns. Being employed then by the University of Arkansas, I contacted the head of the entomology department. I had done some cooperative work with him and asked if he could tell me what they were. He said to send about four of them, and he would get back in touch with me. He sawed one of them in half and sent me a photo that revealed several tiny white grubs/larvae. He identified them as Cynipid Wasp Galls. I doubt that the turkeys knew these contained wasp larvae.

The galls had a tough outer shell, but a turkey's gizzard can quickly grind up such materials in a matter of hours, even objects as hard as pignut hickory nuts.

Numerous other crop and gizzard contents were examined containing unusual objects, such as a nice gobbler I killed on a large property in Mississippi one spring. When I began to clean and skin the gizzard, I observed a shiny white object inside that I assumed to be a soybean. Taking my knife and turning it over, I saw a shirt collar button that I presumed the turkey thought was grit when he picked it up. Once while hunting in the Nebraska pine ridge area just north of the Niobrara River, when cleaning the gizzard of a gobbler killed there, I found a .22 rimfire short hull the gizzard had almost ground up, except for the rim.

The green stink bug resurrection story, however, is one worth pondering. My wife's nephew Jim Brooks and I were hunting in the mountains of Jackson County, Alabama, in an area called Paint Rock Valley. Several days before I arrived, Jim had been at the cabin we used for a camp in a valley between two large ranges of steep mountains. This had enabled him to pinpoint several gobblers based on listening to them gobble from the cabin's front porch. He had seen one of them that he described as being huge.

Being familiar with the "lay of the land," so to speak, Jim said the big gobbler usually started gobbling near a flat knob about three-fourths of the way to the top of the mountain. A long-abandoned cemetery was located on the flat knob, with a dim road curving its way to the top of the mountain. Jim also said that he had heard a turkey gobble in that general area often, so we decided to go there the following morning.

We made it to the old cemetery well before daylight and hoped we hadn't spooked the gobbler or other turkeys on our way up. Looking around, it seemed logical that we needed to get Jim set up within shotgun range of that old road. There were some red cedars and black locust trees nearby. We made Jim a natural blind in which to sit. Because of the terrain and vegetation, I wanted to be behind Jim up a bit of slope about 30 yards away. I found a good place hidden from the direction we thought the gobbler would come and sat down.

After the songbirds began singing, along with some barred owls and crows, the turkey gobbled directly in front of us. He was over the top of the knoll, maybe 150 yards away, down the steep face of the mountain. We also heard a gobbler behind where I had sat down, but our focus was on the gobbler in front of Jim.

Feeling confident about our setup, we waited until the two birds broke their gobbling rhythm. I clucked and tree-yelped. Both turkeys gobbled. The next time the bird in front of us gobbled he was on the ground, not very far over the face of the knoll. At the next two calls I made, the gobbler cut me off, quickly responding. I was confident he was coming. Soon, he gobbled just over the crest of the knoll. Suddenly, there he was. It was like an apparition coming out of the ground and directly toward the old curving road in full strut.

He stopped and gobbled again at about 75 yards. The gobbler up behind us didn't respond. Although unable to continuously see the gobbler in front of Jim, when he was visible, what impressed me was the width and length of the beard. He slowly worked his way toward the road. Once he got there, he popped back into a strut and paraded back and forth, getting closer and closer to where Jim was sitting. There was no need to call at that point. I sat and waited for the shot. But, for whatever reason, Jim didn't think he had a good clear shot.

Some hens started calling down over the crest of the knoll. The gobbler folded up and walked directly back to the edge and over the crest. After that, the gobbler wouldn't answer a call, and in about ten minutes, I walked down to Jim, asking why he had not shot.

After hearing his explanation and decision not to take a risky shot, we decided to find him a better view of the road and make a blind hoping that we might call that gobbler back later. We were both amazed about the length and width of that gobbler's beard. Honestly, I don't think either of us had a lot of hope that we could call him back to that old road, but it was worth a try.

Moving back to our previous setups, after about 15 minutes, I called. The gobbler we had heard up the mountain behind me earlier had moved closer, and he gobbled. Waiting a few more minutes before calling again, he did not gobble, but I could faintly hear him drumming. As the drumming got closer, I slowly turned my head to the right. There he was, about 35 yards above me, in a full strut. As he turned his fan toward me, I slowly moved my shotgun to my left shoulder. As he turned back around, so his head and neck were visible, I clucked with my mouth call. When he straightened up to look in my direction, I shot him.

Jim came on up and told me that was a great shot. After discussing it, we decided to stay there and wait a while, hoping the big gobbler might return to his strutting area along the road. I knew there was a little drain containing water that went down the mountain some 200 yards away. I told Jim we should go over there and gut this turkey so that it would cool. Then we could return to our previous spots and sit and call to see if we could get that big gobbler to come back.

After getting to the small stream of water coming down from a spring on top of the mountain, I opened the gobbler up just below the bottom of the breast, removing the intestines and organs. Then, I slit through the breast sponge and removed the crop. I wanted to see if he had eaten anything that morning. After removing it, I slit it open, revealing an old acorn, a few grass leaves, and a green stink bug. Using the point of my knife and turning that stink bug over, it started moving its legs. We sat there and watched as it progressively began moving around, and ultimately it walked out of that crop! That gobbler must have just eaten the stink bug shortly before I shot him, and the stink bug had experienced a resurrection opportunity.

After washing the parts I wanted to save and putting them into a plastic bag, I removed three baseball-sized stones from the bottom of the spring-fed stream. Those were placed inside the gobbler for cooling off the breast meat.

We were going back up toward the old cemetery discussing where we felt Jim should sit. Then, we found him an old stump about 20 yards from the curve in the road and assembled a natural blind. Going back up to where I had been earlier, I found a shady place on a rock to place the gobbler and covered him with some red cedar branches.

At that point in the day, about 10:15, we waited for about ten minutes, and I called a couple of times. At the second call, a turkey gobbled down over the knoll crest in front of us. Then, shortly, he gobbled closer and appeared suddenly, coming over the crest of that knoll. It was the same big gobbler with the paint-brush beard, and he was alone!

He strutted across that knoll directly to the road and began drumming up and along that road right in front of where I thought Jim was. I enjoyed the exhibition that old gobbler was putting on and expected to hear Jim shoot any time. After some delay… "KABOOM!" then putt, putt, putt, and with wings flapping loudly, we watched him take flight over the side of the mountain. It was hard for me to believe that Jim had missed him when he was so close.

Jim showed up on the road; I joined him and asked what happened. He said he had no idea as he thought he had it right on the gobbler's head and neck when he shot. We looked carefully for any sign of a hit, and there were no feathers nor blood, so I asked Jim where he was sitting when he shot?

He had moved while I was getting set to what he thought was a better spot. When I looked there, I found a red cedar limb an inch in diameter that, although not in his line of sight, was right in front of the muzzle of his shotgun. It had taken the full charge of Jim's shot, leaving the gobbler unscathed but scared. We were both sorely disappointed. Yet, we had enjoyed a wonderful morning of hunting action and had the privilege of observing that huge gobbler and the resurrection of a green stink bug.

Many years ago, I hunted in the Catskill Mountains of New York several times with a professional colleague and friend, Mike Zagata. At that time, Mike was Commissioner of the New York Department of Environmental Conservation. We stayed as guests at a premier trout fishing lodge that had a substantial amount of property. Some of the property was mature timber, but a good bit was grown-up pastureland. The first evening after arriving at the lodge and meeting other hunters and guests, we determined where we would hunt before dinner.

We had a little time, and as it was just getting dark, I walked out back where a steep mountain rose behind the lodge. Owl-calling, I stimulated a bird at the top of the mountain to gobble. Since we had already planned to hunt another area a few miles away the following day, I simply filed in my memory where I heard that turkey gobble.

Our plans were for me to call for Mike the first morning. We heard a couple of gobblers on a misty, drizzling morning but couldn't seem to get either of them cranked up. We kept moving around and calling and finally got one response. He was not too far from the edge of where the mature timber started, so we found a place near the edge to set up. I began calling, and at the second call, the bird gobbled. The gobbler came out of the mature timber and moved down into the old grown-up pasture below us before working his way back up in our direction. He finally came into view about 30 yards away, and Mike killed him.

We admired the bird, talked about the hunt for a few minutes, and then, being wet, decided to take Mike and his bird back to the lodge. On the way there, I began thinking about getting up the mountain behind the lodge to see if that gobbler I had heard the evening before was still around.

After locating an old road that headed up in the right direction, I drove up as far as possible until it ended at an old home place. I hoped that it was not too far from where I had heard the gobbler the evening before. It had started raining a little heavier now, so I put rain gear back on and started walking toward the peak of the mountain.

After walking a few hundred yards uphill, I could see the top of the ridge. Moving upward, I found myself on a predominantly beech and sugar maple hillside. After looking around a bit, I soon found a small opening, and with virtually no understory cover in those mature woods, I located a large maple and sat down. The opening was about 25-30 yards downhill, and after sitting down, I noticed beech nuts all over the ground. Most of these were beginning to sprout. Waiting a bit as it continued to rain steadily, I called a few times on my mouth call but got no response.

After about half an hour and hearing nothing but the rain falling on my rain gear, I had that feeling that something was looking at me. I slowly looked to my left out the side of my face mask as far as I could turn my head but saw nothing. Then turning slowly to the right, I finally could see out the corner of my face mask. A big gobbler was standing and looking down toward the opening below me, about 40 yards up behind me. All I could do at this point was freeze in place, not move, and wait and hope that he would somehow work himself into range. Not being well hidden, I feared he would spot me and spook.

After what seemed like 20 minutes, I could see him walking downward, out the right corner of my face mask. He passed by me almost within arm's reach. My trepidation was that he would surely spot me and spook before I could get a shot at him. Amazingly, he walked right by me, never looking around, apparently focused on that opening.

After reaching the edge of the opening, the gobbler popped into a strut. With his fan in my face and his vision obscured, I got my shotgun to my shoulder undetected. When he stepped forward a few yards and raised up out of a strut to look around, I dropped him.

I shook the rain off of my gear, noticing it was 11:30. I walked down, placed my carrying strap on the big gobbler, and headed back to the lodge. Later, when I started processing the gobbler and removing his crop, I noticed it was bulging with beechnuts. I later counted these and found that he had 122 mostly sprouted beech nuts that he had eaten that morning which surprised me!

I have learned other biological observations of how quickly a gobbler's emotional state can change. While displaying vivid red, white and blue coloration on the neck and head, it can change immediately to a dull gray for various reasons. The changing coloration of their head and neck and their actions are a direct influence of some stimuli. When you can observe this change in coloration, it helps determine what might happen next, and often they don't tarry long if it is because they have been spooked.

Several years back, I guided a couple of hunters/clients at Vermejo Park Ranch in northeast New Mexico. Both these guys were younger than me but relatively robust in size. From the first hunt, it became evident they could not climb up the mountains, primarily due to the altitude and their physical condition. Therefore, I had to plan accordingly and locate birds in the canyon floors or nearby meadows that we could hunt.

The first morning we tried to work a gobbler on the side of a mountain, but he did not want to come down, and my clients could not climb far enough up for us to call to him effectively. Fortunately, we spotted a gobbler that was alone that afternoon, but he just would not come close enough for a good shot.

After the gobbler departed, I suggested we drive on up the canyon and try to find another bird. We drove maybe a half-mile and took a dim road going up out of the side canyon. After about one-quarter mile, I spotted two gobblers and some hens about 250 yards up the side of the mountain in a small meadow.

The turkeys did not seem to have noticed the truck, so I backed it down the old road out of sight over a bit of hump. The two clients quickly gathered their gear, and we headed up to see if we could get one of those gobblers to respond to calling. There was a little branch with running water that paralleled the road, and we were able to slip along, out of sight, getting almost directly below the birds.

Once we were across the branch but still well below these birds, we could see them most of the time. A good bit of scrub oak brush was scattered not too far above the branch, so we crawled up using the oak brush as a visual barrier. After finding a couple of places where my clients could sit and see the birds if they came down, I moved down behind one of the men to call.

My first call was a loud one on a mouth call and watching through binoculars. I could see one of the birds turn and gobble. After waiting maybe five minutes, I called again, saw one of the birds gobble, and watched as the hens began moving down from the meadow.

The hens were maybe 15 yards ahead of the gobblers. We could see them occasionally as they worked their way around the oak brush. As they got closer, we could see a dominant bird strutting and the subdominant bird walking behind him, following four hens. I motioned to the two guys to stay where they were sitting and stay still because the turkeys were coming right down toward us. They got the message.

Sixty yards up the hill from where we were set up, there was a little open flat spot with some oak brush in front of it. There was also some brush to the right of it. The turkeys came down and stopped on the little flat area.

The dominant gobbler was resplendent with his blood-red wattles, brilliant blue head, and neon white skull cap. He certainly put on a display for those hens and us. The subdominant bird would occasionally go into about a half-strut before slicking down and watching. The hens seemed oblivious to the dominant gobbler's active displaying.

Calling softly, the hens looked my way, but they, too, stayed on that little flat, pecking and feeding. At that point, they were so close that I chose not to do a lot of calling for fear of them getting spooked before coming into range.

This displaying just out of range went on for about another 20 minutes. I decided to see if the hens could be called away from the gobbler as he was unlikely to leave the hens. I changed calling tactics to just clucking softly and purring. If they could be enticed to come closer, the gobbler would follow. Since both clients were sitting where they could see the turkeys if they came down off that little flat, I slid backward down toward the branch and started a soft cluck and whine routine.

Two of the hens slowly started down our way, but the other two stayed with the gobblers. Sliding backward a little further, I continued the clucking and whining sequence. After that, the other two hens came around the oak brush. The gobbler, still displaying brilliantly, suddenly realized that his hens had departed. His head and neck immediately turned from red, white, and blue to a dull gray.

He came out of a strut and followed, walking around the oak brush down into range where one of the clients shot him at about 25 yards, just before he was about to go into strut again. Unfortunately, the other client could not get a good shot at the subdominant bird, so he passed on taking a risky shot.

The next morning in another canyon, we stopped the truck with these same two clients after driving down the canyon about one-half mile. We all got out to listen just as it began to get light. We must have heard 20 gobblers, but all of them were roosted high up on the sides of the mountains. We waited and listened for a while. I heard a gobbler near the edge of the canyon. Moving down in that direction, I stopped the truck about 300 yards back, got out quietly, and listened.

He gobbled again and was up in a tight little cove not too far from the canyon edge. One of the clients felt like he could climb with me if we took our time, so we headed up to get above the gobbler. After about 15 minutes, we were above that little side cove.

I found him an excellent place to sit, and I began to call. The turkey immediately gobbled back. He seemed to be walking back and forth along the other side of that cove but would not come any closer. After about 30 minutes, we decided to go on up the canyon and find another gobbler.

We soon spotted a strutting gobbler with some hens down in the canyon floor, so I told one of the guys to get out of the truck while we were in a gully. Then after backing the truck up so that it would remain out of sight, the two of us started working our way along the edge of the woods to a closer calling spot. Within about 300 yards from this group of birds and across the open canyon floor, we found a place to sit and started calling.

Once we got set up and started calling, another gobbler on our side of the canyon began gobbling at every call and soon came into view. He came on up the canyon about a hundred yards, getting closer and occasionally strutting, until he got into range, and the client shot him. Then, driving up the canyon, we didn't spot any more gobblers. Since we just needed one more gobbler for those guys to be limited out, I decided to go back to where we had worked the first gobbler.

We turned around, drove back to within a quarter of a mile, parked the truck, and the client who still needed a bird joined me. We took our time and worked our way upward to get above where the gobbler had been before. Getting reasonably close, we located a parallel ledge around the side of that mountain and followed it to where we wanted to stop and set up. We looked for a good setup for him and found one about 30 yards back from the edge of that cove. I dropped down below him so that I could see partially down into the cove. Once in place, I called and immediately was answered by a gobble. Watching and realizing he wasn't very far down below us, I called softly. The next movement I saw was that gobbler with red wattles flashing through the oak brush as he ran straight up that steep hillside toward us. Motioning to the client, I pointed out where he should have his gun aimed and that the gobbler was coming fast. I saw him shoulder his shotgun. That gobbler popped up not 30 yards from the edge of the steep ridge, stopped to look for the hen, and the client nailed him.

Talk about a quick hunt and a complete change of emotions by a gobbler. Earlier he would not budge from his strut zone, yet an hour or two later, he almost ran us over after I called just twice to him. My speculation on this is that he had some hens with him earlier and didn't want to leave them. Later, however, finding himself alone, he ran straight up that steep ridge.

An examination of gobbler crop and gizzard contents, where fall hunting is allowed, is also enlightening. Depending on the time of day the gobbler is killed, it may show a much greater diversity of vegetative matter and insects. Over the years, such examinations have revealed seeds and fruits of various plants, trees, and animal matter. Of course, where croplands are available to turkeys, they will eat waste grain not harvested.

Some turkey crops examined where food plots are within their range often reveal clover blossoms and leaves and other available grass leaves. Some people plant chufas, which turkeys love to scratch up and eat.

Out west, Merriam's gobblers taken in afternoon spring hunts have often revealed a crop full of dandelion greens, heads, and blooms, as they are among the first plants to green up in the spring. This reminds us again that turkeys are opportunistic omnivores when it comes to food items. It is worth a little effort and close examination to explore these biological observations.

Another biological observation worth checking out is the hormonal advancement of the testes in spring. Often, when the peak of the gobbling season is later than usual, I have noted in looking at the testes that they sometimes will only be about the size of the end of your little finger, roughly jelly bean-sized. In addition, the coloration will be pale yellowish-green. In contrast, if it appears that the peak of the season is early, most dominant gobbler testes will be bright yellow and swollen to about the size of the last joint of your thumb or larger.

Often, if two people are hunting together and a dominant and subdominant gobbler come in together, and both are killed, the subdominant bird's testes will not be as bright and yellow as the dominant bird's testes are. This doesn't necessarily imply that these birds will not gobble or come to the call. It can, however, alert the hunter that later in the season is likely to be better hunting with more gobbling, breeding, and nesting activity.

The gobbler testes are located internally, tucked into an area above the intestines just under the point of the breast bone up next to the backbone. If you have never eaten turkey testes butterflied, battered, and fried (also called turkey fries), you have missed a real gourmet treat. This is especially true if you have found some morel mushrooms and fried these up to go with the turkey fries.

Note: Most turkey processing plants usually sell these if you know what to ask for. But don't ask for butter balls; ask for turkey fries.

CHAPTER 11

Trophies or Memories?

Some turkey hunting purists reading the following will likely disagree strongly with my opinion of what makes a trophy gobbler. Any gobbler taken in a fair-chase hunt that gobbles to and or responds to my call is a trophy. Whether it is a mature, long-spurred, long-bearded old gobbler or a jake with a four-inch beard, to me, it is a trophy.

Admittedly, it is illegal to kill a gobbler in my present home state that doesn't have at least a six-inch beard. With that being the regulation, we don't shoot jake gobblers in Mississippi. However, in other states where it is legal to take a jake, I have no regrets and make no excuses as those jake gobblers sure do make great meals. A little explanation, though, might help those who get upset at the idea of killing a jake gobbler.

Over the years dating back to the late 1960s I worked at planning out my annual leave to hunt a few days with friends or colleagues in other states. Some years this has enabled me to hunt ten or more states in the spring.

These hunts usually start in the south, then move north and west as the seasons open later. That means, except for my home state, buying a non-resident hunting license in every one of those states is necessary. This gets expensive and might be considered prohibitive as these non-resident licenses range from about $175 to almost $400 annually.

Fortunately, my wife is both tolerant and forgiving, and she understands that those fees are used to manage and sustain wildlife in those other states. She is also aware of how much these spring hunts with friends and colleagues are enjoyed and treasured.

Regarding harvesting jake gobblers, sometimes when a jake gobbler comes to my call and is killed, there may have been only a couple of days available to hunt. It is certainly appreciated when some very nutritious and organic meat is taken home or shared with those in camp. Others who enjoy such meals are the landowners if hunting on private land.

Further, most population studies have shown that adult gobblers are more likely to be killed during the spring season than are jakes. In addition, as most turkey hunters know, there will be a few days to a week, sometime during the season, when the hens are going to stay with the gobblers all day long. They do very little gobbling during this time when they have a harem of hens and stay with the group during that peak of the breeding season.

In travels from state to state, if you are there for just a few days during those peak periods, you are likely to hear very little gobbling from mature birds. If you are able to watch a gobbler with hens, you may see subdominant gobblers following them around, hoping for a chance to breed one of the hens if the boss gobbler's attention gets diverted. Even these subdominant gobblers are reluctant to gobble much during this peak breeding period.

Although fortunate to have killed a good many large, long-bearded, and long-spurred gobblers over the years, my motivation has never tempted me to enter one in the National Wild Turkey Federation's (NWTF) record book. However, in earlier years, a few prizes were won from local sporting goods stores for checking the biggest turkey that season. This was when you had to take a turkey to an official check station personally. Most states now rely on either mail-in, online, or phone check systems. As stated earlier, admittedly, I am very opinionated and likely will be considered a dinosaur by some who consider my justifications.

For those who obtain satisfaction from having their name associated with killing a record-book turkey, that is their choice. It reminds me that people who know I have turkey hunted for a long time often ask me, "How many turkeys have you killed?"

They seem surprised when my answer is that I honestly do not know. Earlier in my hunting days, I kept count for a few years. Yet when people would ask me to tell them the number, I would observe their reaction and sometimes be concerned by their response. They either perceived me to be a game hog, poacher, or bald-faced liar.

Since those early days, I have not kept count and have no idea how many gobblers have been called up and killed. Over the past 55 to 60 years, I can remember a few springs when I killed 11 to 14 gobblers. This did not include those called for family members, colleagues, friends, or clients. My memories are not of the numbers of birds killed, but the hunts, either alone or with someone else. Recalling those experiences, observations, and times shared with others is what's important.

CHAPTER 12

Mistakes, We All Make Them

A classic example of gobblers getting spooked occurred in north Alabama with my wife's nephew Jim Brooks and his friend Keith Jennings. The circumstances were unusual since we got the bird into range yet failed to get a shot. We tried to work a couple of gobblers early. I was along to do the calling but could not pull the gobblers away from their hens.

We had, however, heard a gobbler several times on another mountainside about a half-mile away. So, about 9:30, we started up the mountain, following an old dim logging road toward where we thought we had last heard him. After getting about 300 yards up the mountain with Jim and Keith behind me, I caught a glimpse of some turkeys. They were directly up that steep face of the mountain about 80 yards above us. I motioned quickly for Jim and Keith to stop and get down to the ground. Crawling over to them, I told them that there was a gobbler and several hens above us on a little flat ledge. We located a good place for Jim to set up with Keith close below him but on the other side of the old road.

Sliding down the hill from them, I planned to call and see if we could pull the turkeys into range. After the first soft call on my little slate, the gobbler turned and gobbled down toward us. However, the gobbler and hens stayed pretty much in the same area on that flat ledge, with him continuing to strut. Moving further down the mountain, I called again, this time a little louder.

The gobbler responded and, with a couple of hens, moved down among some large boulders on the right side of the road. They slowly started moving downward, adjacent to the old road. Jim had his gun on his knee and aimed toward the gobbler, which was close by now. I could see both guys, the gobbler and three of the hens. The gobbler and one hen moved closer.

I expected to hear Jim shoot any time when suddenly, the hen closest to the gobbler sort of ran her neck out and froze in place. She was very alert, with her neck stretched out, and head pointed down like she had spotted something. I noticed Jim trying to do something with his shotgun when the hen and gobbler suddenly broke and ran back up over the hill, as did the other hens. I sat still for a couple of minutes, then called again, but got no response. After a few minutes more, I walked up to Jim. Keith had already moved toward him as well.

Truly puzzled, I asked Jim what had happened. He had forgotten to chamber a shell in his semi-auto before sitting down. When he attempted to shoot the gobbler, all it did was click on an empty chamber. That is likely when the hen went on point and, as Jim tried to chamber a live shell, they both spotted the movement, became alarmed, and fled. Keith, too, was frustrated because as the birds got close to Jim, he could not see the gobbler due to some large boulders.

Regardless, it can happen to anyone and happened to me one morning in Tennessee when hunting with my friend Jim Byford on some timber company land. I had not hunted the area before, but Jim had, so we drove by it on a public road the afternoon after buying our permits. Jim showed me where he would park and a place about a quarter-mile up the road where I could enter by climbing up a steep road bank to the ridge. The next morning, we arrived well before daylight. Jim went into the woods where we had parked. After getting my gear out, I thought that since I would be walking up a public road for a quarter-mile, my shotgun probably should not be loaded until I got up in the woods.

Walking to my entry spot, I climbed up a steep road bank and walked about 80 yards up the hill to a flat spot. I got my face mask and gloves and put them on before walking up the ridge another 100 yards with my shotgun slung on my shoulder. It had started getting light, and a few birds were singing, so I stopped and owl-called. Two gobblers answered. One was not far away across a hollow and on the east side of a ridge near the top. The other was up the ridge above and behind me on the east side of the ridge.

I dropped down into some brush on the side of the ridge, found a good place to sit, and listened to those two gobblers for the next ten minutes or so before calling softly. Both gobblers responded. The one across the hollow from me flew down, and although not able to see him fly, I knew from the sound that he flew down toward me when he gobbled again. I waited a bit, then called softly, and he gobbled down in the bottom of the hollow.

Placing my shotgun on my knee, I soon caught a glimpse of him as he partially hopped and flapped across the little branch at the bottom of the hollow. He then disappeared behind some brush and briars before appearing directly in front of me, just out of range but closing. He moved up the side of the ridge a bit and stopped about 30 yards away, and when I pulled the trigger, all that could be heard was the click.

I realized immediately that in my effort to be cautious, I had forgotten to load my shotgun. The gobbler was alerted at the click but didn't spook. I attempted to open my shotgun and put shells in the chambers as he moved up the ridge and out of sight. Once the gun was loaded, I stood up, hoping to see him again, but he was gone. A lesson not forgotten. I learned that before you call to a turkey, have your shotgun loaded!

If you are a hunter and it has never happened to you, that is great. But I suspect Jim and I are not the only ones who had forgotten to load our firearms before we started hunting.

CHAPTER 13

Hunting Ethics

Admittedly, not everyone will agree about hunting ethics. That is certainly their prerogative, but to me, it is a very personal and necessary commitment. The best description of ethics I know was written by Aldo Leopold in *A Sand County Almanac* back in the 1940s. It reads:

"A peculiar virtue in wildlife ethics is that the hunter ordinarily has no gallery to applaud or disapprove of his conduct. Whatever his acts, they are dictated by his own conscience, rather than a mob of onlookers. It is difficult to exaggerate the importance of this fact. Voluntary adherence to an ethical code elevates the self-respect of the sportsman, but it should not be forgotten that voluntary disregard of the code degenerates and depraves him."

It would be lying if I said that I did not make mistakes in my younger days and often failed to consider hunting ethics. After reconsideration, I was reminded not to make those again. On growing older and becoming more experienced, my ethical code, based on a better understanding of Leopold's quote above, has helped me pass that code forward. It has been especially critical to get that message understood and adhered to by my sons and grandson and hopefully, by example, with friends and colleagues with whom I have hunted.

The hunting ethics a person adopts are dependent on their attitude toward being responsible for their actions, good or bad. It depends on how they value the experience, the appreciation they have for the game they are pursuing, their concern, if any, about the sustainability of the species, and respect, or lack thereof, for what is considered fair chase.

In discussing my ethics about hunting, most of these mentioned are responsibilities determined after much personal thought and consideration. For example, some activities like hunting over feed or bait may be perfectly legal within some respective state wildlife agencies' regulatory declarations, yet not for me. Even if declared legal, that does not make it ethical according to my code.

Although absolutely my ethical guidelines, this does not mean they condemn or are intended to criticize others who hunt according to published regulations. It is, however, a personal decision that everyone who hunts, fishes, or traps should take time to consider seriously for their own benefit and satisfaction.

It is essential to conduct myself ethically, whether hunting alone, with family, professional colleagues, or friends. Hopefully, they have developed their own ethics and are willing to take responsibility for their actions. My primary question about hunting any wildlife over bait or supplemental feed is why you would hunt an animal you love in a manner that you know is not fair chase? Such disrespect for the quarry, in my opinion, degenerates and depraves one's conduct.

Changing gears, I have hunted pretty much across most of North America and on several other continents. It has been my privilege to harvest game species ranging from the size of a mourning dove to a greater kudu to a moose and virtually every other game considered suitable for fair chase hunting and eating. All of these hunts were enjoyable, enlightening, and memorable. For most of my adult years, however, the challenge of hunting wild turkey gobblers in the spring became my most intense passion. Throughout my working years, spring gobbler hunting is what my annual leave was primarily saved for.

The following observations, stories, events, and memories are not chronological nor cited by exact location, primarily because I failed to record them. They are, however, actual examples of real hunts, observations, camaraderie, and ethical experiences remembered over the past 60-plus years. Throughout these and many other unmentioned hunts and events, the desire to learn has drawn me closer to understanding the depth of these observations. What is currently being seen, felt, heard, smelled, and otherwise experienced is what keeps me focused. Becoming a naturalist requires being alert constantly and focused on what is happening within the environment, and remaining eager to learn as a participant. Hunting and the studies of wild places and wild things are essential elements of my being. Some would consider them frivolous and undisciplined. Others would argue that they are, without question necessary, require great discipline and are responsibilities that many people today have never considered.

With that said, my focus will be directed toward observations made while spring gobbler hunting. Although similar observations have been made during hunting, trapping, and angling for other species, it would be impossible to describe them all in one book.

The following observations are an integral part of my effort to share why turkey hunting became a true passion. The emphasis on this magnificent game bird in no way belittles the passion others have for other species. As I continued to learn more about them, it increased my appreciation and respect for the quarry. It further increased my determination to only do it based on personal ethical convictions, with often no audience to cheer me on or admonish me. It reminded me that my conscience would guide me forward when hunting alone with no referee but the Almighty looking on. That personal conviction has constantly reminded me that integrity is what we do when no one else is looking.

Some brief explanations about spring gobbler hunting follow. There are significant differences from state to state about specific regulations regarding what is not legal in that respective state. It is vital when you plan to hunt other states to obtain a copy of the state wildlife agency regulations well ahead of time and adhere to these laws. For example, some states require early applications for permits; the bag limit of birds that can be taken is different, and most states have early youth hunts before starting the season for adults. Some other essentials to understand are that some states require physically putting a tag on a turkey as soon as it is killed or reporting it before moving it. The responsibility for checking a turkey can sometimes be an onerous challenge.

Currently, most states today have gone to a mail-in, online, or telephone checking system. There is usually a defined starting and stopping time listed when you can legally kill a gobbler. Many states have shotgun and shot size restrictions; most allow archery, some allow crossbows, and some allow rifles.

One of the most frustrating restrictions required by a good number of states is morning-only hunting. Although no scientifically acceptable or legitimate biological justification for this restriction is provided, some states continue to maintain it, apparently as tradition. I have hunted and studied wild turkeys and their management for many years; the morning-only hunting restriction seems ridiculous and unjustified, basically eliminating half the time to hunt.

These explanations and professional opinions are shared after having hunted turkeys in most of the contiguous United States and Mexico. Additionally, some of the following observations and stories were from hunting in morning-only states, and others were from where all-day hunting is permitted. It is imperative to become familiar with regulatory requirements where you plan to hunt, and these may change from year to year.

CHAPTER 14

Personal Dilemmas

Let's discuss fair chase ethics about turkey hunting and hunting in general that some will question. It should be clear that these ethical decisions are not being dictated to anyone else. When hunting with others, if they are observed doing something unethical or unsafe, it may require stopping and discussing before continuing the hunt. If they are unwilling to change their actions, I choose to avoid hunting with them in the future and terminate the hunt immediately if I feel it necessary.

Over the years, I have been hit with shotgun pellets and had two great hunting dogs shot by others due to carelessness. Such action usually ends my willingness to hunt with those people again. Although it may be legal in some states, my code will not allow me to shoot a gobbler out of a tree, nor a ruffed grouse or other gamebird. I also choose not to hunt out of a pop-up blind or ambush a gobbler that has not come to my call. I elect not to use motorized decoys nor a recording device to call a gobbler into range. I do not shoot at flying gobblers, even though it is probably legal in many states.

Not caring to ambush or otherwise kill a gobbler not called is my decision, as is choosing not to shoot a gobbler being called in for someone else. This latter decision has resulted in many gobblers walking, running, or flying away that could have easily been killed. Most often, when calling for someone else, if they are an experienced turkey hunter, my shotgun is left in the vehicle. Exceptions are made for guided hunts, when calling for youngsters, first-time turkey hunters, or if a bird is wounded. My hunting success has become increasingly determined by the observations made and the enjoyment of sharing them with whom I hunt.

Indeed, my success is not dictated by the number of animals killed.

Some questionable hunting techniques are being touted in outdoors magazines and some of the "snuff film" and outdoor TV shows. These include hunting practices that encourage methods of killing a gobbler that are both dangerous and unethical.

Examples are shooting turkeys over bait or feed in front of a pop-up blind, ambushing a turkey by crawling behind a turkey fan (real or manufactured) into range and shooting the bird, use of motorized decoys, and shooting them at long range with a rifle. If that is their choice and manner of hunting such a magnificent bird and is legal where they are hunting, then it is their decision. I would hate to have to admit that was the only way I could kill a turkey gobbler. It is not fair chase nor how turkey hunting should be conducted.

Those folks who crawl behind a fan into ambush range are taking a real chance at getting shot in the face by someone who mistakes that fan and painted gobbler's head on front for a real turkey. With the lethality of some of the modern shotshell loads, in my opinion, it is not worth the risk. These techniques are legal, unfortunately, in most states, but are they genuinely fair chase? As Aldo Leopold so eloquently stated in *A Sand County Almanac* (1948):

"I have the impression that the American sportsman is puzzled, he doesn't understand what is happening to him. Bigger and better gadgets are good for industry, so why not for outdoor recreation? The sportsman has no leaders to tell him what is wrong. The sporting press no longer represents sport; it has turned billboard for the gadgeteer."

How relevant for today's hunters, many of whom strive to have more and more gadgets every year.

For example, how many hunters employ multiple trail cameras to document when a deer, turkey, or elk shows up to the bait pile in front of the camera? The primary reason is not to spend very much time hunting. It seems the purpose is primarily to avoid learning hunting skills and exerting effort. Is this fair chase? These baited camera sites increase the potential threat of infectious disease transfer to both target and non-target wildlife, i.e., Chronic Wasting Disease (CWD) and Bovine Tuberculosis (BT), to name a couple.

I have talked with people who use trail cameras extensively and most justify that they do it primarily just to see the animals, and to know what is coming to the bait site. If you believe that, I have some ocean-front property in Kansas that you might be interested in purchasing. What they want to know is what time the critters arrive during daylight hours. If you have 800 trail camera photos before the season comes in, and you know within an hour or less when the animal visits each bait pile, where is the thrill of the chase? Is this hunting? Maybe to some, but to me, it is NOT fair chase.

Is there any doubt the outdoor recreation industry Aldo talked about in 1948 has not acknowledged the demand for the multitude of gadgets available today? Amazingly to me, people are willing to pay premium prices for these gadgets and gizmos even though they likely do not need them.

Look at the next outdoor or hunting catalogue you receive and scan the advertisements devoted to the sale of trail cameras, automated feeders, feed, attractants, remote motorized decoys, wind machines to tell which way the wind is blowing, ozone machines, scent-free clothing, and numerous other gadgets and devices. Are hunters that gullible? Sadly, many appear to be, and the idea of fair chase hunting is not their primary objective.

It seems like many hunters are simply trying to short-circuit the skills and knowledge they should be trying to learn. They instead continually pursue the next "silver bullet" gadget. Maybe, their fundamental objective is to see who can own and carry more gadgets and widgets on their next hunting trip. The question here is who is being exploited aside from the public trust wildlife resources?

Although others regularly hunt from a pop-up blind, I do not and will not do this. I do not feel that it is fair chase hunting if it eliminates one of the turkey's two primary means of survival—their vision and ability to spot movement—that such blinds provide. Depending on a make-shift natural blind or just finding something large enough to break up my outline has worked well for many years. Even if the gobbler spots you and spooks, at least you gave it a fair chase effort.

CHAPTER 15

Your Decision

As a hunter, you decide to take a shot at a gobbler called into range or pass on it for various reasons. Hopefully, a passed shot occurs because you are not 100% sure you can kill the gobbler or have some safety factor concerns. From experience, I have learned that if you know your firearm, load, and effective range, once you have a gobbler where you know you can kill him, it is your decision.

A memory of a hunt that occurred years ago in Arkansas stands out where I passed up shooting a gobbler only because of my strong friendship with a hunting buddy and professional colleague. Some people will not understand, but it was my decision then, and I have never regretted it.

In those days in the early to mid-1970s, the bag limit on turkeys was three gobblers in the spring and three either-sex birds in the fall. It was getting pretty late in the spring season, and I had killed two gobblers before taking a trip to California to make a presentation at a conference. My best buddy, who was a great turkey hunter, had experienced one of those seasons when everything just seemed to go wrong for him. Although hunting hard and often, he still had not killed a gobbler. He had made a few mistakes, had gobblers spooked off him by other hunters, and missed a couple, and had not been able to carry one home.

When I returned from my trip, it was on a Friday, and the season closed the next day. Wanting to catch up on his hunts, I called and visited with him to see if he was going that last morning and offered to go with him if he wanted me to. He said he would love for me to go with him, but he would prefer hunting by himself. He had a gobbler he had worked several times that he wanted to kill, and I could possibly take a bird too and use my last tag. We planned on our meeting place and time and met the following morning going in his truck. Hunting on the Ouachita National Forest west of Little Rock, we split up when we got there, each going to a different location.

We left his truck well before daylight, and he indicated which side of the mountain he was going to be hunting on. I went the other direction, although not having hunted that area before. We had agreed to meet back at the truck about 11:00. He was hunting on the north side of the mountain, so I hunted on another mountain about half a mile to the south of where he was hunting. I hoped I could hear him if and when he shot.

Once the birds started singing, I owl-called and listened intently but heard no gobbles. Waiting for about five minutes, I started crow-cawing loudly and heard two gobblers respond at my second attempt. One was not too far away down the side of the mountain, and the other was down a long, deep hollow back toward the branch and to the west of where I had crossed it earlier.

Moving toward the closest bird, I was able to get set up before he left the roost. He gobbled several more times in the tree, then flew down and gobbled once to my call. Shortly, he headed up and over the top of the mountain, either going out of hearing or quit responding. After moving toward the crest and calling again with no response, I decided to see if I could get close enough to the other bird to hear him gobble.

By the time I got down the side of the mountain, staying about halfway above the branch, it was about 9:30. I found a little open glade, made a sparse blind, and decided to set up and call for a while. Hopefully, he might hear me and would respond. On my third call, I heard a gobbler both behind and below my setup. Confident in my setup, I stayed quiet for about five minutes, then yelped softly, to which a gobbler responded. It sounded like he was directly below me, less than 150 yards away. He stayed pretty much at that same location for about 30 minutes, gobbling occasionally and moving back and forth down the side of that ridge. I decided then to sit quietly for about 15 to 20 minutes and see what happened. In about five minutes, he gobbled much closer and not too far below where I sat. The next thing I heard was him drumming directly across that open glade. Then he stepped out into the glade at about 45 yards in full strut. He was right at the edge of some blueberry bushes and scrubby oak brush.

With my shotgun resting on my knee, I knew he would be moving closer, so I just waited and watched as he strutted and drummed. Suddenly, I heard a noise to my right, up the hillside—a sound I had never heard before. Wondering just what it was, I knew it was not the gobbler that I could see. From the oak brush to my right, a male roadrunner marched out into the glade and repeated that sound. The best description I can think of is a "rattley-whoof-zoom" sound that he repeated about every 45 seconds. When making this sound, he would quickly raise his tail high, call, then slowly lower it while simultaneously puffing his feathers out. The gobbler paid him no attention whatsoever and continued strutting, coming to within 35 yards of me. The roadrunner soon ran out of the clearing, and I heard him make that sound a couple of more times.

By this time, I had my shotgun shouldered and looked down the barrels ready to take a shot at the gobbler. Having not yet heard my buddy shoot, I just could not force myself to shoot. The gobbler strutted in the glade for another ten minutes or so, coming out of strut to search for the hen he thought was somewhere around. Then, he walked up the hillside out of sight. Waiting a few minutes, I just had to call softly one more time. I looked at my watch, and it was about 10:15.

The gobbler did not gobble but strutted and drummed right back into that glade like he was begging to be killed.

Admittedly tempted, I just was unable to shoot him unless I heard my buddy shoot first. The gobbler folded up in a little bit and walked on back up the hillside, and I unloaded my shotgun. Without question, I had that gobbler in easy killing range longer than any other I ever remembered, but I am still glad not to have shot him.

I got to my feet and walked quickly back toward where we had left the truck, arriving at about 11:30. Thurman was waiting for me. He told me he had worked the gobbler he went to for quite some time but could not get him into killing range. He asked me if I had heard anything, and I told him about the two I heard. Telling him in more detail about the roadrunner exhibition, I ignored mention of the gobbler called into range. We remained best of friends until his death in December 2019.

We hunted together many more times over the years and shared numerous good times, but I never told him the complete truth about that morning. In hindsight, I am so glad I did not. I don't think I ever revealed this story to anyone other than my wife, who knew my friend well. Killing another gobbler was just not that important to me, considering my best friend had hunted so hard that season but had not been able to kill one.

Some who read this might say my killing this gobbler would have made no difference, but they do not realize the bonds and respect that long-term hunting buddies share. Even today, it still seems right to me that I did not shoot that gobbler because of our friendship.

As I mentioned before, shooting a turkey out of a tree is not something, in my opinion, that is ethical. I have, however, had many opportunities to do so. There have been three hunts when I have had gobblers fly up into a tree in sight and range. In each case, they sat in the tree for several minutes or more, looking around before flying down. One even flew into the tree above where I was sitting. Over the many years

I have turkey hunted, there have been many opportunities when I could see gobblers in the tree, in range but chose not to shoot. Most while they were on the roost. Some would see that as missed opportunities, but it is my decision.

While living in Arkansas, my buddy and I would apply for a permit to hunt on the Ozark/St. Francis National Forest WMA between Marianna, and Forrest City, Arkansas. The locals call it Crowley's Ridge. It is a prominent ridge of loess soils positioned northeast to the southeast toward the confluence of the White River and the Mississippi River. The ridge itself is characterized by predominantly hardwood forests and deeply eroded loess soil gullies. It is excellent turkey habitat. This particular spring season, my friend arrived there about noon, rented a motel room for us to share, and had done a little scouting.

When I arrived later in the afternoon, he suggested we go back and scout until dark. We drove in my truck to the western border of the ridge, crossed a railroad track, and proceeded up the ridge on a sandy road. We went by a large recent clearcut to the east on the way up and later reached a fork in the road. He said to take the right fork, and we drove on another mile or so. "Let me out here," he said.

I turned around and drove back just past the fork where there was a place I could get off the road, stopped, and parked. Walking down and across a couple of the deep gullies, I came to a long ridge and began to walk along it. It was getting on toward evening, and I crow-cawed loudly and heard a turkey gobble nearby. Not wanting to spook the bird, I sat down and, in a few minutes, saw four long-beard gobblers across a gully. One or more of them gobbled often, and I followed until close enough to hear them fly to roost.

Getting back to my truck at dark, I turned around, drove back, and picked up my buddy. He had roosted a gobbler as well, so we both felt pretty confident about our chances the next morning. We got up and left well before daylight. I drove him to his spot, turned around, and headed back to where I had parked the previous afternoon. Sadly, by the time I got back to that spot, three hunters were getting out of two pickup trucks. I just drove on by, and before long, I was back near that clearcut. I located a place to park as it was starting to get light in the east.

Gathering my gear, I began working my way through the clearcut toward mature woods I could see on the other side. About halfway across the cutover, I heard a train whistle coming south along the track. Continuing to walk, the next time the train whistled, I thought I heard a gobble in the direction of the mature woods ahead. The train had whistled a couple of more times by the time I was into the mature woods, and it enabled me to course two gobblers that sounded close together.

Daylight was coming fast, and these birds were across a gully on a fairly large ridge. I moved quickly, got across, found a big oak tree on the peak of the ridge, and sat down. Within a minute, a gobbler sounded off about 150 yards above me. Another gobbler answered him only about 90 yards across a gully to my left. Still on their roost, these two birds gobbled back and forth at each other for about ten more minutes.

Finally, not having called to them at all, I clucked softly and tree-yelped one time. Both gobbled. The bird across the gully flew and landed in the tree I was leaning against, not 50 feet over my head. I could see his long beard and wondered just what was going to happen next. Before long, I heard several hens cackle as they flew down toward the lower side of the gully. Both birds gobbled, and the one above me sailed off and down through the ravine to those hens.

The other bird stayed on the roost, so I waited probably two or three minutes and softly clucked, then heard him fly down straight out in front of me. Not able to see him, I could hear him begin drumming as soon as he was on the ground and thought he would come out the top of the ridge. I soon realized he had moved just over the crest to my right. There was a slight saddle about 20 yards in front of me; it sounded like he was working his way there. With my shotgun on my knee and watching for him, I caught some movement very close. There he was, only about 15 yards to my right.

He walked toward a huge oak tree. As his head went behind that tree, I slowly swung my shotgun barrels to the right slightly, but he froze behind that tree. His tail feathers, rump, and the back of his wings were visible. It seemed like he stayed there for 20 minutes, although it was more likely a minute or so. I then saw him move forward slightly, and his beak and eyes came poking around the side of that tree, looking directly at me. Decision time! Thinking back, the only thing I can think of that alerted the gobbler and stopped him behind the tree was the sound of my clothes rustling as I moved my shotgun into position.

Although seriously thinking about shooting at the top of his head, I knew how quickly he could draw it back, and I would miss. So I waited. He finally pulled it back, took a couple of steps, and walked right out in front of my gun barrel. As he straightened up, I shot him at 12 yards. He was a big mature gobbler with a huge beard and long spurs. The sight of his beak and eyes poking around the side of that tree trunk are still etched in my memory many years later. Since that experience, I have had two others that flew up into trees and watched a while before flying down. One of these came to the call after flying down, and I killed him. The other just walked away, seemingly uninterested after not being able to see a hen.

Whether turkey hunting or other game, at some point, hunters face a dilemma about the decision to shoot or not. I have often commented that turkey hunting likely requires more hunting and less shooting than any other hunting activity I know. Regardless of the quarry, becoming a fair-chase hunter requires serious responsibility and commitment that some, unfortunately, seem to have forgotten. I must admit I have taken a few shots wounding saplings, brush, briars, or trees before realizing how dispersed the pattern becomes. Following those early learning experiences, I have passed up a lot of potential shots at gobblers. Some of these birds were called back later, and some were never hunted or heard again.

CHAPTER 16

Confessions

Remembering Aldo Leopold's message about the code of ethics a hunter either adopts or ignores requires me to think about how I would feel if I ignored my ethics. I am convinced that it would come back to haunt me and prevent me from sharing that story and memory with anyone else. Clearly, state wildlife agency regulations must be adhered to by ethical and responsible hunters, but even doing our best, mistakes can happen.

My worst mistake happened in the early 1970s when the spring gobbler limit in Arkansas was three gobblers, but only one could be taken per day. That year, while on a couple of scouting trips, before the season opened, I located two gobblers in an area I had hunted previous years. I watched two mature gobblers, eight hens, and four jakes for about 30 minutes on the second trip. One gobbler stayed in full strut, except when the other gobbler, or the jakes, got too close to the hens.

Following that observation, it was pretty easy for me to determine where I wanted to go on opening day. I felt confident that I would not encounter other hunters since the area required about a mile and a half walk, mostly uphill, to get to the location from where I wanted to listen.

Leaving my truck early enough to get to the area before daylight, it promised to be a beautiful opening day. I thanked God, as always, for the privilege and opportunity and found me a place to wait and rest until the woods started to wake up.

As dawn began to show some pink rays of sunlight to the east and songbirds began singing, I made a long, drawn-out, barred owl call. Two birds gobbled. One was just down and around the side of the ridge that I was on, maybe 250 yards away, and the other was considerably farther.

Having made it to the top of the ridge above a small, somewhat open, saddle I moved closer to see down the slope along with most of the saddle and set up. It was the same saddle I had observed those turkeys in before the season. I waited there and hoped when he left the roost; he would move up toward the saddle.

Both birds gobbled several more times. After about ten minutes, the one farther away either stopped gobbling or flew down and was out of hearing. Shortly afterward, the closer bird gobbled, and he was definitely on the ground to my right but still over the side of the ridge.

Moving around to face where he was gobbling from, I called softly; he gobbled right back and was closer. The direction he was coming from had some nearly waist-high blueberry bushes and small, brushy oak saplings that I expected him to go through or around. I got my shotgun on my knee with it pointed to that area.

His next gobble was very close, so I mounted my shotgun to my shoulder just before spotting his neon white skull cap and red wattles coming through the blueberry bushes. He continued upward until he was about 25 yards below me, raised his head and neck and at my shot, he disappeared. Jumping to my feet, I ran down toward where he lay. About the time I spotted him, I heard wings flopping behind and below where he lay.

My heart sank, thinking I had possibly killed a hen that had been behind him. On closer inspection, it was not a hen but another gobbler. Apparently, a sub-dominant bird had been following the gobbling bird that I shot. Having not previously seen nor heard him, I did not realize he was there. He had taken enough of that charge in the neck and head to kill him.

After making sure they were both dead, I sat down and pondered the situation, recognizing that I had just broken the law according to state regulations. Certainly not intentionally, but I was still guilty.

It was still early, so after some prayer and a lot of thought, I convinced myself to take both birds, walk out to my truck, find an enforcement officer, and turn myself in. I placed my carrying strap over the neck and legs of the first gobbler, and took a bootlace from one of my boots and made a carrying device so I could carry one bird out on each shoulder.

Fortunately, most of my walk back to the truck was downhill. After unloading my shotgun, I placed a bird over each shoulder and started walking with wings flapping on both sides. I did not encounter another hunter or an enforcement officer, and after arriving at my truck, I placed both gobblers in the back.

The local enforcement officer for that area lived in the tiny town of Perryville, which was only about 15 miles away, so I headed into town. Knowing where he lived, I drove up to their home, but his truck was not there. After parking in the driveway, I walked up to the front door and knocked.

His wife came to the door, and after introducing myself, I asked her if she knew where Cookie, as most everyone affectionally called him, might be. She said she was not sure but would see if she could contact him and for me to come on in and have a cup of coffee. It was only about 8:45, and in a few minutes, I could hear her talking with him. She said he would be home in about 20 minutes.

I offered to go back and sit in my truck, but she insisted I stay inside until he got there. Cookie soon arrived and immediately asked me what was wrong. My answer was that I had messed up earlier that morning. He asked, "You didn't shoot somebody, did you?" I quickly responded that it wasn't that bad, but I had made a serious mistake.

We sat down on the porch swing, and as accurately as possible, I described just how the situation had occurred and why I had decided to bring both gobblers to him and plead guilty. Knowing this was a clear violation of the regulations, I prepared for him to issue me a ticket.

He said, "Let's look at them." So, we walked over to the back of my truck, and he carefully examined both birds. He then went to his vehicle, retrieved a clipboard, and went back to the porch and sat down. While he was writing something on the clipboard, I suggested he take both turkeys and give them to someone else, but he declined.

He then stated that those were the first gobblers he had seen that morning. After checking both turkeys, he told me he would not write me up for a violation. Blurting out my sincere appreciation, I also told him I did not want to put him in a delicate or precarious situation and would gladly pay the fine.

He said, "If I thought for a minute you had done this on purpose, I would write you up. Your effort to bring those birds in and admit your mistake is proof enough for me that you had an accident that could happen to anyone who turkey hunts."

He then told me to take both gobblers home with me and for my family and me to enjoy them. He asked that I not tell anyone about his decision. He continued, "I know you would not have taken the chance without considering the consequences. I trust what you have told me is true." Sadly, Cookie Rankin passed away several years later after being diagnosed with terminal cancer.

These examples describing my actions based on ethical decisions certainly do not make me a saint, and we are all subject to making these or similar mistakes requiring some soul-searching. They illustrate why these and other hunting memories are treasured when reflected upon and why the action taken at that time was seriously considered.

Although it is not something I enjoy doing, over the years, occasionally, if you care about yourself and others hunting with you, it becomes necessary to admonish a fellow hunter.

Most of these occasions have been while hunting with someone not having previously hunted with before. Most commonly, it was because they handled their firearm in a manner that endangered themselves and others hunting with them. Although clearly, that is not the only reason.

A couple of examples come to mind. One was when two guys I knew, but had never hunted with, wanted to join me on a hunt to a WMA in Alabama that had become an annual trip for me. Without going into explicit detail, the WMA we were going to hunt on only allowed morning hunts, although you could scout in the afternoon without a gun. With these guys not having hunted the area before, I helped them both find places to hunt the first morning where I had encountered birds in past years. After going to another site, a gobbler came to my call, and I shot him at about 10:00 that first morning.

It was hot, so after returning to camp, processing the gobbler and getting the meat on ice, I decided to go down to the creek and bathe before taking a nap. Just before leaving for the creek, these two guys pulled in, and both had heard gobblers but had not been able to get them into range. I told them where I was headed, and they both decided they would prepare themselves some lunch. I took my bath in that cold creek, hustled back to my tent and, seeing their truck gone, assumed they had gone into town or were doing some scouting.

About 4:30, I heard their pickup arrive. By this time, I had dressed and was thinking about going out to roost a gobbler. Going over to visit, the younger of the two told me to look in the back of the truck. There were two jake gobblers he had ambushed with a .22 magnum scoped rifle they had brought with them. I was furious at this violation of the law. I was also furious at their ignorance or lack of concern for my relationship with the WMA wildlife manager and local enforcement officers I had become friends with over the years. Immediately, I told them in no uncertain terms that they needed to pack up their gear and leave before the biologists or enforcement officers found out what they had done. They both started trying to justify their actions which infuriated me even more. I reminded them again of the consequences if they didn't leave immediately. They realized this was no idle threat and started packing and loading their stuff in the truck. My last words to them were to never approach me again about hunting with my friends or me. I don't think our paths ever crossed again, thankfully. To this day, it still bothers me that they did this without consideration for me or for the resources they claimed to care about. My confession is that I probably should have turned them in to the authorities.

The second situation was not as severe but still reminds us that we sometimes forget how our actions impact others. It, too, occurred on this same WMA a few years later. I had hunted or fished with both of these guys before and thought I knew them much better than the other two I just described. Both of these guys were older than me, and both were very accomplished turkey callers and hunters with years of experience.

We arrived the afternoon before the season opened and got our camp set up. One of the guys started cooking up some fish, hushpuppies, and beans he had brought along in a huge ice chest in the back of his truck. He also had an ample supply of beer in that ice chest. My other friend nor I drank beer, but we enjoyed the dinner. With some maps of the area and feeling pretty sure they would hear or locate a gobbler in those areas, I pointed out a place for each of them and directions on how to get there.

The following day, they went in their truck, and I went in mine to an area suggested to me by the area manager. Two of us killed gobblers that morning. The guy who cooked the fish had worked a gobbler but could not get it into range. The next morning, they went back to the areas they had hunted the previous morning, and I went to a place that required a long walk. Again, the same two of us killed gobblers, but sadly, for whatever reason, the other guy could not close the deal, although he did hear and work a gobbler.

Although turkey hunting is not a competitive sport, it became apparent that this guy was getting a little cranky and frustrated. After lunch that day, I saw the area manager drive into his office and maintenance building. I walked up and visited with him, asking about some different areas where he had seen birds earlier. He told me about a place that no one else hunted because it was difficult to access. It was near a vacant house that was about 100 yards off the highway, and he had seen a large gobbler there recently.

The manager said an older lady who owned the property might let us leave our truck there and walk through her property to get to the WMA property line if I asked her. With his directions, I drove over and visited with her, and she kindly gave us permission. Since it was still a couple of hours before dark, I decided to scout it and drove over to the old house and parked.

After walking past the house and an old garden site, I began moving up a pretty steep ridge of mature hardwood timber to a knoll on top that looked down toward the creek. The timber type was predominantly oak, hickory, and yellow poplar. However, at the top of the hill, a flat area about a half-acre in size had a huge magnolia tree almost in the center. Not wanting to possibly disturb any birds using the site and noticing a good bit of turkey sign around that big magnolia, I slipped over and sat down by it. The creek was only 200 yards over the knoll, and I could see two small ridges that led down toward the creek.

Not having called at all, I heard some turkeys flying up to roost near the creek just before dark, then I heard a gobbler fly up close by. I saw him in flight just before he lit on a huge, flat, oak limb about 60 yards down the ridge to the right. Once in the tree, he was visible and had not seen nor heard me.

Sitting very still, I waited until it got completely dark and began crawling back toward the way I had come up the ridge to the knoll. Because he was so close, I tried not to make any noise. I crawled about 80 yards before going over the side of the ridge and being able to stand up and walk back to the truck.

Knowing exactly where that gobbler was roosted, I felt we could get in there quietly before daylight. Arriving back at camp, I asked our friend who had not yet killed a gobbler if he was interested. If so, we would go there in the morning. We parked his truck in the old house place yard and slipped quietly up the back of the steep hill to the knoll.

Getting near the place where we needed to set up, I told him where the gobbler had roosted and gave him his choice of where he wanted to sit. He chose to sit at the base of the big magnolia as it was close to where he should see the gobbler when it got light. I slipped about 35 yards away and found a place looking at another ridge that dropped off toward the creek. The two ridges were only about 60 yards apart. I felt confident the gobbler, once on the ground, would come up one or the other of the ridges. We sat quietly, waiting for it to get light. About the time the birds started singing, a barred owl called down near the creek. The turkey gobbled right where I had seen him go to roost. He gobbled several more times on the roost, and we both could see him as he moved around still on the roost.

Shortly, I heard several hens fly down toward the creek bottom. He gobbled once more, then pitched down to them. We could see each other, and both called, prompting the bird to gobble. He was clearly down in that creek bottom with the hens. We took turns afterward calling, and he would gobble every time but stayed in the bottom.

Motioning to my friend that we should not call for a while, we both stayed quiet for about ten minutes, and then I motioned him to call again. When he did, the turkey gobbled closer and was coming up the ridge in front of me. Soon, his drumming indicated he wasn't far down the ridge. About that time, a hen came up over the ridge directly in front of me and started walking toward the big magnolia tree. Behind her, I could see a gobbler fan. As she went by me, about 30 yards away, the gobbler came up to the top of the ridge to the knoll.

I then heard the hen putt, as she had spotted my friend. As she started walking back down over the side of the knoll, the gobbler came out of a strut and KABOOM, my friend made a very long shot, and the gobbler went down. Because it was such a long shot, we both jumped up and ran toward the gobbler. The bird had started flopping, but the shot had broken his neck.

We admired the gobbler, discussed the thrills of the hunt, placed my carrying strap over his neck and legs and walked back down over the hill to the truck. On arriving at the truck, he handed me the keys and asked me to drive us back to camp. After placing the gobbler in the back of the truck, he reached into his big ice chest, pulled out two beers and a soft drink for me.

We headed back toward camp. About halfway there, he finished off the first beer, rolled down the window and started to throw that beer can out. Objecting as graciously as possible, I suggested that he should place the can in the floorboard instead. Then at camp, we could dispose of it by placing it in the garbage bin.

As he was several years older than I, it was evident that he didn't appreciate being admonished about throwing that can out. He threw it on the floor, opened his second can, and neither of us spoke again. Back at camp, I took the empty cans and disposed of them in the garbage receptacle.

After about ten minutes, when he finished that second beer, he walked over and placed it in the garbage can. At that point, not expecting an apology, I asked him, "How would you feel if someone from this state came to Arkansas and threw out beer cans or other trash in the areas where you like to hunt?" He didn't respond immediately but, after a few minutes, admitted that he would not like that.

After our other friend arrived, we had lunch, he cleaned his gobbler and reiterated the details of the hunt. Later, he thanked me for putting him on that gobbler, apologized, and admitted he had not thought about how trashy it was to litter the roadside. We finished our hunt a few days later. We all took at least one more gobbler before heading home. We remained friends afterward and hunted and fished together for several years before my family moved away. I never remember observing him litter or attempt to throw refuse away again.

CHAPTER 17

It's Not A Competition

It has been my good fortune to have hunted over the years with many good turkey hunters. I have also hunted with some who were still novices, as well as first-time turkey hunters. Some attributes are essential to enjoy the hunting experience fully while hunting with them, whether as a guide or sharing a hunt where you go together but hunt individually.

The first is to understand that hunting is not a competitive sport, except to compete with yourself and not with others you hunt with. A second one is that they are careful and responsible in handling their firearm. The third is that they show up at an agreed-upon time and are not always late. Another is that they understand not every hunt will be easy, nor will every hunt result in a gobbler harvested. And, finally, there are no guarantees in turkey hunting. Therefore, complaining when things do not go as planned will not help.

For many years, when sharing hunting and fishing trips with a good guy and friend, I recognized early on that he was very competitive. He wanted to kill his limit first, or catch the biggest fish, or otherwise somehow feel he had beaten you, even when you made clear you were not competing with him. I explained several times over those years that I was in no way competing with him, only with myself. However, it took years for him to understand and begin to enjoy the hunt and the memories without competition.

Another is when you take a long trip hunting with someone, regardless of how good the hunting is, and they are constantly griping about something, it will be a bad experience. Whether it be the place you are staying, the food you have access to, or someone else who is hunting with you, it makes for a miserable hunt. For example, a few years back, a long trip was made with three other guys for a hunt. I had hunted with two of them in the past, but none of us had hunted with the other guy.

This new person constantly complained, and if he was not complaining, he was bragging about something of little interest to anyone. By the time we all got back home, we vowed never to make that mistake again. This fellow made an otherwise enjoyable trip very difficult.

Hunters need to understand that everything will not be perfect on every hunt, and most of us have experienced numerous unpleasant distractions on trips. Indeed, everything is not necessarily going to happen as we might have preferred. Therefore, working to make the best of the situation is sometimes a struggle. However, it is better to avoid getting cranky or disagreeable and enjoy the experience as much as possible. In my opinion, a good turkey hunter must be flexible and willing to stay focused, regardless of how tough it might get.

Regarding staying focused, in recent years, I have often guided people who insisted on taking their cell phones with them. Regardless of how hard you try to keep them focused on the hunt, the temptation is too great. They just cannot resist checking their e-mail, text messages, or playing games or when they think they have the phone turned off, they get a call at just the wrong time.

While guiding a youngster some years back, we had set up in a good spot. However, it had a knob nearby that gobblers would sometimes come up the back and be virtually on top of you before seeing them. After getting set up and calling, two gobblers answered. It sounded like they were together to our left. From that direction, we could see a bird approach well before they got too close.

After getting a second set of gobbles to our left, I motioned for him to be ready as they were coming in. Not planning to call anymore and hoping he would stay focused, I watched for them to appear. They did not come in right away, and when checking on the youngster, I found him either playing a video game or texting someone. I motioned for him to put that danged phone away and be alert because those gobblers would show up soon.

It couldn't have been more than a couple of minutes afterward when I saw three big gobblers that had circled and were coming up over the knob. I turned again to see if the boy was ready to shoot. He had that cell phone out again. By the time I could get his attention, those three gobblers were on top of us, spotted the boy and vanished before he could shoulder his gun.

The cell phone problem reminds me of another incident when hunting with a veteran hunter and friend. We had hunted together often in previous years, never with any issues. However, this particular morning we had not heard many birds. For whatever reason, we could never get set up right on the one gobbler we worked for some time.

We followed the gobbler up and down some steep hills and hollows, never really getting him very close. Finally, the gobbler got down in the bottom of a hollow, and we could tell then that he was with a few hens. We then backed away, circled and came into the hollow about a quarter-mile below him.

Setting up almost in the creek bottom, I called and finally got him cranked up again. We moved to the base of a side gully that came down to the branch bottom. With my friend positioned to see up the ridge, I moved off to the right behind a bit of mound below him. After calling, the turkey gobbled up the ridge above us on the hillside. He was not far. Lying down below the bank, I clucked one time. Although the turkey did not gobble, we soon heard him drumming. I expected him to shoot as the drumming was getting closer. Suddenly, my friend's musical-toned cell phone rang loudly. You know the rest of the story. The gobbler disappeared, and we never heard him again.

Over the years, several folks I've guided have drifted off to sleep or must have been in a coma. After a long hunt, when the gobbler finally came into range, my hunters were unaware that the turkey was there. By the time the gobbler had come close enough for a kill shot, it was too late. A couple of times, I have heard hunters snoring, and I woke them up.

Although never having gone to sleep while hunting in my younger days, I confess that it happened to me one afternoon a few years back. It was a delightful day, and I had been outfoxed that morning. Slipping back into the area about 3:00 that afternoon, I made a quick little blind and called a few times over the next half an hour. My blind was comfortable, and I enjoyed the beauty of the day. After not hearing anything for a while, I decided to try one of my loud cuts, followed by a gobble on a tube call. Nothing responded, so I waited about ten minutes and did it again.

Hearing nothing, I inadvertently drifted off to sleep. I truly have no idea how long my doze lasted, but guess what? On awakening, a big gobbler was standing directly in front of me, not ten yards away. As our eyes met, he turned quickly before I could get my shotgun to my shoulder, and he was gone!

That is the only time in my life I have ever gone to sleep while hunting. Presumably, that has been because of my heightened anticipation and focus. I have friends, however, who will take a short nap while working a stubborn bird, then wake up and sometimes get him started gobbling again.

Aside from our family members, one of several favorite turkey hunting friends I have enjoyed many great hunting trips with is Jim Byford. Jim is one of those guys who does not complain, is always on time, and is willing to experience the good times and the bad without grumbling or getting cranky.

We have hunted together just about every year since

the early 1970s, and I cannot remember how many times we have "doubled," with both of us killing gobblers the same morning. This occurred when we were not hunting together or even hunting in the same area. We have shared some great hunting experiences, especially in Tennessee and Kentucky.

One I remember vividly was in a pasture mixed with wooded hills and gullies. We had gotten there later than planned. By the time we got started to the area we wanted to listen from, we saw a gobbler fly down on top of a hill in the pasture and start strutting. We dove down into the upper end of a hollow that ended in the edge of the field, into some multi-flora rose and honeysuckle vines.

We found a place to sit after cutting and removing some vines and called, expecting the bird up on the hill to gobble. He did not, but we heard one from behind us, and he was close. Calling softly again, he gobbled, then a bearded hen ran right in front of me, putted loudly and flew. The gobbler gobbled again to my immediate left. Jim was to my right, so he could not see the gobbler until I shot and the turkey started flopping.

While calling to that bird, another bird had gobbled up over the hill to our left front. Knowing the area better than Jim did, I suggested he head up that way, and I would catch up with him. I took my gobbler and shotgun to the truck and hurried up to the top of the hill, catching up with Jim. An old dim road ran around a point of woods, mostly Virginia pine, but between the pasture and some other good timber. I called to pinpoint the bird, and the gobbler answered almost behind us. There was another small pasture there, and that is where he sounded to me. I suggested that Jim get right next to that old road where he could see out in the pasture, and I ducked down in a little gully to be out of sight. However, that positioned me where the road dipped, and a curve in the road was visible. Calling again, this time, the gobbler had moved closer and was coming up the old road.

When the gobbler first came into view, my first reaction was he was enormous. He was trotting up the road toward where Jim was hidden. The front of that big gobbler's breast, shaking back and forth as he ran with all that breast sponge under the breast feathers, was almost comical. Shortly after going out of my sight, he showed up 15 yards in front of Jim in the pasture. Coming out of strut, the gobbler realized something was not right, turned and started to walk away when Jim fired.

We both jumped up and were astounded at that gobbler's size. That big bird had a huge beard and long curved spurs. After I congratulated Jim, he picked up the huge gobbler, and we walked to the truck and drove back to our cabin. We weighed both turkeys. Mine was a nice 22 pound plus gobbler with good spurs and beard, but Jim's gobbler weighed over 26 pounds, by far the biggest wild turkey either of us had killed at that time. Over the years, we have killed gobblers on the same morning many times but never such a large gobbler as this one.

Another enjoyable and fun hunt was in north Alabama with my wife's nephew, Jim Brooks, and his friend, Keith Jennings, when I called up their first gobblers. We had some classic hunts together in the mountains in Jackson County and some other places. One hunt came in early April when a massive killing freeze hit those mountains that severely damaged many trees and other vegetation that had already greened up. That freeze was so severe it virtually eliminated any hard mast crops that fall. We had planned to hunt that morning and fortunately had some warm clothing with us as it was 22 degrees when we left the cabin.

As we started up the mountain, I remarked that it was probably so cold that turkeys would not gobble early. Prophetically, we did not hear a bird until about 8:15, and that bird was a long way off on some property we did not have permission to hunt. We had walked up a curving old

Jim Byford with his 26-pound Kentucky gobbler (right)
next to the author's 22-pound bird.

mountain road that went toward the top of the big mountain, stopping and calling periodically.

Finally, just below another curve to the right that went around a bench, a bird gobbled. We moved up, getting Jim up as close as possible to where we thought that gobbler might come around that bench. After getting him set up behind some downed timber to see the roadway, I informed Jim that my position would be below him about 20 yards. Once in place, I called, and we were rewarded with multiple gobbles, but the ridge up to the bench was so steep I could not see anything above where Jim was hidden.

Several birds gobbled right above Jim on the bench at the next call. Some or all of them gobbled at each call again, but they stayed up on the bench. Shortly, some of them started fighting. The very loud noises they made included a lot of purring and gobbling mixed with wings beating and a heck of a racket.

Crawling up to where Jim was, I told him to move up carefully until he could see some of that flat in front of the bench. Then, I planned to go back down the mountain in increments of about 30 yards at a time and see if they could be enticed to come closer to Jim. Finally, he was able to carefully move to where he could see most of the bench. What he eventually saw was five mature gobblers with one dominant bird.

Moving downward, I called, and after each move, Jim said they eventually started working their way over toward him. However, it was probably 35 minutes before they finally got into range. He then shot the big dominant bird. Because we did not have any working scales, we made some photos then took the gobbler to the nearest community that had scales. They showed that the gobbler weighed 25 pounds and 14 ounces.

As we drove across those mountains that morning, it looked like the mountainsides had been aerially sprayed with herbicide as all the former green leaves were now brown. This had been a heck of a hunt, and Jim had killed a giant gobbler. I told Jim if he had ever thought about getting a gobbler mounted, that would be the one. But he declined, and we cleaned the gobbler back at camp after taking a few photos.

Jim Brooks with his giant gobbler.

CHAPTER 18

Patience and Persistence

Where I grew up, and until well after leaving home for college, there were very few deer or wild turkeys within 50 miles. Then, after getting older and with more mobility to go where there were turkeys and deer, I quickly observed that turkeys particularly seemed to be located in very remote places.

Another recollection about the early days of turkey hunting is that populations seemed to be relatively sparse even where you could hunt them. If you heard a bird gobble and called one in, it was usually a mature gobbler, and you rarely saw or heard other turkeys.

It is easy to remember the first jake gobbler I ever called up; even though I knew it was a legal bird, I was unsure because of no visible swinging beard or brightly colored head and wattles. Nevertheless, I sat there and watched him walk off. Continuing to turkey hunt, mainly in the spring, but occasionally in fall when such seasons were allowed, were real learning experiences for me. They enabled me to understand more and more about some of the critical factors associated with hunting such a mystical and elusive animal.

As most experienced turkey hunters will tell you, we learn as much or more from those we did not kill as those we occasionally take home. So, possibly, some observations from hunting experiences might help explain how things can go wrong.

Frequently, hunters are responsible for these miscues, but some are unexplainable. Once, before a morning hunt, I had roosted a big gobbler, and it had flown up close to me. I waited until black dark before slowly crawling away. My purpose in staying so late was to prevent him from hearing or seeing me. I returned well before daylight the next morning when, about 150 yards from where I had planned to set up, I stopped, took off my boots and sneaked in my socks to get into position.

Everything went well, and I got into position under the spreading limbs of a giant American holly tree in the black dark. It was a beautiful morning, waiting and listening to the sounds of the impending wake-up. Knowing that I was only about 70 yards above the gobbler boosted my confidence. He had gone to roost in a big yellow poplar tree below me.

As other birds began singing and the morning light grew progressively brighter, he gobbled right where I expected, yet I could not see him. I heard two or three other birds gobble in the distant mountains, but this bird had a deep gravelly and raucous voice. I guessed that he was an old gobbler because he challenged those birds immediately. First, he gobbled probably 20 times on the roost with no hens heard with him, then he broke his rhythm of gobbling.

It had become light by this time. I could see him stretch, fluff up, drum up the limb, and start looking down. I decided to make a soft little cluck. He gobbled immediately and turned on the limb, looking directly toward where I was. Not flying down yet, he gobbled another time or two, so I scratched out a very muffled tree yelp. This prompted him to fly down within 60 yards and start strutting up the hill directly toward me.

Already having my shotgun across my knee pointed in his direction, no movement would be necessary as he came closer in range. Killing him now as he progressed seemed a sure thing. Then, when he had gotten to about 50 yards, there came a thunderous crashing noise directly up the hill behind me. Something big fell from a tree, hit the ground loudly, and the gobbler immediately turned, ran down the mountain a few steps, and flew.

Frustrated by what had just happened, I got up to see what had fallen and spotted a large raccoon sort of shaking itself. It then started waddling up the mountainside away from the huge white oak tree it had just fallen out of. But, as most turkey hunters have learned over the years, the only sure thing about turkey hunting is that you never know what will happen. Nor can you anticipate what kind of unique observations you might have the opportunity to witness.

There have been many other occasions when things beyond the hunter's control have occurred to mess up an anticipated spring gobbler hunt. These include 4-wheeler disturbances, trees or big limbs falling, other hunters slipping in and scaring the gobbler, bobcats or coyotes sneaking in on a gobbling turkey, a squirrel jumping down near a strutting gobbler, and a herd of buffalo deciding to run by while you were working a turkey.

I have experienced all of these and likely other disturbances not always recognized while working a turkey gobbler. A hunter cannot anticipate an unusual or extraordinary event while working a gobbler from one hunt to the next. Sometimes, if the gobbler has not seen you when it spooked, you can try staying where you are, be patient, and allow some time for things to settle down before moving or calling again. This is especially true if you do not have another gobbler to work. The turkey that spooked might settle down later and be willing to respond.

Turkeys, like other wildlife, are exposed to a diversity of disturbances, many that may be natural yet only temporarily alarm them. In trying to describe the reactions of a gobbler in spring, I have often said they are like a loose ball of exposed nerve-endings that can be triggered by any number of sounds, actions, or sights they encounter. Thank goodness their sense of smell is virtually non-existent.

Occasionally, like the Garth Brooks country song "Thank God for Unanswered Prayers," a blind hog does find an acorn. For example, one hunt I remember well occurred in the mountains of north Alabama. After hunting a bird a couple of mornings with an escort of apparently willing hens each time, he followed those hens when they gathered to him and went mute.

The second afternoon while scouting, I heard him go to roost on the face of a bluff over a creek. So the following day, I slipped in, circling and getting directly above his roosting spot. Setting up between a couple of trees and a hollow place in front of a big rock seemed to be a good location, and I could see the area well. Thankfully, he gobbled lustily at wake-up time, and a gobbler way up the mountain gobbled back once or twice.

After gobbling several times, the bird I roosted flew down and started slowly working his way up the ridge above the bluff. I could occasionally see him taking a few steps, then strutting. Finally, calling very softly to him one time after he was on the ground, he gobbled loudly and continued toward me. He soon was in range to shoot, but his head and neck were behind a small American holly tree. I waited with gun ready, knowing he would soon reveal his neck and head for a clean shot.

Entirely focused on that gobbler, I heard a whistling whoosh of flapping wings, and a hen turkey flew in and lit on the ground not three feet from my elbow. She immediately spotted me, putted and flew, at which the gobbler ran back down the mountain and flew off the bluff. It is very likely I could have killed the gobbler by shooting through the top of that little holly tree, but I did not want to take a chance of crippling him. So, very disappointed, I sat there for a while, licking my wounds.

Finally, remembering the gobbler up the mountain above me, I decided to move and get set up looking up the steep mountain. I then called to see if a response could be aroused. After cutting a couple of times loudly on a diaphragm call, sure enough, a gobbler answered, but he was way up the mountain. I waited a little longer, called again, and he answered closer. I was not yet able to see him because of the steep slope of the mountain. After about 15 minutes, there he was, finally appearing above me and stepping up on a log approximately 35 yards. I shot, and down he went. Because it was so steep, he started flopping and rolling down the side of the mountain. I knew that my shot had broken his neck, so I was not in any hurry to get to him.

Getting up then, I walked to where he lay. Upon turning him over, I discovered he had four beards of varying lengths totalling over 23 inches in length. Had I taken a shot at that first gobbler earlier that morning, I would not have killed this multiple bearded bird. When he was dressed, I noticed numerous spur marks on his thighs, breast, and back, but he

The author's four-bearded gobbler taken in Jackson County, Alabama.

still weighed over 21 pounds. I have killed multiple bearded gobblers before, but none with four in total were that long.

There are many other examples of having gobblers spooked or scared away, but one that sticks in my memory occurred in West Virginia. That was a hunt with a good friend and professional colleague Dan Stiles, a former U.S. Fish and Wildlife Service biologist near the Potomac River. Dan's place was not too far from a little community called Paw Paw, where he had a cabin. It is a very remote and mountainous area, just above the river, and there was a regularly used railroad tunnel up the mountain from his place. His ownership of property was less than 100 acres. It mainly consisted of a couple of ridges with a dim road that paralleled the railroad tunnel. We had enjoyed many hunts there, but this one spring, it had been raining for four days, and we had not heard a single gobbler.

On the afternoon of the fourth day, I finally got a bird to gobble at my crow-cawing about 5:00 p.m. He was across the old road off of Dan's property. I tried to talk Dan into going with me the next morning and setting up across the road on the edge of his property. He declined as he wanted to hunt a different ridge where he had heard a gobbler before the season.

Therefore, the next morning with it still raining and drizzling intermittently, I went back to the area, and Dan went to his spot. With rain gear on and very sparse cover on those steep, hardwood hillsides, I searched as it got just a little lighter for a place to set up.

Finally, I located a couple of twin oaks that had sprouted from an old stump. I found a few shadbush limbs with some green leaves emerging, cut them and placed them in the ground in front of me. Then I got into my hiding place, hoping to hear the bird gobble. For over two hours, although attempting to stimulate something, I heard not a single gobble. The persistent drizzle was running down the back of my rain suit, and it was getting colder. I decided to call again, and from my right, just over a little ridge, came a muffled gobble. I could tell the gobbler was close. Pretty soon, scrunching around to face the direction from which he had gobbled, I could hear him drumming.

Shortly afterward, I spotted the very tip-top of his head and fan but not enough to risk a shot. He moved slowly, and soon I could barely hear him drum. Then, suddenly, here came the rumbling sound of 4-wheelers and shouting as three machines roared and sputtered up the old road below me. All three 4-wheelers had a couple of young men riding on them as they sped by. Obviously, that gobbler vanished.

They drove up to where a log had fallen across the road and began jumping over the roadside with the machines roaring and them hollering and laughing. After about 15 minutes, tiring of this activity, one hollered out, "Hey, let's go down to the river." Fortunately, they did, roaring back past me. They never looked up in the woods but thankfully moved away until they went out of hearing. Not only was this disturbance discouraging, but frustrating. Already wet and cold, I had very little hope of calling that gobbler back.

With this being the only gobbler I had heard in four days of wet hunting, I decided to try to stick it out for another hour or so. Now it was almost 10:00 a.m., so shivering a little, I called pretty loud on a diaphragm call but heard nothing.

Waiting another ten minutes or so, I called softer this time and purred, still no gobble. Shortly after calling, though, I spotted some movement out the ridge in front of me. What was that black object moving about 85 yards out the ridge?

Focused in that direction, I watched and soon recognized a big gobbler slowly walking toward me. Hoping my rain suit camo pattern was good enough to keep him from picking me out, I snuggled back in between those trees, with the little branches in front. Although he stopped and peered at my setup a couple of times, he did not waver.

Slowly, he kept advancing until he was in range, and when his head and neck went behind a tree, I was able to get my gun on him and shoot when he came out. An hour or so before, I would not have thought it possible but often patience and perseverance pay off, especially when working the only game in town.

Among other hunts that proved persistence pays off, one occurred in the Land Between the Lakes area in Tennessee many years ago on my first ever hunt there. I met some colleagues with the Tennessee Wildlife Resources Agency (TWRA) the afternoon before the season opened at their campsite and settled in.

The author with gobbler taken near Paw Paw, West Virginia.

They took me to an old road that was closed on top of a ridge and suggested I scout it. They agreed to return and pick me up at dark or shortly after that. After walking a mile or so, drifting off on finger ridges that branched off the road, I found some fresh scratching and gobbler tracks.

After crow-cawing a few times, two gobblers answered down near a small branch, and they seemed to be together. I followed as best possible the direction they were headed and luckily roosted them just before dark. I did not observe any other hunters, so I felt pretty good about my chances the opening morning.

The following day they dropped me off again before daylight at the old road, and I got near where the birds had roosted. At the appropriate time, I owl-called, and both gobblers responded. It sounded like they were in adjacent trees about 90 yards away. They gobbled quite a bit, and when the rhythm of the gobbling changed, I clucked, then tree-yelped softly, and both gobbled raucously.

I did not think calling more would help since no hens had been seen nor heard, and they soon flew down almost in range. I called softly, they both hammered back, and I could see them coming up the ridge. They were side by side, very close to each other. Fearful that a shot at that moment might cause both to be hit, I waited for a clean shot at one or the other. Then suddenly, something started crashing down the ridge behind me. It turned out to be another hunter. All that noise scared the gobblers in the other direction before I could fire a shot.

Frustrated, I got up to confront this guy when I heard three shots across the branch the way those gobblers had run. That made me think there must be two hunters, one on each side of me, who tried to slip in on those gobblers. So, as politely as possible under the circumstances, I explained to the guy when he came up that you cannot run a gobbler down.

He swore that he had not heard me calling to those birds and apologized for scaring them off. After that brief interruption, I decided to go across the branch where the other hunter had shot three times. I located the guy (actually someone I knew well but will not name) frantically searching for one of the gobblers he claimed he had knocked down with his shots. I helped him scour every gully, treetop and brushy area around for about 30 minutes, but we found no sign of the gobbler.

With this early disappointment and knowing the guys would not pick me up until about 11:00 a.m., I decided to venture further into the area and see if I could locate another gobbler. It was about 8:30, and after walking another half-mile or so, occasionally stopping to call, I finally got a response some distance away. I moved nearer, looked over the habitat and realized there were two connecting ridges with a little saddle between them. The cover, however, was pretty sparse on top of the ridges. Searching around, I located a spot not too far from that saddle, cut a few red buckeye branches, placed them in front of me, and called.

On my first call, the gobbler answered, still some distance away. I waited about five minutes and called again, a little softer this time, and he answered closer. By this time, it was about 9:45. In a few more minutes, there he was across the saddle, at about 70 yards in full strut. He put on a show for about 20 minutes on that hillside, strutting and occasionally gobbling in a very muffled tone. There was no need for me to call, as the gobbler knew where the call had come from, and I could see him, so I waited. Finally, he began moving into the saddle to go across toward me.

Eventually, he got into range at about 30 yards, where I had a clean shot. At the shot, I saw a small tree about two inches in diameter topple over between me and where he had been. I jumped up quickly and ran over to him. Luckily, however, enough of my pattern had penetrated his head and broken his neck that he was not going anywhere.

Two encounters with other hunters aside, the morning's activity had not been expected to turn out this way. Thankful, I carried the gobbler back to the meeting place where the other guys picked me up.

These few examples are not the only times turkeys have been spooked off, or I spooked them off myself, and most of them were not killed. In my younger turkey hunting days, I was a run and gun hunter who covered a lot of territory. Most likely, I scared many birds while moving around; some were seen, and others were not observed.

Eventually, I realized the places turkey gobblers liked to spend time in and changed my tactics accordingly. Of course, the more you know about the area you hunt, the better your odds are of being where he wants to be at some time during the day. Sitting and being patient may often be more productive than running and gunning.

Another example of something spooking a big gobbler that should have been killed occurred in south Alabama on a WMA called Kinterbish Creek. I hunted this cooperatively managed area annually for over ten years. Each spring, I would plan for about five days of hunt time. It had excellent turkey hunting on it for many years until the paper company progressively converted much of it to short-rotation slash and loblolly pine plantations.

Fortunately, it did not have much hunting pressure for a public WMA, except for a few local hunters. Most of the locals did not get too far from the limited roads that traversed the area. Regardless, the limit of turkey gobblers in Alabama was five per season, and that spring had been a perfect gobbling year.

Through good fortune and experience hunting the

area, I had come to know pretty well from spring to spring, where a gobbler might be found. Part of my success was the willingness to do a lot of walking to get to them. That particular spring opening week had been great. I had killed a gobbler each of the first four mornings.

Feeling pretty confident about where a fifth one might be, I planned to limit out before returning home. So that fifth morning before daylight, I walked down a rutted-out sandy road with a bridge out for approximately two miles. My urgency was to get to a place on a creek where several birds had been found in past years. I felt confident no one else had walked that far in to hunt the area.

Sure enough, at gobbling time, I heard two birds gobble and quickly realized one bird was the dominant gobbler or that the other bird had gathered some hens and quit gobbling. So I crossed the creek to set up and call to the gobbler thought to be the dominant one down the creek about 200 yards. There was a fairly open flat between us, so I sat on the edge of the flat and began calling.

The gobbler answered every call I made, and I was sure he would come in. Regardless, he stayed about 75 to 80 yards away for well over thirty minutes. I decided to shut up, sit still, and watch for him by giving him some time to anticipate what was happening with that hen. He stayed about that same distance away, and occasionally, I could spot him through the creek bottom vegetation.

After about 20 minutes of not calling, I could see him working his way closer. He was almost in range. I already had my shotgun on my knee pointed in his direction, so I did not need to move, but suddenly he spooked. He was running away from me, and not wanting to risk a crippling shot, I just sat there. In a minute or two, I saw something moving from pretty close to where he had been when he spooked.

It was a big bobcat, carrying something in its mouth.

Knowing what poor scent capability bobcats have and how movement-oriented they are, I just sat still. He was slinking by me at about 15 yards, and as the big cat got closer, I could see he was carrying half of a cottontail rabbit. He never saw me nor smelled me and walked on up the creek carrying that rabbit. It is unknown if he was stalking that gobbler or just by chance walked close enough to spook him.

Many encounters over the years with bobcats and coyotes scaring gobblers have convinced me that most of them were stalking either the gobbler or the caller. Because the coyote's sense of smell is so acute; they usually smell you before getting too close.

These examples convince me that a spring gobbler hunter needs to remain flexible, be willing to try something different, and learn to be patient and persistent.

CHAPTER 19

The Good, The Bad and The Ugly

As previously mentioned, it is a fact that you cannot kill a gobbler if you are snuggled in bed or your sleeping bag. In my case, when the season is in, I often have limited time to hunt in any one place and have usually paid for several expensive non-resident licenses. For many, years I hunted from eight to fourteen states every spring, and most were limited to a few days in each state, often hunting with professional colleagues or friends.

Occasionally, by trying to include a hunt in with some work-related travel, I could only hunt a day or two, so in that situation, you have to go regardless. The extremes, of course, are hunting in snow, torrential rainstorms, severe wind and cold, or lightning storms and tornados. Although it does not make me sound too bright, I have hunted turkeys in all of these situations.

Many years back, a non-resident had to apply for a permit to hunt in Illinois. I had not hunted in Illinois for a few years. In planning to lead a regional research committee meeting at the Max McGraw Wildlife Foundation near Dundee, Illinois, I noted that it would be during the Illinois spring gobbler season. Therefore, I made application early and, fortunately, received a permit.

Unfortunately, other factors interfered with my plan "A" before heading there, and I only had one day to get to the central part of the state and one morning to hunt. So, I contacted a biologist friend of mine with the Illinois Department of Natural Resources and asked if he knew any place close by where I might squeeze in a morning hunt. He said he did and would meet me at the motel in the little town he recommended. He took me to a small piece of private land, less than 100 acres adjacent to a hunt club, and pointed out another small area across the road of about 40 acres.

There was no time to scout, but I planned to get there early the following day and walk in before daylight. Fortunately, I had packed a camo rain suit and other hunting equipment. Because, on awakening the next morning at 4:00 a.m., the rain was coming down in buckets, with little hope of letting up.

With some trepidation, I headed out to the area. There was a dim sandy road going into the property, so I slowly worked my way into this hardwood-dominated property. About three-fourths of the way in, I flushed a hen out of a tall pine. I decided to stop and listen nearby, although it was pouring rain and pelting off the rain suit like hail. Finding a sparse clump of young oak seedlings that had sprouted up around an old stump, I settled in and listened to it rain.

It rained incessantly until about 10:15, and by that time, after calling some, with no response, I had almost given up on hearing or seeing any other turkeys. Then, getting to my feet, I carefully did a little visual observation of the area, noting that there was a bit of a mound that sloped up to the highest spot on the property to my right. It was about 200 yards away.

Getting over to the mound, I found a place to hide with some blackjack oak and an occasional bur oak encircling the mound without a lot of understory vegetation. At that point, I decided to sit there and do some calling until noon when in Illinois, you had to quit hunting. Although it had continued to drizzle, the hard rain had stopped, and at least I could see a little better, although it was getting foggy.

A slate, box, or typical friction call would have been useless. So instead, I had a diaphragm call and an aluminum pot call with a glass striker that, out of desperation, I thought might make a decent yelp. I would call first on the diaphragm about every five minutes or so, then with the aluminum pot call, which didn't sound too bad considering how soaked everything was. I watched down the slope and to either side as far as possible for anything moving.

Then at 10:55, below me and slightly to my left, something red moved. Soon, I could see the red wattles coming up the slope toward me. It turned out to be three long beards, possibly siblings, that never made a sound. They did not strut or display at all but advanced until a clean shot was taken at about 30 yards. I did not know for sure that those birds were coming to my call, nor did I care. I was just so delighted to see those gobblers.

I quickly jumped up, shook the water off and headed to the rental car. I needed to get checked out of the hotel by noon and check the turkey. The drive over to Max McGraw to get ready for the meeting the next morning was at least warm and dry.

After arriving at Max McGraw and checking in, I then cleaned that gobbler. The chef there was kind enough to allow me to process, wrap and place the gobbler in their freezer until I was ready to leave. It wound up being a memorable experience, and I considered it a good hunt despite the poor weather, but there are bad hunts as well.

More recently, after having hunted eight states, taken 13 mature gobblers myself, and called in seven more for other colleagues and youngsters, I had agreed to come back to Illinois. I came not to hunt for myself but to call a gobbler for friends, Laura Andersen, and her husband, Chris. Laura and I worked together for several years doing Conservation Leadership for Tomorrow (CLfT) Workshops around the country.

Laura and Chris wanted to learn something about turkey hunting. So, after leaving Columbia, Missouri, where I had taken two nice gobblers, the last in a driving rainstorm, I drove over in yet another downpour to southern Illinois. The place I was to meet them was at a camp just north and west of Cairo. I arrived at the camp, got my gear unloaded and visited with Laura and Chris, neither of whom had ever turkey hunted.

There are quite a few scattered parcels of the Shawnee National Forest north and west of the place we were staying, so after purchasing yet another non-resident license and permit, we drove around some in the continuing rain. Primarily, we were looking for a likely place to walk in the next morning where we would not be competing with other hunters. However, the season was coming to an end, and they had not scouted, so we did not know exactly where to go.

Before dark, we saw an old road crossing a small branch or creek where we could park the vehicle and walk towards some steep hills in the distance. It looked from the road like turkey habitat on both sides, so we decided to try that area in the morning.

The three of us, wearing rain suits and rubber boots, crossed the branch, which had become much deeper by morning. We headed upward toward some fairly steep ridges, occasionally stopping to catch our breath as we climbed.

We made it near the top just before daylight. By walking ahead, I found that about 80 yards farther up the hill, a sizable grown-up powerline crossed the mountain.

The old road crossed the powerline. I walked upward, finding that the woods opened up considerably. I recognized that the top of the main ridge would provide good visibility and calling location. Laura and Chris came up, and we walked to the top of the flat as it was just getting light.

After I crow-cawed loudly, a bird gobbled back across the powerline down in a steep ravine. The powerline itself was grown-up in briars, weeds, and saplings, especially near the top. In looking around, there was a side ridge facing down toward the hollow where the bird had gobbled. It sloped downward through some mature oaks and yellow poplar trees. We quickly made each of them a sparse blind and got seated.

My hope was the gobbler, if he came, would cross the powerline and walk up one of the open ridges toward where they sat. So, after getting them positioned, I sat down at the base of a big oak tree near the ridge's peak but directly above and between where the two of them sat.

It was time to call, and the turkey gobbled maybe 100 yards below them. He had crossed the powerline and appeared to be coming right up one of the ridges toward Laura and Chris. I waited a short time then called softly but got no response. Deciding to sit quietly, I fully expected the gobbler to walk up soon so one of them could get a shot. It had quit raining, and I felt sure the gobbler was coming, not having heard any hens.

Suddenly, there he was to my immediate left, about 35 yards away, having side skirted around where they were. He popped into a strut, then slowly worked his way across the peak of the ridge. Soon, I heard the gobbler drumming behind me and around to my right as he moved away.

Knowing that neither of them could see the bird, all I could do was call and hope he might circle and come back across the top of the ridge in range of Laura and Chris. Unfortunately, he continued skirting around the ridge behind me to the right until he went out of earshot. We waited for 20 minutes or so, and although I called several times, he did not respond or show. Close, but no cigar and neither of them saw nor heard him drum.

Later that morning, as we scouted and occasionally called, we realized there was a green plot on some private property almost at the base of those ridges on the powerline right-of-way. Using my binoculars before we headed back to the truck, I glassed the plot and spotted a huge gobbler in full strut with two hens. Being limited to morning hunting only, we decided to get some lunch and scout some new territory.

By the time we got back to the truck, it was raining again, so we headed back to camp for a rest. Later we drove miles and miles around the national forest's scattered parcels. We neither saw nor found any place we liked better than where we had been, and the roads were getting nasty. We did see some turkeys on private land but had no permission to hunt them. It constantly rained the next two days. Even though we tried to hunt, nothing happened, except we were getting very wet and cold as the temperature dropped.

The evening before the final day of hunting, I went back to the first area we had hunted. I found a way to stay in the forest but get reasonably close to the green plot at the bottom of the ridges. The next morning we sneaked around the edge of the forest boundary following our plan and crossed the powerline right-of-way, getting settled before daylight. It was drizzling; after daylight, I tried owl and crow calling, yelping loudly several times. While having trouble hearing him, both of them said a gobbler answered me several times. But, alas, thunderstorms began again right after daylight.

After about an hour, we talked it over and decided to move them to a spot across the powerline, placing them on the crest of little humps. Those spots would enable them each to see down toward the green plot and back the other way, hoping the gobbler might show up later in the morning. Unfortunately, both sides of the ridge adjacent to the right-of-way were choked with multi-flora rose thickets. We took our pruning shears and diligently cut away and pulled out thorny stems so that both could see better from their spots.

After getting them into place, I backed down the hill below Laura and started calling. At the second call, two gobblers answered—one in the woods above us on the hillside and the other down toward the private land.

At each call, they seemed to be getting closer. Being behind and below Laura, I could not see the gobbler myself, but I did see Laura raise her gun to her shoulder, and she held it there for quite some time. Finally, both birds gobbled very close, and one gobbler sounded like he was right on top of Chris, so I waited for one of them to take a shot.

Unfortunately, neither of them shot. Chris said later he was waiting for Laura to fire, and then he was going to shoot. His gobbler left following a hen. Laura thought the gobbler she was looking at was a little too far, and she did not feel comfortable taking a shot. They both had finally seen gobblers up close, and though neither shot, they had a great time, considering the circumstances.

I do not remember working harder trying to call in a gobbler for anyone in such a period of rainy weather and unfamiliar territory. To Laura and Chris's credit, they were both troopers, never complaining, and willing to follow my hunches and suggestions in our effort to get them gobblers. Sadly, having hoped to get at least one of them a gobbler, I had to admit defeat. This is an example of some of the bad, but it can get worse.

Now the ugly. Many years ago, hunting in the Ouachita Mountains of Arkansas, my buddy, Thurman Booth, and I had both killed a gobbler the first day. However, the weather changed, and thunderstorms raged for the next day or two. Even though we had hunted hard, neither of us had heard a bird. On the fourth day, he let me out that morning at a promising spot, and he went to another area. He planned to pick me up at noon. Again, neither of us heard or worked a bird that morning. As we headed back to camp, he mentioned a bridge/culvert had washed out earlier that spring.

I knew the road, and since it had not yet been fixed and accessed an area into some remote mountains, I gave it some thought. Having taken birds there in past years, it occurred to me that it might be an excellent place to spend the afternoon. Although we knew severe weather was predicted in the area that evening, we agreed that he would put me out at the washed-out culvert and pick me up at dark. I had water and snacks in my vest to sustain me till dinner. He did just that and went on to camp.

After crossing the stream below the washed-out culvert, taking my time, I walked up the old road. On the way, I spotted indigo buntings, goldfinches, other colorful birds and emerging flowers along the roadsides while moving up the mountain. Finally, I reached the mountain peak about 2:30 p.m., having made some small side treks off the main road to look for sign on the way up, and called a time or two.

Not too far from the peak, I scared a hen in the road and assumed she was picking up grit. Farther down on the sides of the road, I had seen three old dusts, and one place where a gobbler had strutted in the road. This sign encouraged me about a possible encounter with a gobbler before dark.

I decided to sit down on the peak, eat one of my snacks and drink a little water. While sitting there with a majestic view of mountains for miles, I noticed some lightning, heard distant thunder and saw a black cloud headed in my direction. I pulled my rain gear on as the wind was picking up and swirling as it headed my way. One thing about forest service roads leading up slope, they always pull out pretty good bar ditches for drainage. They had done so on this road as I began looking around for shelter from the storm.

There was no shelter nearby. Unfortunately, I watched the approaching storm become a tornado. It would drop and seemingly jump back up, scattering debris in its path and bouncing up and down as it crossed over those ridges and mountains. Not knowing exactly where it would hit, I started searching for a place to get lower than the mountain peak.

Just back down the road, I had seen a dug-out area where the dozer pulling out the ditches had left about a three-foot-wide cut that sloped downhill. I decided to get into that cut that did not have any big trees nearby and hope not to get blown away. By the time I got on the ground, it was lightning all around. The rain was coming down in a deluge, and the wind was howling. Getting into the ditch and covering up as best possible, I could only hope and pray that it passed without coming directly over the top of me.

It passed by with a roar like a locomotive and then got eerily quiet.

The wind died, and the storm moved on to the east. It appeared to have passed less than a half-mile to the north, as it was easy from the peak to see mangled trees and debris on the mountainside below. By that time, it was 4:35, and it had pretty much gone out of hearing. It was a weird situation as there was no wind, the rain had stopped, and no birds were singing or moving around. I decided to begin walking back toward the washout; being muddy, wet, and cold, I needed to move around a little to warm up.

On getting back to the washed-out culvert area, I found a place to cross the flooded stream and saw my buddy arriving. He had brought me a sandwich and a soda that I truly appreciated. Once in the truck, he said a tornado hit one of the largest marinas on Lake Ouachita earlier that afternoon. It had caused severe damage to several homes and businesses in the area. I then shared my story and my thanks for being alive.

In my younger days, I witnessed how devastating such a storm can be. We experienced a tornado where I was raised in Alabama on November 23, 1957. I remember the lengthy and costly effort to repair our home and replace the outbuildings we lost. I recall another case of having a lightning storm so close to me that my shotgun was left leaning against a tree while I moved 50 yards or more away until the storm passed.

These are examples of the ugly we sometimes find ourselves in when hunting.

CHAPTER 20

Don't Call Too Early

In the late 1960s or early 1970s, I learned a lesson about calling to a gobbler on the roost too early in the morning. I was hunting on what was then called the Ferguson Ranch property west of Little Rock, Arkansas. Having hunted it before, I knew there was a saddle between two mountain ridges that had proven quite productive.

The saddle was approximately 70 yards across at its most narrow part. Not having an opportunity to scout the area the spring before the season, I slipped into the saddle well before daylight and listened. I sat down about in the middle of it and waited in the hope of hearing a gobbler.

As a faint pink ray in the eastern sky began to show, a gobbler thundered out to the south of the saddle, on the east side of the ridge, probably 150 yards away. It was still dark on the ground, and it sounded like the bird was slightly uphill from me. So I slipped quietly up the ridge face to the south and found a big tree to sit in front of as he gobbled a couple of more times.

After settling in, excited at how close he was, I gave a soft cluck on my mouth call. He gobbled back immediately, then flew down within 45 yards of me. I was surprised as I glimpsed the movement of him flying down and could barely make out his profile as he strutted by me at about 25 yards. However, it was still too dark to see his head and neck enough to shoot. In my excitement, I failed to think of trying to cluck him out of a strut, afraid he might spook since he was so close. Instead, I sat very still as he worked his way down to the saddle and watched as the area became more sunlit and visible.

When the gobbler got to the saddle, he strutted to the bottom level and proceeded to display and serenade the world with his thunderous gobbles. The gobbler was strutting right around the area where I had first sat down before I heard him.

Without my moving, he would likely have come to that strut zone anyway. Instead, he strutted back and forth along the saddle, almost coming close enough for a shot but not quite in range. Not being able to move forced me to wait until he strutted back away from me in the saddle and to call very softly, to which he gobbled.

This strutting exhibition continued for at least 20 minutes. Then, suddenly, the bird came out of strut, putted loudly, and flew up into a pine tree in the middle of the saddle. I was not sure what had alarmed him for a minute or two. Then I spotted movement on the ground.

A coyote walked up from the west side of the saddle and started sniffing the ground where the gobbler had been strutting. I could see both the coyote and the gobbler in the tree above. The gobbler and I watched without making a sound. The coyote walked around below him, sniffing and looking up at the gobbler. Had my position been upwind of the coyote, he would likely have smelled me and vanished.

This standoff between the gobbler and coyote continued, with the coyote looking up occasionally at the gobbler. The wise old bird was not alarmed that the coyote knew he was up in the tree. The coyote continued walking around sniffing and daring the gobbler to fly down for another 30 minutes. I was amazed at his patience. Finally, the coyote started walking back to the west, occasionally stopping to look back until he disappeared.

Looking at my watch, it was about 7:30, so I decided to wait another 15 minutes before calling to the gobbler. I hoped he was over his scare from the coyote and would fly down and come toward me after such a long time sitting up in that tree. On calling softly, the gobbler looked my way but did not gobble. Instead, he began to walk out the limb, looking down like he would come to the ground. Then, after another minute, he turned away and flew down over the crest of the saddle to the north.

I called. He gobbled but started moving up the mountain to the north, occasionally stopping to gobble. I got up and tried to follow him, hoping that he would turn around and return to me. Sadly, the gobbler eventually went on over the top of that mountain, and I never heard him again.

The lesson is that you should not call to a hot gobbler while it is still too dark to see on the ground. Occasionally, turkeys will fly down in the dark before you can see clearly. That anticipation of getting to a willing hen makes gobblers sometimes do crazy things, like fly down in the dark. It has been evident to me for years that a coyote will stalk a gobbling bird, as well as a hen that is calling. Based on the evidence observed, I am confident that they often are successful, especially if they can get close enough to the bird before being seen.

On several occasions, I have watched coyotes out west stalk gobbling birds. Once I observed a strutting gobbler that almost waited too long before taking to the air. His hesitation enabled the coyote to jump up and pull out a couple of tail feathers as the gobbler flew off. Hens seem to be more observant and become alarmed very quickly when a coyote shows up anywhere near them.

A friend of mine sent me a video several years ago where a guy videotaped a strutting gobbler and five hens. He had set out one of those early hard plastic hen decoys in the strutting area. As he was filming the hens and strutting gobbler, the hens became alert, looking at something to their left, and then walked away quickly. When the photographer panned around, he spotted a coyote slinking in toward the gobbler. It seemed as though the gobbler was paying no attention to the coyote. He continued videotaping as the coyote got closer. The gobbler finally spotted the coyote and flew away.

The frustrated coyote then focused his attention on the rigid plastic hen decoy. Crouching down, it made a mad dash, trying to clamp its teeth around the neck of the decoy that was firmly staked in the ground. As it reached out to grab the decoy by the neck, its teeth could not penetrate that plastic. It so startled him that he ran off about ten yards and looked back at the decoy spinning around on the stake. The coyote studied the decoy like he could not believe what had just happened. He soon realized it was a fake hen and walked away with head and tail down, obviously confused.

CHAPTER 21

Know When to Hold 'em and Know When to Fold 'em

As previously mentioned, some turkeys that, depending on the emotional state and how many hens they have with them, sometimes will not respond to a call. However, there are other times when you may encounter one of the "kamikaze" gobblers who come running to the first call they hear. A lot depends on how much patience and persistence you have. If you can avoid making a grave mistake, it may just be a matter of time before that gobbler decides to check you out.

Sometimes you can determine by their behavior or the coloration of the head and neck if they will potentially make that fatal mistake. Sometimes, you need to "fold 'em" and try to get him to work another day, or forget him and find another gobbler to hunt.

A good friend whom I had enjoyed hunting with for many years called me several years back as he occasionally did when he had encountered a problematic gobbler. I listened carefully to his description of the interactions he had experienced and asked an occasional question for clarification to help me understand his dilemma. Occasionally, after one of these discussions, I would suggest different techniques he might try. Sometimes, my advice would be to forget that gobbler and find another one.

One particular discussion we had was about a gobbler that would usually respond, seemingly interested in the calls. Then, however, it would just go mute and disappear. So, it seemed appropriate to ask him how many days he had already spent hunting this bird. When he said ten, my immediate response was it was time to "fold 'em." Mark that one up. Hunt him next spring if he is still around, but forget that gobbler this spring and find another one.

Being somewhat stubborn and opinionated like me, he said that he would kill that turkey before the season was out. My suggestion to him was based on my opinion that the gobbler had patterned his calling and hunting style. So, I encouraged him to find another turkey. After the season was over, he admitted that he hunted that gobbler 21 times and never got a shot at him.

Although having interacted with some turkeys like that, the most I ever hunted the same gobbler was eight mornings, not on successive days. Since arriving at that conclusion, I decided never to expend more than two or three days hunting the same bird. Sometimes you need to know when to hold 'em or know when to fold 'em and move on.

An example of knowing when to hold 'em occurred with a big gobbler that a friend, Ray Rinker, and I hunted on a mountain in Virginia known locally as Paris Mountain. It was a rugged area of private land above the Shenandoah River. We had permission to hunt, but it also was hunted by others. Because we both hunted other places, we usually did not hunt that area until later in the season. However, this particular year, we had each killed one gobbler elsewhere before going together to Paris Mountain. The weather had been great for several days, so after checking by phone with the owner, we went up on a Saturday morning, about three weeks into the season.

Most of my Saturdays had been used up guiding at Quantico, so I was looking forward to hunting with my friend. We arrived early enough to get to the top of the mountain before it got light and heard two gobblers, one way below us and one on around the mountain. So, we decided to hunt together and go to the gobbler below us, staying about 200 yards above him because of the very open hardwood habitat. The bird gobbled several times. Finally, we heard hens answering him below, and sure enough, he flew down to those hens and quit gobbling. We tried to drop down some, get closer, and get him to gobble, but we never heard him again. So, we decided to go toward where we had heard the other gobbler and, if not successful there, come back and try the first gobbler again.

That mountain is very steep, and it took us at least 30 minutes to get anywhere near where we thought we had heard that bird gobble. We looked for an occasional morel mushroom on the way there. Spotting something on the ground that looked out of place, I stopped and dug it out. It was a nice Case Trapper XX, a two-bladed pocket knife that had been there long enough for the blades to get slightly rusty. Ray indicated he would like to have the knife and would clean it up and keep it, which was fine with me.

After getting on the side of the mountain where we thought we had heard the gobbler earlier, we stopped and called, getting an immediate response about 300 yards away. We carefully worked our way about 150 yards closer and decided to call. We quickly decided that if the bird came, Ray would shoot. Therefore, backing up about 30 yards behind him, I called again. The gobbler responded but seemed to be in the same place as before. We sat for a few minutes, and when calling again, the gobbler responded. He appeared to be in the very same area, except maybe a little further to our right.

Ray came back to me and said he would try to work his way down the hill to the right as it seemed the bird had found a strutting area he did not want to leave. Agreeing on that strategy, I moved straight down the hill about another 50 to 75 yards, found a place, and kept calling occasionally. On getting set up there, I could see the edge of a small opening.

At first notice, I did not realize exactly what it was.

Getting out my little slate call, I waited about five minutes and called softly. The gobbler hammered back very close but to the right where Ray had moved. Sitting tight, I could not see the bird but pretty soon could hear drumming near the opening. I expected to see the gobbler any second or to hear Ray shoot.

Instead, in less than a minute, the turkey gobbled again without being called to, but to my right. By this time, it became apparent that the little opening was a narrow grassy, power line right-of-way that came around the side of the mountain. The gobbler was strutting up and down that power line opening.

Expecting to hear Ray shoot any second, I sat still. Instead, the drumming got louder, and pretty soon, I could see two big gobblers working their way from the direction of the power line, directly toward me. They were inside 30 yards to my left, then went behind some small pines allowing me to get my shotgun up.

As soon as one of them cleared that cover and raised his head, I took the shot. The other gobbler flew by me close enough that I could feel the wind from his wings. He had a massive beard and was probably the dominant bird that had done all the gobbling. Ray came up and said he almost had them in range a couple of times but could not get a shot. After that, we left for home and split up when we got back to Highway 50, where he had left his truck. Him with a knife, and me with the gobbler.

During the last week of the season, the then Director of the U.S. Fish and Wildlife Service, John Turner, called and wanted to know if we could take his son hunting the last Saturday of the season. I told him to let me check with the landowner up at Paris Mountain because there were at least two gobblers up there.

Ray had already told me he had limited out near home and would not be going that Saturday. After checking with the landowner and getting his approval. I called John and suggested we plan on meeting at Upperville, Virginia, at 4:30 the following Saturday morning. On Friday evening, however, John called and said that his son had appendicitis and was in the hospital.

Still possessing one tag and having already loaded my gear and shotgun in the truck, I decided to go by myself. Arriving very early, instead of going in the usual way, I walked around the backside of the mountain up a different ridge, straight up the mountain. Hoping not to flush any birds, I soon made it to the top.

It was still black dark on getting to the top. Surveying that knob, I recognized an old house place with part of the base and chimney still standing. I sat down on that old chimney base and waited, thanking God as always, for yet another day in wild places and listening to the night sounds.

I heard some coyotes in the distance. The whippoorwills were still calling. Then, as those first pink rays to the east showed up, I began hearing several different songbirds. These ranged from wood thrushes to cardinals to mourning doves. Next, I heard a fox bark, then some Canada geese down toward the river honking. I fully expected to hear a turkey gobble but did not. I sat there for probably another ten minutes or so. Finally, after crows cawing and owls hooting but hearing no gobble, I decided to move back to the north along the top of the ridge.

After having gone maybe 80 yards, trying to creep, a bird gobbled almost straight below the knob from the house place where I had been. The bird sounded like it was about 150 yards down near a fold in the ridge.

On a hunch, I decided to move to the north another 75 yards, then try to drop down just above a bit of a crest that ran around the side of the mountain. Even though it was very late in the season, at this elevation, aside from an occasional thicket of mountain laurel, there just was not much ground cover. I searched around for a good place to set up on the steep hillside. Noticing a place where some tulip poplar sprouts had come up around an old stump, I worked my way into them and faced back toward the gobbler.

I waited maybe five minutes, then clucked softly, getting an immediate response from where the gobbler had been the first time. Thinking that he should be on the ground since it was good light now, I realized that he was still on the roost. I did not call for another few minutes. Before long, he gobbled again. Right after that gobble, I heard two or three hens leave from a tree between me and the gobbler and fly down the side of the mountain. They even cackled a little as they left the roost. I figured then the gobbler had flown down with them, and the hunt was over.

I waited about five minutes and called softly on my slate. The gobbler cut me off with a loud gobble. He was definitely on the ground in front of and below my setup. It sounded like he was slightly under the crest of the ridge about 75 yards down the side of the mountain. He had moved my way and seemed to be coming closer.

Pretty soon, he gobbled again almost directly below and to the right of the direction I was facing. As quietly as possible, I began moving around to the right to see the crest below me. I waited for seemingly another 15 agonizing minutes, and he gobbled again, straight down and over the ridge.

At this point on that very open mountainside, I expected to see him any moment. After a few minutes, he came over the crest in full strut. It was like he had emerged from the ground. Then, he came partially out of a strut and looked directly toward me, causing me to think maybe he had spotted me. Then, however, he proceeded to strut up the hill from the crest. His strutting brought him to about 65 yards below me. He turned, like he was on a pair of roller skates, and strutted back down to the crest.

Then, he quickly whirled around and repeated that same strut pattern back toward me. This time when he turned and put his fan toward me as he strutted back down his zone, I glanced at my watch. It was only 7:35. About 20 yards below me and directly between us was another small clump of sprouts around an old stump. It had some deer-browsed stems of green briar about three feet tall mixed among them. By this time, having gotten my shotgun up on my knee and aimed in the right direction, there was nothing to do but wait.

The gobbler continued to parade up and down that strut zone for the next 25 minutes, stopping at the top each time and peering intensely toward me. Hoping my camo clothing prevented him from realizing that this clump was a hunter, I sat nervously.

Finally, after at least 20 more struts back and forth, it was clear that he was not likely to get any closer. Evaluating the possibilities and expecting him to spook any second, I considered a move but was very reluctant to do so for fear of him spotting or hearing me.

Not having called to this gobbler since he appeared over the ridge crest, it was evident he knew where the call originated. So ultimately, I decided that the next time he put that fan in my face, I was going to try to slide on my rear end down his way, keeping low to the ground.

Doing this only while he was strutting downhill was a huge gamble. Each time he got to his turnaround point, my only option was to freeze in place and hope he did not spook. Amazingly, in five more struts, I had slid almost to the clump of green briars and sprouts. Freezing in place again, I waited for another turnaround and slid again, pulling myself up enough to get my shotgun aimed in his direction before he turned and started back up his strut zone.

My estimation now was that my maneuvering had gotten me to about 45 yards from his stopping and turning point. Having a diaphragm call in my mouth the entire time, I had fought trying to make a call in this situation for fear of spooking him.

Finally, however, I decided to make a soft purr just before he reached his turnaround point. He quickly strutted about five yards closer, raised his head, and I fired. He went tumbling and flopping down the hill. Jumping to my feet, I hurried to him as quickly as possible with legs that were almost asleep from being cramped up so long.

He was a magnificent gobbler. My load of 7 ½ copper-plated shot had fatally broken his neck and macerated his head. In this case, patience, some confidence based on experience, some knowledge of gobbler behavior, and a whole lot of luck paid off.

What a hunt! Throughout the entire ordeal, my thought was that something is going to spook that bird. However, aside from patience, persistence, the gobbler being visible, and luck, taking a chance moving the only way I could had paid off. Having thought about this particular situation often, I can only speculate that he was so focused on his displaying and the noise he made while strutting that he neither saw nor heard me when I moved.

Looking at my watch, it was now 8:30 and what a morning! I went over to his strut zone for my observational interests after placing my carrying strap over his head and legs. His strutting up and down that area had pretty much swept that zone clear of leaves and loose debris. His wingtips were worn down significantly from a great deal of strutting activity during this season.

Had this gobbler not remained in sight for such a long time with no more gobbling than he did, I would typically have gotten up and left. But, remembering that scenario where my original sitting spot was, I am amazed that he did not see me while scooting on my rear end to get closer. I halfway expected him to spook. There was, of course, no way of knowing if this was the gobbler that had flown by me a week earlier, but he sure had that same heavy beard. And, he was definitely in the same general territory I had hunted the previous Saturday.

Virginia gobbler taken 1982 near Winchester.

CHAPTER 22

The "Gobblingest" Turkey

Admittedly a slow learner and not remembering my lesson with that gobbler on the old Ferguson Ranch in Arkansas, I made the same mistake one more time. While living in Virginia, and with our season over, I had bought a license to hunt in West Virginia, where the season was still open. Although near the end of their season, I had not found an opportunity to go until the last two days.

A friend had told me about a small WMA not too far across the line from Winchester, Virginia and suggested it would be worth a try. He provided directions on how to get there. So the afternoon before the last day of the season, I drove over and found a place to park. I planned to sleep in the back of my truck and started scouting about 3:30 p.m., as it was morning hunting only there.

I walked a mile from the truck in those steep mountains and decided to drop down and walk parallel to a small creek. About 4:30, I crow-cawed loudly and was a little surprised to get a gobbler to answer not too far away. Immediately, I sat down and listened as he continued along the other side of the creek, occasionally stopping to gobble.

That bird progressively became more and more vocal, gobbling about every couple of minutes but moving downstream. I followed the gobbler probably another half mile before he started moving up a steep slope of a mountain to the west, continuing to gobble.

Staying a safe distance, hopefully downslope from him, I started climbing up that mountain. In places, it was almost too steep to climb. It was beginning to get dark on the mountain when it became clear the gobbler had reached a shelf almost at the top of that mountain. The shelf was not too far above, so I sat down.

Within a few minutes, I heard him gobble, then fly up to roost. As soon as he got on the roost, he started gobbling again. Realizing it was vital for me to get down that steep mountain and find my way to the truck, I started creeping and sliding down to the bottom.

Fortunately, it was a clear night with a full moon. Walking away, I continued to hear that bird gobble until I went out of hearing. On arriving back at the truck, I ate a quick snack and got in my sleeping bag. With the alarm set at 4:00 a.m. hopefully, I could find my way back to that area before daylight.

When the alarm went off, I quickly gathered my gear and headed out with the moon helping to illuminate my travel. Acknowledging that it is hard to believe, but when I got back within hearing distance, he was gobbling in the black dark! There is no way to prove it, but I firmly believe that bird gobbled all night long.

Regardless, as he continued to gobble, I started climbing and pulling my way up that steep slope, going to the north of where I thought he was roosted. I finally made it up to that shelf before it got light. With him gobbling so often, it was not hard to tell when he was about a hundred yards or less from me. Vegetation on the shelf, which was pretty flat, was predominantly blueberry bushes, briars and hardwood trees. It was just beginning to get light, and the gobbler was very close.

He continued to gobble, although I was unable to see him. But I could tell exactly where he was in the tree. Completely forgetting the lesson that I should have learned from that Ferguson Ranch hot gobbler, I made a real soft cluck on my mouth call. The gobbler immediately gobbled, flew down toward me, and quickly started drumming. Within a minute, I could occasionally make out his form as he worked around those blueberry bushes and green briars.

It was still too dark to see well, and I could not see his

head and neck. He occasionally came out of strut, then started drumming again. He passed by me at about ten yards. I probably could have killed him since he was so close, but I did not want to chance potentially hitting him in the body, missing or crippling him.

He drummed on by me and started toward the top of the mountain, probably another 50 yards higher than the ledge. He continued to gobble often. Finally, when he was on top, I began working my way carefully to get on the same level as him.

He had proceeded to the south on reaching the mountain's peak, along the top, which was a fairly open ridge. I crawled up to a big scarlet oak tree, got myself settled, then called. He thundered right back. I could soon see him coming back toward me. My confidence level went up immediately. On he came, stopping to gobble sporadically until he was about 60 yards out.

At that point, he seemed to stand up on his tiptoes and glare right at my hiding spot. I had my shotgun already on my knee and was waiting until he got in range. He continued to strut and gobble in a small circle without getting any closer for about ten minutes. There was no telling how many times he had already gobbled that morning. Finally, he came out of a strut and started walking back to the south, still stopping to gobble every so often. I got up and followed, somehow not spooking him, although he was not all that far ahead of me. I located a place where dropping down the slope a little would enable me to work my way around in front of him. It was very steep, however, and took much too long. I finally reached the top of the ridge again. By this time, he had gone on by that area and was some distance ahead, still gobbling.

Twice more that morning, I got that gobbler within 60 to 70 yards and could see him but had no chance to shoot. He must have gobbled 300 times or more. But he would not come any closer than about 60 yards. To my knowledge, he never gathered any hens by his gobbling the entire morning, although he sure gave it an all-American effort. Hunting ended there at noon, so I walked away from him at 11:00 a.m. with him continuing to gobble. Finally, I headed back toward the truck as it was not clear to me exactly where he had led me through those mountains. I did, however, realize that it was going to be a long walk.

That bird continued to gobble until I was out of hearing. On arriving back where my truck was parked, it was a little past noon, and the season was over. Although never close enough to see his spurs, he had a huge paint-brush-wide beard and was a big gobbler. He had likely experienced numerous encounters with other hunters during the season and learned his lesson.

That bird defeated me fairly and squarely, primarily because I failed to learn from my first mistake of calling too early. Since that morning, I have tried not to make this mistake again. I am pleased that old gobbler hopefully lived to spread his seed amongst many hens in that area. Admittedly, though, I have never heard a bird gobble as much as that monarch did. My hat is off to him. Unfortunately, I never had an opportunity to hunt that area again.

CHAPTER 23

Pros and Cons of Guiding

The opportunity to provide counsel about hunting and partial or full-time guidance for the first-time, novice or experienced hunter has mainly been enjoyable. In addition, it is a way to share the fair-chase hunting experience with others, be they family members, colleagues, friends, or youngsters.

In addition, it often gives the person doing the guiding an opportunity to observe things they might have missed if they were intent on killing the animal themselves. Having hunted over the years on my own (aside from early guidance from my dad), this is a welcomed benefit. I can only remember three times being guided by someone else on a hunt, and I have hunted in many places in North America and several foreign countries.

The great majority of my hunting has been the do-it-yourself (DIY) hunt, although I am always eager to listen to recommendations from local people, friends or colleagues when planning a hunt. For sure, having guided others a lot over the years, the experiences helped me understand the need to listen to the guide.

To be a good client, you must realize that most guides will provide you with the best advice, knowledge and suggestions to enable you to have a successful hunt. Many of my early guiding efforts were for family members, then for friends and colleagues who wanted to learn more about hunting, and later, for others who asked. In most cases, we agreed on how we would hunt before going, which resulted in fewer problems.

Considering whom I was asked to guide and being flexible has helped me understand the challenges. Although having guided upland game bird hunts, rabbit and squirrel hunts, waterfowl hunts, deer hunts, and other big game hunts, most of my guiding has been for wild turkey hunting.

A couple of explanations might be helpful and should be understood. First, I have guided hundreds of people—the U.S. Secretary of State, the Assistant Secretary of the Department of the Interior, the Director of the U.S. Fish and Wildlife Service, CEOs of national organizations, senior military officers, senators, astronauts, professional colleagues, friends, family members (young and old) and others.

These guided hunts were never planned with an understanding that compensation was expected. Although some of the people I guided may be referred to as "clients," this does not mean they paid me. The explanation is that except for two locations, my guiding was for people who asked me to take them or for whom I volunteered.

For many years, the two places where I guided clients turkey hunting were at the Quantico Marine Base south of Washington, D.C., and the Vermejo Park Ranch in northeastern New Mexico. Concerning the Quantico situation, the Natural Resources Manager, Colonel Bill Windsor, contacted me for some on-site review of their management practices and the benefits for turkeys. This occurred not too long after we moved to Fairfax, Virginia, in the fall of 1978.

Bill familiarized me with how they assigned hunts and explained their hunting and non-hunting zone classifications during that visit. He also asked me if I might be willing to help him out by guiding some VIPs who came down for turkey hunts. He explained that some were experienced turkey hunters, some novices, and some would be people who had never hunted before. With that invitation and explaining that my "real job" required me to travel a good bit, we agreed I would primarily try to go down on Saturdays, which was their busiest day. In Virginia, Sunday hunting was illegal, and only morning hunting was allowed otherwise.

With that agreement began a long-time friendship that lasted until after Bill retired and the opportunity to meet and guide some people that I likely never would have met any other way. For the most part, it was an enjoyable and enlightening experience.

Over the next several years, it enabled me to become very familiar with most of Quantico's 55,000 acres, excluding some restricted areas. However, as with any situation where you closely interact with people, you will have a few clients who will be unhappy. Sadly, this is true for those individuals, regardless of how hard you try to help them.

Without listing the names of those who never seemed pleased, a few would not follow instructions, could not sit still and be quiet, disagreed with my helping them get into position to hunt or did not safely handle their firearms. These were some of the cons of guiding. A few of these clients were reported to Bill, with my suggestion that he never asked me to guide them again, and he did not.

The pros far outweighed the cons. Most of the people were considerate, did their best to follow instructions, and a number of them became good friends. This is not a one-up name boast, but an exceptional person, I truly enjoyed guiding there included former Florida Congressman, Senator, and Governor, Lawton Chiles.

The first time I guided Lawton, when introduced to him before the hunt, he asked me where I was from. I told him rural north Alabama originally but that I had obtained two degrees from the University of Florida, of which he was a great supporter.

We were assigned our zone to hunt that morning. After he moved his gun, vest and other clothing to my truck, we headed out to the zone well before daylight. It was not the best weather we could have hoped for, but I knew the area well and had called up gobblers there before and felt confident we would find a bird. Sadly, for whatever reason, the birds did not want to gobble that morning, but he was an experienced turkey hunter and understood the situation.

When we left the truck that morning, I noticed that his shotgun was an Ithaca semi-automatic 10- gauge, a very heavy gun, but one he seemed used to carrying. As we moved from one ridge to another, trying to stimulate a bird to gobble, it became evident that he was falling behind as we headed up a ridge.

Not wanting to over-exert him, we stopped, found a place to sit down and caught our breath. He was at least a decade older than I at the time, so he welcomed that opportunity. As we visited, I questioned why he was carrying such a heavy shotgun, and he said that he liked the killing power of the 10-gauge for turkeys and geese.

He then asked about my over/under (guides were encouraged to carry their shotgun in case they had to chase down and kill a crippled bird). I explained that it was a 12-gauge, three-inch magnum modified to make it a turkey gun. Many years back, a good gunsmith friend had cut both barrels to 23 inches long and sleeved both barrels. These sleeves were designed for shooting a very dense pattern of small copper-plated shot into a 30" circle at 40 yards. Afterward, I had silver soldered a sling swivel to the bottom barrel, added a sling swivel to the buttstock, and camouflaged the entire gun by spray painting it with woodland camo colours.

He asked to see it, so I unloaded it and handed it to him. After throwing it to his shoulder, he remarked how light it was and how well it came to the shoulder. He then asked me if it killed turkeys, causing me to state that it usually killed a turkey every time it was shot unless it was my fault. We talked a while longer about hunts until it was nearing 9:30

and warming up.

Before moving, I suggested we swap shotguns with me carrying his 10-gauge and him carrying my gun. We walked over to another ridge and decided to call a few more times before quitting. We crossed a small branch, and when we got to the top of the next hill, I started crow-cawing as loudly as possible. I tried to simulate a mob of crows chasing after something, like a hawk or owl.

Before stopping crow-cawing, he pointed, and we both felt we had heard a bird gobble one time in that direction. We discussed how far, and Lawton thought it was maybe 200 yards. We quickly found a place for him to sit, took a couple of dead tree branches and propped them around him to break up his outline. Then, I whispered for him to watch out the ridge to his left and that I planned to get behind him.

After getting set, I called a couple of times softly to see if the turkey would respond and heard him gobble in the direction where we thought he had been. Lawton got the gun up on his knee and pointed it toward where the gobble had come from. Waiting a few minutes, I just clucked one time very softly, and he gobbled very close. Within a few seconds, there he was, strutting up the ridge toward us. He stopped about 25 yards directly in front of Lawton. He shot, killing the gobbler cleanly.

We both got up and made sure the bird was down for the count. After he flopped a few times, Lawton came over. He said, "Man, I like that shotgun of yours. Would you sell it?" Thinking he was just joking, I put my carry strap over the legs and neck of the gobbler; we unloaded our shotguns and walked back to the truck. It was a nice 3-year-old gobbler with good spurs and beard, and Lawton was pleased to carry him over to the check station and check him in. I offered to clean the bird for him, and he politely said no. He asked me again about selling him my shotgun, to which I declined but did suggest he did not need a 10-gauge shotgun to kill a turkey.

We went our separate ways, and a few days later, I received a call from Lawton's top staffer Gene, asking me to meet Lawton at a nearby restaurant in Fairfax for dinner that Friday evening. We had a nice dinner, and he asked me about fixing him up a shotgun like mine. By this time, Remington was making their Model 1100 semi-automatic in a 12-gauge three-inch magnum with a 26" barrel, fitted for screw-in choke tubes.

We discussed it and agreed he should buy one of those, then get an aftermarket choke tube to shoot dense patterns. It would effectively do the job and weigh about three to four pounds less than his 10-gauge. He thought that sounded like a good idea, and as it was near the end of turkey season, I did not expect to see or hear from him for a while.

However, in a few days, Gene called me and asked me about fixing up a gun for Lawton. I was unsure what this would entail but agreed, telling him where we lived and asking if he could bring it over. We decided on a time, and he came by the following evening. He brought a new, in the box, Remington 1100, 12-gauge, three-inch magnum with a 26" vent rib barrel and screw-in choke tubes. I queried Gene about what Lawton wanted me to do to it, and he said for me to add sling swivels, paint it camo and tell him what choke tube he might start with as a recommendation. So, in a couple of days, I did just that. I took the new shotgun, fitted sling swivels to the buttstock and fore-end cap, then leaned it up against a tree and spray-painted it camo.

I had some aftermarket turkey choke tubes for a Remington, so I screwed one of those in it and told Gene to have Lawton pattern it on paper at 30 and 40 yards with number 7 ½ copper-plated shot. If he could not locate 7 ½ copper-plated shot, then use Winchester XX number six, copper-plated shot, which was readily available. So, Gene came over and carried it back with him.

Lawton called in a few days saying it patterned great with copper-plated number six-shot and asked how much he owed me. Of course, there was no charge and we turkey hunted and visited several more times at Quantico before he retired and moved back to Florida.

Although he invited me to come to Florida and hunt with him, unfortunately, I could never do so. However, Lawton and I communicated periodically and remained good friends right up until he passed away. His "go-to" turkey gun was that 1100 Remington that I fixed up for him. This is the kind of pros that make guiding an absolute pleasure, and fortunately, I was able to make similar friendships with numerous others while there and elsewhere.

There are many other stories, mostly good but a few bad ones, I could share about guiding a diversity of people over the years on turkey hunts at Quantico. Moving on, however, I need to share some experiences from the other place I guided for several years.

That unique place was Vermejo Park Ranch in northeastern New Mexico. Without going into the details of how and why my involvement with this venture began, in essence, I was invited to come out to Vermejo to do a turkey management/hunting workshop with friends Jim Clay and Tommy Duvall.

We did the workshop for the first-ever managed spring gobbler hunt there, and it became an annual event. At that time, the ranch was owned by a large oil company, which I think was Pennzoil. It covered more than 565,000 acres, mostly in northeastern New Mexico but some in Colorado as well.

Careful planning enabled me to take annual leave their opening week of turkey season, and I travelled there, did the workshop and then guided two hunters for up to five days if needed, for Merriam's gobblers. My perks included enjoying great food, meeting new friends, and having the opportunity to kill two gobblers myself after my clients got their two. Then, if time remained, I got to go trout fishing in their fantastic lakes while enjoying the spectacular scenery. It was an excellent opportunity to learn more about the Merriam's subspecies, see lots of diverse wildlife, plus hunt and fish in some of the best habitats in the west.

Again, for the most part, the pros far outweighed the cons. Still, a couple of cons described below are likely experienced perhaps in different scenarios by anyone who guides many people. This is especially true if they have never met before the hunt. Again, it is not necessary to identify these folks by name, but the experience is worth noting. When hunting Merriam's gobblers, the habitats they occupy are fairly open with tall steep mountains, deep canyons and broad valleys. Early in the season, these birds will usually have hens with them, except for just at daylight when they have not flown down yet and gathered their harems. Even if someone is an experienced turkey hunter for other subspecies, the Merriam's does not always behave or react in precisely the same way. Therefore, the client must listen to the guide and try to respond accordingly if physically able.

The guide needs to assess the client's physical capabilities and wisdom to follow what the guide suggests to help them get their turkeys. Clearly, at the elevations found in that part of the west, many people can quickly succumb to physical exhaustion or altitude sickness. Therefore, the guide must determine the client's capability, and for some clients, it may be impossible for them to climb up the steep slopes. That makes it challenging to be at the same level where the gobblers roost at fly-down time. This necessitates hunting the canyon floors or walking out ridges that can be driven to, and roads are fairly limited over most of the area.

One particular client, at that time, was probably in his mid-60s and was in no condition to climb up those slopes. He, too, hunted with an Ithaca 10-gauge semi-automatic and bragged that he could kill a gobbler at sixty yards. We discussed it, and I strongly encouraged him to wait until a bird got within 40 yards before shooting.

We located a big gobbler with at least 25 hens and a few jakes across a vast canyon. Unfortunately, the only way to get there was by walking at least a mile around a curve and back up the other side through a deeply eroded gulley. Knowing he could not make it that far, I dropped him off in a small gully with a few primarily dead cottonwood trees around the ravine.

It was about 400 yards from where we had seen the gobbler and hens across the canyon. So I drove the truck on about a quarter-mile and stopped. Then, staying in the edge of the canyon and gully, I worked my way back to the client. We found a place to sit and made a little blind of dead branches in front of him, and I started calling.

By the time we got situated, it was about 10:30. As we watched, the turkey gobbled at the first loud call, but some of the hens headed into the woods above the canyon floor. The gobbler stayed in a strut in the same place, although I expected him to follow those hens. We were positioned where we could see them and had binoculars to watch them react to the call. The second time after calling, a few more hens headed up the slope, and the gobbler turned and gobbled back in our direction. This went on for some time. At every call, more of his hens headed out of the canyon.

After about 40 minutes, the gobbler had a couple of hens and one jake gobbler left in the canyon floor with him. Calling a little more often, he gobbled then started moving in our direction. He never wavered, and each time after calling a little softer, he would gobble, pop into a strut and come closer to us.

The gobbler went out of our sight a couple of times because of dips or mounds between us. Yet, when he re-appeared, he was still headed in our direction. As the gobbler neared the 75-yard mark, I reminded the client who had his shotgun pointed toward the gobbler not to shoot. The turkey was committed to coming on over where we were. I planned to wait until he got about 40 yards, and then he could shoot when he was ready.

We watched the gobbler head in our direction, still strutting. Then, all of a sudden, somewhere between 55 to 60 yards, the client shot, knocking the gobbler over. But, the bird got up and ran back the way it came almost immediately. Then, I urged the client to shoot again before it ran out of sight, but he said his gun had jammed. Jumping up and running after it was my only option at that point. I hoped to get close enough to the gobbler dragging a wing, to shoot him and put him down. It seemed like he was gaining on me for a while, but eventually, after about a 200-yard chase, I was close enough to kill the gobbler and did so.

After waiting for him to quit flopping and me to catch my breath, I picked the gobbler up, walked back over to the client and handed him the bird. Asking why he did not wait until the bird got closer, he replied that he always killed them at that range and did not understand why that one ran off after he shot. I finally got his jammed gun unloaded and then walked to the truck, came back and picked him up.

He never said thank you, and I thought maybe he was embarrassed at having shot and crippled the gobbler. When we got back to the lodge, he asked me if I might be able to fix his shotgun. Reluctantly, I agreed to try to fix it and borrowed some tools back at the lodge and took the gun apart. I discovered what was broken and figured out how to replace the recoil washer and get it operating again. I later walked it over to his room, and he took it without again even saying thank you. What made this even more unpleasant was over-hearing him that night at dinner, telling people at the table about this fantastic shot he made on that gobbler.

Oh well, you will meet clients like this one or worse if you guide long enough. My only salvation was asking that he be assigned another guide for the rest of his hunt. It was discreetly handled by the wildlife manager, who coordinated the hunts and paired up clients with their guide.

The most common mistake some clients make is shooting at birds too far. In that open country, it is hard for some people to judge the range. Another is not firing when they have an open shot or trying to move to get a better shot, rather than waiting.

The Merriam's subspecies will tolerate a little more movement than will the Eastern or Osceola subspecies. However, they have excellent vision and hearing and are familiar with predators trying to catch them. Therefore, movement does trigger an escape reaction, though not usually as quickly as the Eastern or Osceola subspecies.

Those clients who had killed a few turkeys and thought they were expert turkey hunters were often the most difficult to please. Nevertheless, guiding enabled me to enjoy some remarkable and rewarding experiences over those 15 or more springs on the Vermejo Park Ranch. The opportunity to observe western wildlife up close and personal, from songbirds to eagles and red squirrels to elk, bear, cougar, mule deer, antelope and bison, as well as to experience fantastic trout fishing, was great. In addition, I have never hunted any other place in North America with such a density of wild turkeys as some of those canyons.

Although it might appear from these descriptions that turkey hunting there is easy, the primary reason that ranch can support that kind of hunting pressure is that it is so large.

Another nice thing about Merriam's gobblers is that they will gobble all day long during the spring. Rio Grande gobblers are pretty much the same way. Generally speaking, it is uncommon to find Eastern or Osceola gobblers that walk around gobbling all day. Looking back, I cannot remember a single year guiding at Vermejo where my clients did not kill their two gobbler limit.

The author (right) with a client and Merriam's gobblers
at Vermejo Ranch.

CHAPTER 24

Attributes of Good Hunting Partners

It is truly a blessing to have turkey hunted with many fine professional colleagues, long-time friends, and some family members, which are, of course, always memorable. I have, however, also hunted with many other good people with which it was a pleasure to share hunts. This is because they enjoyed the hunt, had a positive attitude, were attentive, and handled their firearms safely.

Of family members, I hunted the most with my dad for many years. He did not start to spring turkey hunt until he was into his late 30s but truly enjoyed the challenge until his health prevented him from continuing.

Most of the first dozen or more gobblers that Dad killed were called for him before he had enough confidence to call his own birds. Having given him several different kinds of calls, I tried to help him develop enough confidence in his calling to succeed. It was because I recognized that he would appreciate it more than having me call a bird in for him. Although he never gained much confidence in diaphragm calls or box calls, he did develop some skills using a slate call.

In Leeds, Alabama, a gentleman named Earnest Black, Jr. made a really sweet little box-like call. However, unlike most box calls, instead of using the call sides to generate the sound, he placed a small peg-type striker in the lid. On the call floor was a piece of slate the peg sat on and was scraped across to generate the sound.

It operated somewhat like a box but provided a more consistent sound than either of us could do with a regular box call. Mr. Black called it the Combination Turkey Call. Ordering a couple of these for Dad, I hoped that before the next spring season opened, he would have gotten proficient at making a good cluck, yelp, and purr with one of those calls.

I had planned that next spring to try to locate a gobbler for Dad not too far from the road, wanting to let him begin the season on his own. However, just before the season opened, the timber company which had recently bought the land we had hunted for years started building new roads into the area. They planned to remove the entire existing stands of mixed pine and hardwoods for conversion to the planting of short rotation loblolly pine.

While doing some pre-season scouting, my buddy, Thurman Booth, and I had walked down some of these new roads. The timber company had opened new territory we had not previously hunted. We found lots of gobbler tracks

Combination Turkey Call. The author's father's favorite call and the one he used to call in his own gobbler.

on some of these roads. Fortunately, this was before the cutting crews had begun harvesting timber.

Therefore, before the hunt, I had decided to go with Dad the first morning in these newly opened areas. If that did not work out, I would turn him loose on a gobbler or two I had located earlier that would be easy to get to.

The first morning we hunted, it was cloudy and drizzling rain. Dad and I headed out from camp, and I mistakenly took another new road rather than the one planned. Finally, I found the right road and drove in where the new road dead-ended at a creek. It was still drizzling and beginning to get a little light. When we stopped, Dad said, he did not believe turkeys would gobble that morning.

Going into the woods a short distance, I made a long, high-pitched owl squall that was responded to by at least four gobblers! Looking over at the truck, Dad had his window partially rolled down. He, too, had heard them. I came back to the truck and told him to get out quietly, gather his gear and let's go. By this time, at least six gobblers were gobbling at each other on both sides of the creek.

I asked him which of the birds he wanted to go to, and he said the one straight across the creek sounded the hottest. So, we found a place to wade across and headed up the ridge. Before getting there, we realized that the gobbler was well over the ridge. Once we got to the top, we also realized there was a natural bowl ringed with big pines and that gobbler was roosted in one of those pines on the backside of the bowl.

The top of the ridge was pretty narrow, so we found Dad a good place to sit. I dropped back down the side we had just walked up but close enough to see and motion to Dad if needed. As soon as we got set, I cackled one time like hens flying down and thought I heard seven different gobblers. One was very close, off to my right.

I stopped calling, and they gobbled back and forth for quite a while at each other. Dad could see over into that bowl. He soon motioned to me that he saw the gobbler fly down. The turkey gobbled on the ground, and the others responded. Then, Dad motioned to me that the bird was headed away.

That prompted me to cackle again, followed by a yelp, and a gobbler down the creek about 100 yards went nuts gobbling. Additionally, the one to my right started drumming very close behind me. Then, hearing a bird fly, I looked up to see a gobbler land on top of the ridge within ten yards of Dad. He waited, letting the gobbler walk away a few yards, then killed him. The bird behind me flew by, very close, and sailed across the creek at the shot.

Getting up, I walked up to where Dad was standing with his gobbler. First, we discussed all the gobbling we had heard. Then, since it had now become legal to take two birds per day, I asked him if he heard that bird down the creek that had gone crazy gobbling when I cackled. He said he had and thought the bird would run out of breath before he stopped gobbling.

We stood there a minute, and I decided to cackle again to see what might happen. Immediately, that gobbler cut me off. We both thought the bird was not too far down the creek, but it sounded like he was on the other side. I asked Dad if he wanted to get set up and see if I could call that gobbler in. He replied that he had enjoyed enough excitement already, so why didn't I give that gobbler a try, and he would meet me at the truck later.

I headed to the creek, found a crossing place and walked on up a slight ridge about 85 yards down the creek. I located a little place to set up and call from, and a thunderous gobble answered the first call right across the stream and up a bit of drain coming down into the creek.

Without waiting very long, I cackled at him. That bird

cut me off gobbling. The next thing I heard and saw was the gobbler flying across the creek. He landed about 20 yards from me, and when he straightened up, I shot him.

When he quit flopping, I gathered him up and walked back up the creekside to the truck where Dad had already placed his gobbler in the back. Looking at my watch, it was just a few minutes after 7:00, and we had already killed two mature, long beards. It was a hunt to remember. We had lucked into the mother lode of gobblers that morning.

The next morning, I led Dad up a ridge to a somewhat flat knob with many white oak acorns. Turkeys had been actively scratching in this area, and it was not too far from the road. We made Dad a blind. We had carried him a bottle of water and a boat seat cushion to sit on. I planned to leave him there and see if he could call up a gobbler on his own without having to walk a lot. I was going to hunt a ridge about a half-mile across the valley from him. I did not hear a gobble back his way as it was pretty windy that morning, and I had not heard a gobbler either but kept hunting.

About 8:15, however, I heard Dad shoot, so I went to the truck and drove back to where we had walked him up the ridge and headed up to check on him. He was still sitting in the blind we had made. When he saw me coming closer, he stood up, grinning. "Did you get him?" was my obvious question. He said, "I shot, didn't I?"

He then proceeded to tell me the story. Not too long after daylight, he thought he heard a bird gobble to the west of where he was, so he got his little Combination Turkey Call out and yelped four or five times. After that, Dad said the gobbler gobbled right back and began to get closer each time he called. My advice to him had been to call softer as a gobbler got closer, and if he thought the gobbler was committed, just to quit calling and sit quietly.

He said he had not called nor heard a gobble for a long

The author's father's gobbler he called himself in Arkansas
with his good friend Thurman Booth.

time, so he decided to cluck once. When he did that, the
gobbler thundered back just to his left, but where Dad could
not yet see him. He said he was so excited that he dropped
his call but got his shotgun up on his knee just as that gobbler
came up over the top of the ridge. Dad shot him at about 25
yards.

He was a great gobbler, with a long beard and with one
and three-eighth-inch spurs. Following that confidence
builder, he was able to hunt alone more often and, in later
years, called in and killed several more gobblers.

Dad passed in 1989, but my memories remind me vividly
of every turkey hunt we shared over the years, as well as other

hunts for waterfowl, quail, doves, rabbits, and pheasants. It seemed we both were less on edge while hunting than being around each other during other activities. When not hunting, he was inclined to maintain that fatherly admonition to have me do everything his way, and occasionally the sparks would fly.

Dad never had an interest in deer hunting but loved hunting upland game birds and waterfowl. His early guidance enabled me to learn a lot about the value of hard work and honesty. However, he was not particularly pleased with my choice of a profession and was not hesitant to let me know.

Without a loan or support from Dad or elsewhere, I worked my way through college, along with my wife's help, after we were married in 1962. Before passing away, he apologized for his misunderstanding and told me he realized that I made the right decision. For him to admit that was not only a surprise but was deeply appreciated. Dad was a very opinionated person who had survived the Great Depression, some debilitating illnesses, and a six-year military commitment in Europe during World War II.

Among family members I took hunting were our two boys, Kelly and Mike, when they were youngsters. Although they enjoyed dove, squirrel and deer hunting, they did not particularly like to walk long distances. So, after a few run and gun hunts in the mountains of Virginia chasing gobblers with me, they both quit turkey hunting.

They enjoyed camping out and squirrel and deer hunting which we did a good bit. But they chose not to turkey hunt with me anymore. Our younger son Mike had devoted himself to work and sharing the gospel after college, and for probably 25 years, had not hunted at all. Marriage, work, and church involvement had consumed most of his time. He, his wife Christine, our older son Kelly and our grandson, Brooks, all loved to eat wild game and fish. So, every time they visited us, they would always take some home with them.

In 2016, during a Christmas visit with us, Mike said, "Dad, let's plan a spring gobbler hunt." It was great to hear him express that interest. We began making plans. He and his wife lived in Long Beach, California, at the time, so he planned to fly into Memphis, Tennessee, the day before the 2017 spring season opened and booked a flight accordingly.

We both purchased our licenses online ahead of time. I picked him up at Memphis, brought along a couple of turkey guns, gear for us both and some food to take to my friend, Jim Byford's, cabin near Kentucky Lake. We drove over there from Memphis, arriving after dark.

Having hunted the area before, I knew where I wanted to take Mike the following day. Jim was going to hunt another piece of property that he owned nearby. So we arose early and left to drive around to the top of Jim's property. We parked and walked about three-eighths of a mile to the area.

Mike is left eye dominant, so he has to shoot from his left shoulder. With that in mind, I gave him my over/under shotgun, and I took a semi-auto with me. We got to where we wanted to listen from plenty early. Describing to Mike the lay of the land, I suggested where we might hear a gobbler sound off at daylight.

We found a place to set up before we even heard a gobble. When we did hear one, the gobbler was downhill on a steep slope to our right. I told Mike to move into position where he could shoot. I then got behind and to his right a little to give him some room to move around if he needed to. Shortly, as it got more daylight from the east, a gobble rang out, and the bird was a little farther downhill than we had thought. Otherwise, it was in the right direction for our setup. He was the only bird we could hear. He gobbled on the roost a good bit, then flew down and gobbled again. I called, he answered, and shortly we could tell that he was moving uphill toward us but a little farther to the right than expected.

As the gobbler got closer, Mike grinned every time the bird gobbled. We both expected to see him within a few minutes as he worked his way toward us. He had just gobbled again, not more than 80 yards or so away. But, we could not yet see him. Shortly, I heard something moving directly behind us. Turning slowly and through the side of my face mask, I could see eight gobblers coming down the ridge behind us.

The author's youngest son, Mike (right), with his Tennessee gobbler while hunting with Jim Byford.

Knowing that Mike could not turn around far enough to get a shot, I just whispered to him not to move. We waited, and finally, one of them began putting sharply. Eventually, they all turned and headed back over the top of the ridge about 60 yards uphill. As soon as they went out of sight, I got Mike to turn around and get his gun on his knee.

Moving behind him, I turned as well and started clucking and yelping softly. Although afraid they were gone for sure, I saw that white skull cap and red wattles pretty soon. A gobbler was coming over the top of the ridge toward us. I whispered to Mike to keep his gun on that gobbler's head and neck, and I would tell him when to shoot.

Although clearly still wary and moving cautiously, the lead gobbler continued down to about 40 yards, then raised his head and neck straight up, and I told Mike to shoot. He did, and the turkey went down. Some of his buddies flew up and sat back down as they were following the one Mike shot. However, being so proud that Mike had gotten that gobbler, I did not even consider shooting one of the others.

We admired Mike's gobbler, a two-year-old. He placed my carrying strap on his neck and legs, and we took our time walking out to the truck. We drove back to camp, cleaned the gobbler before we went in, and waited for Jim to return. It was a great morning for sure. While we were waiting, Mike said, "Dad, when you get ready to give up your turkey guns, I want that over/under." My response was, "It is now yours, Son, it is my pleasure to pass it on to you."

Although we hunted hard the next day, we never heard nor saw a turkey, though we knew several other gobblers were on the property. Before we started hunting, I had informed Mike that this was a pretty unique area and that since it was about mid-April, there were two things he needed to watch out for.

The first of these was timber rattlesnakes which were

common in those mountains. Second, Mike needed to help me watch for scarlet tanagers, which usually show up about mid-April. It is always a pleasure to watch them forage in the hardwood treetops for insects. Although we did not see a timber rattler, we did see scarlet tanagers, both male and female, and got to watch them flit around from treetop to treetop.

We were blessed with another observational treat at one of our setups on a steep hillside above a creek when we looked up to see a hen and drake wood duck fly in. They both lit very near us in some large mature trees, and she began checking out cavities for nesting. The drake sat patiently on a limb nearby, and the hen went into a cavity, sometimes staying a couple of minutes. Then apparently not pleased, she came out and flew to another big tree. She inspected several cavities, with the drake simply waiting. It reminded me of a country song, "Waiting on a Woman." After checking two or three holes while we watched, they flew out of sight as she did not find one that suited her.

The next morning, we went to a place that had a long curved harvested cornfield between two ridges. I did not carry a shotgun. I wanted to call another bird for Mike. We went to a brushy point in the lower part of the field where Jim had killed and worked gobblers in the past.

We made a hasty blind just as it began to lighten up in the east. We faintly heard two or three gobblers in the next couple of hours, but they were all seemingly around the curve of that field and about half a mile away.

About 9:30, Jim suggested we go into a little community nearby, get a good breakfast, and come back that afternoon. So we walked back up the side of the ridge until we found the road that we had walked down when we came in before daylight.

We were probably within 100 yards of the main road

where we had parked when a hen woodcock fluttered up immediately in front of us and flew off over the side of the road. Telling everyone to stop and not move, I scanned the weeds and grass in that old road and spotted a woodcock chick. I pointed it out to Jim and Mike, then saw another one, then another one, and unfortunately, a dead one that one of us had accidentally stepped on. Those chicks were so well camouflaged and had frozen when the hen flew off that they were tough to see even though standing almost directly over them. Mike had his cell phone, so he took some photos of them, although it is still hard to pick them out.

We went on out, hoping the hen would gather the three chicks and move on. We carefully walked around the three live chicks and carried the dead one some distance away.

We had a great breakfast, came back, and Jim let Mike and me out. He was going to hunt another area that afternoon. We were going to go back to that field area, closer to the curve where we heard birds that morning.

We found a good, shady spot, took a nap, and then prepared to go back down the ridge, watching carefully for the woodcock and her chicks. Almost down to the edge of the field, I suggested that Mike walk on ahead as a call of nature hit me, necessitating a stop.

Even though it was only about 2:30, I decided to yelp fairly loudly and was immediately answered by a gobble. The gobbler sounded like he was at the same level on that hillside as we were but to our left. Finishing up hurriedly, I caught up with Mike and told him, "Let's try to get on down close enough to see the edge of that field." I hoped to locate a place to set up so that Mike would have a clear view of the field.

Having taken a hen decoy with us that afternoon, we quickly found an excellent hide about 20 yards above the field edge. I got Mike set up, sneaked down to the edge of the field, and looked up and down the field.

About 65 yards to our left, there was a brushy point that jutted out into the field. I planned to sneak out and set the decoy up about 20 yards into the field to be easily spotted. The decoy stake went into the ground, and I set the hen decoy on top. I immediately looked back to my left, and there was a big gobbler. He spotted me and vanished back the way he had come. Sneaking back up to Mike, I apologized for probably having completely messed us up. He had not been able to see the gobbler that spotted me and spooked.

Feeling bad, I thought about moving, but the setup was in a good place, so I decided to wait a bit and call some more. If nothing happened, we still had time to move before the evening was over. We sat quietly for about 20 minutes or so, then I called and was surprised to get a gobble to our left that sounded about 80 yards away.

We waited a few more minutes, and I clucked, prompting another gobble just around the point to our left that jutted out into the field. Shortly afterward, I could see two gobblers coming around the edge of the field toward our hen decoy. I motioned to Mike, who could not see them yet, to get his gun up and be ready. They were coming fast and were so close that we could hear them drumming and making the soft clucks and chortles that you often hear gobblers make when they are very close. Then, as they came out from behind the screen of briars and multi-flora rose, they stepped right in front of Mike. He shot one just as they raised their heads and necks up after coming out of strut.

After spooking that gobbler earlier, I would have bet that we would not see or hear another gobbler that afternoon, but patience, persistence, and luck paid off. That was Mike's second gobbler. He enjoyed everything about the hunt, the observations we made, and the interaction with our friend, Jim Byford, who also killed a big gobbler that afternoon. Mike had to return home the next day, so that wound up our hunt. Unfortunately, we have not yet been able to arrange another, but we are still trying.

When I first enrolled at the University of Florida in 1962, I met a fellow who turned out to be a long-lasting, excellent hunting and fishing buddy. We hunted and fished together often while pursuing degrees there over the next several years, and even later when we had a chance to visit their place or ours.

My wife and I married in September 1962, and this fellow, named Joel Smith, and his wife, Polly, became very dear friends. They had two young sons, Lynn and Clay. Those kids loved to come out to our place in the country and spend a couple of nights with us when their parents needed a getaway.

One of the primary reasons they liked us was that we had both beagles and bird dogs, and they liked the dogs. Regardless, the kids always referred to a stay at our place as "spending" and often wanted to go "spend" with the Millers. Fast forward some 50 years, when Lynn, a Naval Officer on nuclear submarines, and his wife Dawn moved back to Gainesville after retiring.

We returned to Florida almost every spring to visit Joel and Polly and some of my wife's family who lived there, and to hunt Osceola gobblers. Therefore, we were delighted when Lynn informed us in early 2015 that he would like to go gobbler hunting with me the following spring.

The first year, although we each killed a gobbler, most of our hunts were not classic hunts, as we encountered some two-year-old kamikaze birds that almost ran us over in their rush to find a hen. But, probably, the thing most memorable about our hunts was that we made a set up on the edge of a big marsh early one morning, thinking we would hear a gobbler or two from this spot.

Over the years, having either called up for others or

killed several gobblers from that location, I knew it was a great area. A massive live oak has a large open flat in front of it and a small branch running not too far below. The tree itself is large enough that with a few saw palmetto fronds, you can make blinds where one person can sit on either side, covering pretty much the entire bottom.

We had been sitting there for a few minutes after my first call, and suddenly, I could hear Lynn whispering something which was not clear to me. Thinking he had spotted a gobbler, I called softly on my little slate, and he repeated something, but I could not understand him. He was soon tapping on my gunstock with a stick, but there was no way to see around that big tree.

In about 20 seconds, I heard something running and assumed it was a turkey, so I moved around the tree toward Lynn. He had his cell phone in his hand. He then proceeded to show me photos of a bobcat that had stalked up to within about ten feet of him before realizing something was not right and tearing away. Lynn had taken three photos with his cell phone. In the last one, the bobcat had crouched as if it were going to spring but apparently heard Lynn's phone click and decided to get the heck out of dodge.

The following spring, we hunted together again. Amazingly, very early the first morning, I called, and three big gobblers answered and came directly to us. Somehow the one that was selected to be shot was missed. We watched them fly back down into the big flatwoods, and although we checked for feathers or blood or a crippled bird, none was found. We thought we would make a big circle and see if we could get one of those birds or another bird to gobble, but after about an hour decided to go to another area.

This new area was adjacent to a large pasture with a sand road that runs along the east side for about a half-mile. The pasture had live oak, palmetto, and cabbage palm clusters scattered within it, and it was surrounded by giant live oaks where gobblers were often seen or heard.

My thought was to set up just off the pasture and see if we could get a gobbler to respond. Then, if we did, try and work him out of the pasture so Lynn could get a shot. We made a couple of palmetto frond blinds pretty near the road, and I started calling. Nothing answered for about 30 minutes. By this time it is about 10:00, so for the next call, I cut real loud a few times, then gobbled on a tube call.

We both heard a gobble, but it was quite a distance across the pasture. We waited a few minutes, and I called loudly on a diaphragm call. The turkey gobbled closer but was still some distance away. Waiting a little longer this time, I called softly. Finally, when the turkey gobbled, we could see him, still in the pasture but closing. We thought he would come on out of the pasture. Instead, he stayed in that little pocket strutting and drumming for about ten minutes, then went back in the direction he had come from, stopping to gobble occasionally.

We saw no hens with him, hoping none would join him, so I decided to hit him with some rapid cuts. When he gobbled, we could tell he was coming back in our direction. He came to his same spot and went back three times. We were about to decide he would never come out of that pasture.

The next time, however, he cut me off gobbling after the call, and it sounded like he was coming back. Shortly he gobbled just out of sight behind some thick briars and jasmine clumps, but we never made a sound. Instead, we could see him strut, then raise his head and peer our way several times. Then, he gobbled again and came out of the pasture to about 30 yards from Lynn. Without waiting any longer, Lynn shot him. We took him back to the campsite where we met Lynn's dad, Joel, who took some photos.

In recent years, Florida had made it legal to kill both your gobblers the same day on private land. Therefore, after returning to camp and taking a brief nap, we decided to go out again. This time we went to a different area that, fortunately, because it had been a pretty dry spring, was not flooded. This area had a very open understory of mostly saw palmetto.

We got there around 3:30, found a couple of good trees, built saw palmetto frond blinds, and started calling. We neither heard nor saw any turkeys. So, about 4:30, I decided to change calls and pulled out my old glass call that was pretty high-pitched. Yelping a few times loudly, a gobbler answered maybe 250 yards away. Because he was coming from the direction we walked into the area, we were not expecting a gobble from there.

We could see that direction fairly well, but Lynn had to move around and reposition to shoot back that way. In a few minutes, the gobbler thundered again, definitely closer, and pretty soon in that open understory, we could both see him occasionally. He headed across that open bottom, working around saw palmetto clumps and large trees directly to us. I called one more time when he went behind some saw palmetto, very softly on my slate, and he gobbled.

Then he started strutting on toward us. He finally stopped at about 25 yards to look. Lynn shot him, which limited him out with two big gobblers the first day of the season! We put the carrying strap on Lynn's gobbler and headed to camp. Calling some as we walked out, we did not hear another bird that afternoon.

That evening at dinner, Lynn asked if it would be alright if he went with me even though he could not hunt. He wanted to learn a little more about spring gobbler hunting. Of course, I was glad to have his company. We agreed to go to another area the next morning.

It was a beautiful morning. We hunted all day and never heard a bird gobble, although we did see some hens. I just could not stimulate a bird to gobble, although we gave it our best effort.

Lynn had taken leave for the week, so we headed back the next morning. We set up on a very vocal gobbler early that had some hens with him. After following him around for most of the morning, however, I finally called him in and killed him. After processing the bird and putting the meat on ice, we grabbed some lunch. After that, we took a short nap back at camp and headed to another area we had not hunted.

This was an area where Lynn's dad, Joel, had heard a bird but had not hunted him. It is a big flat that is often mostly flooded, but this spring was almost dry. We found an excellent place to set up where we could see both ways up and down the flat, again built saw palmetto blinds and waited a while because it was sweltering that afternoon. Thankfully, the mosquitos were not too bad. We had the Therma-cells available, if needed. We just sat there quietly for about an hour before starting to call.

I started off calling softly, and after several calls and hearing nothing, I decided to call a little louder. The second loud call I made resulted in a distant gobble, so we waited a bit, and then I called softly, expecting to hear a gobble but did not. I was sitting there thinking about calling again when we heard a turkey drumming from behind me. He gobbled almost in my ear after getting closer. We were both worried that he would spook before we could see him. However, Lynn's position soon enabled him to see the show.

The gobbler came by on my left side and into my view. He strutted by within about ten yards, and I waited until his head moved behind a big oak to get my shotgun into position for a shot. When he stepped out from behind that tree, he was less than 20 yards away, came out of strut, and at the shot, toppled over backward. So, like Lynn had done the first day, I had killed both my gobblers in one day. That finished us both out, so we were through hunting.

It was a great spring season hunting with dear friends. We enjoyed a wonderful treat that afternoon before the gobbler came in, observing a pileated woodpecker pretty much destroy a dead ash tree not too far from us. That tree must have been full of insects or their larva to get so much of his attention. Regardless, he shredded that tree into chips as we watched, flying off and returning several times.

One of many neat things about hunting in Florida is you never know what you might walk up on or see there. It could range from feral hogs to alligators, cottonmouth moccasins, bobcats, or swallow-tailed kites. From warblers to sandhill cranes and bald eagles, the immense diversity of birds is always a treat for me. Several times over the years, I have encountered large alligators up close, apparently moving from pond to pond.

I also killed one of the largest wild feral boars I have ever encountered there. We had all been instructed and encouraged to kill them if we had the opportunity since they cause severe damage to the property. They usually have hog traps operational most of the time to try to reduce or eliminate the damage. We do not shoot other potentially dangerous species, like cottonmouths and diamondbacks, but do try to stay out of their way and avoid unnecessary contact with them. However, it is enjoyable just observing them, and they keep you alert.

Another classic hunt on that property which deserves noting is a hunt made with another of my friends who hunted there. He was in forestry school as I was finishing up my Master's at the University of Florida, and he worked for many years for a couple of large timber companies. His name is Jim Kaufman. He was joining us for a hunt there several years back, and both Joel and I had killed gobblers, but Jim had so far struck out. We went to lunch together that day, and on the way back to hunt, he mentioned that he had heard two gobblers that morning but could not get either of them to work. He told me where he had hunted, and being familiar with it, I volunteered to go with him that afternoon to see if we could get a gobbler to respond to some different calling.

We walked down toward a big bottom along a road. About halfway to where he had heard those birds that morning, he suggested we stop and call. I crow-cawed loudly like crows mobbing a hawk or owl, and a gobbler answered about 150 yards away. The bird was below us and not too far from the road.

Jim decided to find a place across the road, looking down into a fairly open bottom where he could see both the road and the bottom. Not having a shotgun with me, since I limited out that morning, my choice was to just crawl over to a slight ditch. It had become grown up with sapling sweet gum trees and vines. I thought it would be a good hide for me to lean back against the side of the road bank against those saplings.

After Jim got into place, I called softly on my slate. The gobbler answered and was coming from around behind me. I waited about three or four minutes and called softly on my slate. Then, without gobbling to the call, I could hear him drumming up the road shoulder behind me. At that point, I just had to freeze in place. Less than two minutes later, he came down from the roadside and stepped into the road not more than 30 feet from me. He popped into a strut, apparently recognized something was not right, and, putting loudly flew up into a big pine tree about 40 yards below me. Pinned down, I could not move. He kept looking down at me lying flat in that road ditch. Jim could not see him from where he was but had heard him fly. Jim was maybe 50 yards from the pine tree the gobbler was sitting in.

With a long beard trailing down from his breast, that gobbler walked back and forth on the pine limb for approximately 15 minutes. Finally, he leaned over and flew straight out in front of Jim in that flat. While he was flying away, I called to him. Hearing him land, I knew he was not too far, so I called again softly on my slate and immediately heard him drumming. Looking out into the flat, I soon saw him. He was drumming in full strut right between us along a little branch below me, and to Jim's right. It was a relief to me when Jim finally shot as I was really cramped up from having been pinned down so long.

From left to right Joel Smith, Jim Kaufman, and the author with gobbler.

CHAPTER 25

Special Memories

There are so many fond memories of hunts with respected friends and colleagues I have enjoyed over the years. It would take another book to mention and name them. Instead, the following are a few of the many friends and colleagues I have been honored to hunt alongside. Among the many of these remarkable colleagues, apart from Jim Byford, Jim Brooks, Thurman Booth, Joel, Polly, and Lynn Smith, all of whom I have already mentioned, I am recounting some others who were terrific.

These include Chuck Bates and Pete Bromley, with whom I mostly hunted in Virginia. Others like Tom Franklin, Richard (Dick) McCabe, and Wayne Bell, I have hunted with in several states. Others include Wayne Flowers and his son Hunter in Kentucky, and Bill Rooney, whom I have hunted, fished and worked with many times over the past 50 plus years. I hope others do not feel slighted by my failure to list them and the great hunts and camaraderie we shared because they are treasured memories and friendships.

The first of these is a couple of hunts with Chuck Bates, and although we occasionally hunt separately, he enjoys going and calling together most of the time. This hunt occurred not far from the trailer Chuck fixed up for a group of us, commonly referred to as the "Graybeards," to stay in while hunting near Hermosa, Virginia.

We had worked gobblers briefly in two different areas that morning, but both quit gobbling, so we moved to a third area. This area had several mixed hardwood ridges and mature timber drains surrounding a small grassy field. We slipped in on the east side of the field, and after we found a place to sit, we started calling. Two gobblers answered, one deep down in a hollow to the north; and one across the field in a different hollow. Each time we called, both birds gobbled, but neither seemed to be moving any closer. This went on for probably 30 minutes. It did not matter which of us called. Finally, sitting behind Chuck, hoping he would get a shot if one of those birds came close enough, I suggested that we not call for about ten minutes.

We sat silently for a while, and after about five minutes, the gobbler to our north gobbled. So, we waited, and the bird across the field went mute. Then, in just a few minutes, the bird to the north gobbled again, closer. Yet, even in the open hardwood stands, we could not see him. We both thought he would probably come out into the field at the north end. So, we sat quietly for another few minutes. The next time he gobbled, he was back down in the hollow where we had first heard him.

We agreed for me to call softly on my little hand-held slate after a short wait. After calling so softly I was not sure the turkey could hear it, he gobbled right back. We sat quietly, and in another ten minutes, he gobbled closer but still toward the north end of the field. Waiting a bit, I clucked and purred softly, and the turkey gobbled right back. Pretty soon, we could hear him drumming but could not determine precisely where he was.

Finally, after several minutes, we realized that he was just over the ridgeline to the east, and shortly afterward, his white dome and red wattles appeared 40 yards away. He was in a full strut. Chuck, fortunately, had moved around before we saw the gobbler, and when the bird got to about 30 yards, he came out of strut, raised his head to look, and Chuck fired true. He was a nice gobbler, and we had gotten lucky that he came in when he did because it was almost noon, with morning hunting only in Virginia.

One of the other reasons I remember this hunt so well is that I left my little slate and peg call lying on the ground in the excitement. Planning to go home early the following day, I did not realize I forgot my call. This required a phone call to Chuck later to get him to see if he could go back and retrieve it for me. He did and mailed it to me.

One year on my arrival at camp, Chuck said it had been a strange spring, and turkeys were not gobbling much. He had scouted a few in places we had not hunted before. We agreed to give them a try even though he described the area as both rough and thick.

We probably went to four or five different locations the first day but could not get a bird to gobble. The second morning we walked in about a mile to a place where we had both killed gobblers in the past but again could not get a bird to gobble. We walked back to the truck, and Chuck suggested we try a place where he had heard one bird gobble before the season opened. He said it was a very thick area cut over some 30 years before and was predominantly mixed hardwood, with some scattered Virginia pine. We walked into the area, which was indeed thick, and stopped before crossing a creek at the bottom. I called and was rewarded with a gobble from across the creek and some distance up a steep ridge. We quickly hustled across the stream and found a series of ridges that led down toward the creek. It was so danged thick with hardwood brush and an occasional mature American beech tree that it was hard to find a place to see very far.

Finally, we found a little knob jutting out over the creek. Both of us located a place to sit about 30 yards from the end of the knob. Chuck sat down about 15 yards to my right. At the next call, the turkey gobbled sort of behind us and up the creek 200 yards away. We could not move. It was so dense that we decided to keep calling and see if the turkey would come closer.

The next call, he gobbled to the right of Chuck, still up the creek. I thought he would work his way up one of these drains, and maybe Chuck could get a shot. Waiting perhaps five minutes, I called again. When he gobbled, he was directly in front of us over the point of the ridge along the creek. We waited, expecting to see him come over the end of the ridge. Then he gobbled very close to my left.

Looking in that direction, I could see two big gobblers walking across in front of me. I shot one of them at about 20 yards and hoped Chuck could shoot the other one. Unfortunately, he could not get a shot, although he did see the other gobbler. As we carried the gobbler back across the creek and through that grown-up thicket, we discussed whether we had ever killed a gobbler in such a place.

After getting to camp, I quickly gutted the gobbler and hung him in the smokehouse. It was now drizzling rain. Chuck wanted to try another area nearby where he had seen a couple of gobblers strutting in a field a few days before. We drove over to that area, and sure enough, we saw a big gobbler and two hens in the field. We went about a quarter-mile out of sight, got out quietly, and headed down through another grown-up thicket. We intended to get down in the woods some distance from the field, hoping the trio was still there. However, when we got where we could see, there were no turkeys in the field.

Having no shotgun with me, we set up where Chuck could see them if they came back to the field. Backing up into some brush, I sat down. It continued to drizzle rain, but we both had rain gear. After about ten minutes, I called, and a gobbler answered on a small ridge down behind where Chuck was sitting. That ridge rose over a gully that dropped down behind us into some mature timber.

I called softly. The turkey gobbled again and was now closer but to the right of Chuck. I quit calling but soon heard drumming, then Chuck shot. I could not see because he had shot the gobbler down in that drain. But when I got over to him, he said that two gobblers came in together.

It was a great morning hunt with both of us harvesting gobblers located in thick brushy areas where we usually would not even think of hunting. Chuck and I have shared many memorable hunts over the years. These hunts have ranged from Virginia to Newfoundland to the Rocky Mountains, and he remains a true friend, great hunting and fishing companion, and respected professional colleague. We know each other's families, and I appreciate him for his many fine human qualities as well as his hunting and land management expertise.

My long-time friend and respected colleague Richard (Dick) McCabe and I worked very closely for the 23 years my family lived in Fairfax, Virginia. While I worked for both the Departments of Interior and Agriculture until retiring in 2001, those years were great learning experiences.

Dick worked for the Wildlife Management Institute (WMI). We worked cooperatively with the Institute's capable staff on a lot of conservation issues. One of my assignments was working directly with the land grant institutions with wildlife management programs. I became good friends with his father, Robert (Bob) McCabe. Bob was one of Aldo Leopold's first graduate students at the University of Wisconsin. He later became the department chairman, serving in that role for many years until his retirement. The WMI administration supported our extension wildlife and fisheries educational programs for years, and we often collaborated on conservation programs and issues.

Having participated in many North American Wildlife and Natural Resources annual conferences, I also served on the planning committee. My interaction with the fine professionals at WMI and with other cooperators led to great friendships. These friendships were with their Washington office, regional field staff and professionals from different organizations and agencies. Aside from meeting at the annual conferences, the committee met every spring in mid-April for a few retreat and program planning days. These planning meetings usually occurred somewhere in the mountains of Virginia or West Virginia.

Our mornings at this meeting were for recreation, Some of us turkey hunted while other planning committee members fished, or bird watched or just relaxed. Following the morning activity of our choice, we gathered for a good meal about noon, then began looking over the various requested sessions submitted for the following year's annual conference. These were a challenge for our planning committee to select from.

During one of these planning meetings, Dick had asked me to go with him and call to see if we could get a gobbler. The location for this meeting was west of Amherst, Virginia. This area is not too far from the Blue Ridge on some property that belonged to the Franklin family. We were staying at Tom Franklin's future retirement home. Tom's place was only a little more than a three-hour drive from my home in Fairfax, and I had meetings in D.C. that day that was a conflict. So, I planned to drive down early the next morning. The rest of the group moved to the Amherst property the afternoon before.

Arriving at Tom's place in time to get a cup of coffee, Dick said he had heard a gobbler go to roost the evening before on the side of a steep mountain not too far away. We gathered our gear and quickly headed to the bottom of that mountain.

We stopped for me to owl-call, which was answered by a gobble somewhere up the side of that steep mountain. I questioned Dick about how far away he thought the gobbler was. He said it sounded like the bird was near the top of the mountain.

We started walking up the mountain on a curvy, hog-backed ridge probably less than 12 feet wide in some places. It led to a saddle where I thought we could better hear from and pinpoint the gobbler's location.

It was still dark and about 75 yards before we made it to the saddle. Dick tapped me on the shoulder and whispered that he could see a turkey sitting in a tree very close. This stopped us in our tracks.

At that point, I turned to look, and sure enough, less than 50 yards to the south, silhouetted against the skyline, I zeroed in on the gobbler. Thinking he had probably seen us and would spook, I said, "Let's just ease down to the ground where we are and wait and see if he gobbles again on his own." Dick leaned against a tree trunk, but there was no tree near me to sit by or lean on.

Afraid to move for fear of the turkey spotting me, I laid down on my side to watch the gobbler because it was getting light fast. It was windy, and soon the gobbler popped into a strut and drummed out the limb he was roosted on, with the wind nearly blowing him over as he spread his fan. When he reached the end of his strut, he gobbled. It was easy to see him. We hoped the gobbler mistook us for a deer if he had seen or heard us moving up the ridge before it got light. Our best bet was to stay perfectly still and hope he did not spot us and spook.

We stayed in those positions for approximately 20 minutes longer, watching the gobbler strut and gobble periodically. Then I heard several hens below him and further to the north.

I whispered to Dick that if they came up the mountain, they would go close to his roost tree and that the gobbler would likely follow them. The turkey gobbled one more time, then four hens flew down and walked, yelping and clucking, right under his roost tree.

The gobbler looked down, watching them proceed up the mountain toward the saddle. The gobbler then pitched out and flew directly uphill to the hens. As soon as that gobbler hit the ground, he started strutting, but the hens overlooked his displaying. They were about 75 yards above us. With a call in my mouth, I yelped softly, and the turkey gobbled. When he did, we heard something flying to our left, looked up, and another gobbler flew in just below us over the face of the ridge. Not really having a prayer of calling either of those gobblers into range, I whispered to Dick that I would keep calling and see what happened. Calling again softly on the mouth call, the gobbler we could see turned and gobbled straight down toward us and took a few steps our way.

When it looked like he was committed, it was apparent that he would be coming straight down the finger ridge in front of me. I whispered to Dick that if the gobbler stopped and turned his fan toward us, I was going to roll to the right when he saw me put my fingers in my ears if the gobbler came into range to shoot him. Fortunately, the gobbler stopped about halfway before getting into range and strutted with his fan toward us, so I was able to roll over. At that point, I would no longer see the gobbler but hoped Dick would wait until the turkey was in range before shooting.

With my fingers in my ears, all I could do was wait and hope. Knowing Dick was a safe firearms handler and that I was now out of the line of fire boosted my confidence. Finally, the gobbler came straight down the ridge in a full strut to about 25 yards, and Dick dispatched him.

Turkeys flew off the side of the ridge, some directly over us. Once it was possible, I looked up and could see the gobbler was down for the count. What an unbelievable hunt! Had we both not witnessed and been active participants in the entire experience, we would have had difficulty believing it.

To think we had any chance of killing that gobbler when we first saw him and got down on the ground was a huge stretch. Now admittedly, most of us as turkey hunters have gotten closer than we intended on roosted gobblers and been able to watch them on the roost, but not in this kind of situation. All I can say is that if you get caught in such a situation, play it by ear and give it your best shot. Occasionally it works. Dick and I have also hunted several times on his family's Rusty Rock Farm in Wisconsin. Over the years, it was my good fortune to call gobblers for Dick's son and one of his brothers, as well as for Dick and myself on that farm.

We have enjoyed the good fortune of hunting together for other species like upland gamebirds and waterfowl over the years, and we continued to work together on a volunteer basis. We interacted on such programs as the "Conservation Leaders for Tomorrow" from 2005 until about 2018, when health issues prevented my continuing.

My long-time respected professional colleague Pete Bromley, another great friend I had hunted with often, planned a hunt together one spring. I had worked with Pete while he served at Virginia Tech for many years, and later we continued to work cooperatively after he transferred to North Carolina State University. We have also enjoyed several hunts for various upland game species in numerous states and Virginia. Pete is a member of our Graybeard Club; in fact, I think Pete is the one who named the group.

We strived to get together for a muzzleloader deer hunt in the fall and a gobbler hunt in the spring for many years.

In the spring of 2016 or 2017, we planned to hunt in and around Hermosa, Virginia. On my arrival, they had already been hunting a few days. Pete had killed a very severely wounded turkey the day before. As he described it, the bird was very poor and had infected spur puncture wounds deep in the lower breast, back and thighs to the point he had to discard most of the meat.

Chuck suggested that Pete and I might want to hunt together the next morning. He knew a place where a big gobbler had done some strutting near where we could set up. It was an area adjacent to a huge clearcut that had been site prepared. It was also adjacent to a 30-year-old pine plantation that overlooked a creek and a beautiful hardwood ridge where we had both killed birds in past years. Not having been there since the cutover was site prepared, we guessed where we should set up on arriving there. It seemed that Pete should move down about 60 yards above the edge of the hardwoods, with me staying back up the ridge near the corner of the cutover.

We made ourselves a little hide in among the pines. Before it even got good light, a bird gobbled directly below Pete but across the creek on the hardwood hillside. Pretty soon, the turkey gobbled again. That second gobble stimulated a bird back across that cutover area, and it gobbled in return.

The cutover was clean and open, except for some scattered tops piled here and there, and it sloped up to a peak. The peak was back to the east, in the direction where the second gobbler had answered. That gobbler was so far away we could barely hear him, so I did not think there was any possibility he would come across that open cutover. It must have been at least a half-mile to where he was likely roosted along a little branch adjacent to the cutover.

I waited for maybe five minutes and called, and the bird

in front of Pete gobbled. It was on the ground, so I called again, and both birds gobbled back. It sounded like the bird in front of Pete would show up at the edge of the opening in front of him very soon. Therefore, I forgot about the other gobbler until he gobbled closer.

It sounded like he was right out in the middle of that cutover. I turned to see out toward the peak just in time to see a fan appear almost on top, with the rising sun behind the gobbler. What a remarkable sight! It made me wish I had a camera with a telephoto lens to have captured that scene on film.

At that point, it was a guessing game as to which of those gobblers would get into range first, if either of them would. The gobbler in the cutover was probably 200 yards away but soon folded up and started walking on toward me. The bird in front of Pete was closer.

Where Pete was sitting, he could see the gobbler in the cutover, but he was some 40 yards down the hill below my setup. I hoped his gobbler would show up and that Pete could kill him. But, for whatever reason, the gobbler did not want to come across that creek. The bird in the cutover just kept strutting closer, stopping about every 20 yards to look, and then popping back into a strut and coming on down toward me.

Pretty soon, the gobbler was almost in range and stopped to strut behind a dead treetop. I called very softly; he gobbled and came on around the treetops. I shot him at about 40 yards breaking his neck.

Pete joined me in walking out to the gobbler. Both of us were delighted to have witnessed that gobbler coming across that huge cutover. It was only about 8:00, so I placed my carrying strap around his neck and legs, carried him to the truck, and we drove to the cabin. I gutted the gobbler, removed the crop, then took him out to an old, enclosed smokehouse and hung him up to cool out, planning to finish processing him when we returned.

After grabbing a quick cup of coffee, I suggested we hike about a mile to an area where several nice gobblers had been killed over the years. It was a neat place which no one else usually hunted, and there was always a gobbler or two in that area.

We gathered Pete's gear, left my shotgun there at the cabin, and began the long walk around a large pine plantation.

The old roadway led up a hill to a juncture of an old pasture, some beautiful hardwoods that tailed off into a branch, and some younger pines. The road between the pines and hardwoods was to our north, with the grown-up pasture to our east. Walking in, I noticed fresh hen droppings on the ground. We found Pete a place where he could see the old road, the edge of the hardwoods, and the pasture.

I got behind Pete, and once we were both set, I began some very soft calls on my slate. We had been there about 30 minutes without a response, and I noticed that Pete was starting to squirm. Apparently, where he was sitting was uncomfortable, so I whispered to him that we stay another 15 to 20 minutes, and if nothing showed up, we would leave.

Looking at my watch, it was about 10:20. Pete seemed to have settled down and quit moving around, so I called softly again but got no response. Then, since my position was a little higher than Pete's, I spotted two fans down in the hardwoods moving straight toward the road. He had not yet seen them, so I whispered to him not to move. When Pete spotted them, the two gobblers were only about 25 yards in front of him in the old road.

Pete shoots an A-5 Browning 12- gauge semi-auto, and he has to shoot from his left shoulder because of a vision problem. I knew he would have to turn to his left some to shoot, so while the birds were turning their fans in our face, he was able to move but did not shoot. Waiting for him to shoot was nerve-racking.

After waiting a bit, I clucked softly; the birds both came out of a strut, raised their heads, and Pete shot one of them. He explained that he was afraid of hitting both birds with his shot since they were strutting so closely together. We admired that beautiful bird, picked him up and slowly walked back to the cabin, stopping a few times to catch our breath. What a great morning, even if Pete's gobbler and his buddy did not serenade us with a gobble. We now had two gobblers to process.

Pete Bromley with his Virginia bird, Chuck Bates, and the author
with clearcut gobbler from left to right.

Having already mentioned my good friend and professional colleague Tom Franklin, his first gobbler was a story in itself. During his tenure with The Wildlife Society (TWS) and later, we worked closely for many years while other conservation organizations employed him. That first gobbler was called up on a farm owned by his family northwest of Winchester, Virginia.

Although we have enjoyed many hunts together for deer and upland gamebirds and South Africa for plains game, that first hunt we made for spring gobblers was a classic. It was a lesson in patience and persistence. It was obvious to me after that hunt that Tom would likely become addicted to spring gobbler hunting.

We met at an old farmhouse on the property and talked about what part of the farm we might have the best chance of rousing a gobbler. We first went to an area where Tom frequently saw turkeys on the farm but could not raise a gobble. After trying a couple more spots, he suggested going to a ridge that dropped down to a branch.

Beyond that branch was a county paved road and some property across the road that was part of the farm where he had seen turkeys. We got about 100 yards down the ridge below a pasture edge, and it looked like a good calling spot.

Looking around, I suggested that Tom sit down in front of a big oak that had a dead top in front of it that would break up his outline. I found a place about ten yards behind where he sat. Once settled in, I called loudly on a mouth call. To our surprise, several gobblers responded across the paved road and on the side of another ridge.

Carefully, I eased closer and whispered that there was no way we could get closer without spooking them, so I suggested we stay where we were and see what happened. Tom was in a good spot. About 30 yards in front of him, the ridge tapered off steeply. So, if one of the turkeys came up, he would be able to see it as soon as it came over the end of the ridge.

Moving back, I called again, and several gobblers answered. But it was impossible to tell how many there were, as they were still together. In about five minutes, I called again, and it sounded like those birds had crossed the paved road and were close to the branch. Every call I made for the next 20 minutes was answered immediately with gobbles, whether a yelp, cluck or purr. They seemed to be rooted in that branch bottom and would not budge.

I slipped closer to Tom, telling him to sit still, that I was going to back up the hill about 20 yards or so and try to toll those gobblers up the hill. After doing that, they again gobbled from the same place, so I moved another 15 yards back, found a place to sit and called again. This time when they gobbled, it sounded like they had moved a little closer, so I waited a few more minutes. I turned my head up the hill behind me while calling, prompting them to gobble closer.

Although I was some 45 yards up the hill behind Tom, where the end of the ridge tapered off downhill, the crest was still visible to me. I decided they were committed, and I did not call again. Shortly, they gobbled again in front of Tom and began coming up over the crest of the ridge. It looked like there were five of them. Tom shot, killing one. We had probably worked those gobblers at least an hour but finally could toll them up the face of that ridge. We took the gobbler up to the old house; then Tom took it to the check station a few miles away.

We hunted together often for deer and turkey on his family's properties and other places for many years. Tom was a quick study about spring gobbler hunting. Not only was he highly attentive, but he worked diligently to improve his skills and knowledge. As a result, Tom became an accomplished caller and hunter and has killed many turkeys since that first hunt.

We remain great friends, and he has purchased several firearms from my collection over the years. I have definitely missed hunting and visiting with him and others mentioned over the past two springs, and I still hope we can get together for a hunt in the future.

Although I have not kept count, it has been my pleasure to call up many gobblers for first-time hunters, young and old, over the years. However, before taking them on their first turkey hunt, I always caution them that turkey hunting is addictive.

Another good friend I helped experience the rush of spring gobbler hunting is Wayne Bell, from Annandale, Virginia. Wayne worked for the U.S. Forest Service, and we first met at a seminar I presented in the old Forest Service building on 14th Street in Washington, D.C. My purpose was to help promote the 1983 Yearbook of Agriculture, titled Using Our Natural Resources. Serving on the National Wild Turkey Federation (NWTF) Board of Directors at that time, I had co-authored a chapter in the Yearbook titled "Return of A Native: The Wild Turkey Flourishes Again."

The chapter was a way to honor a long-time friend and colleague, Herman "Duffy" Holbrook, a veteran U.S. Forest Service biologist. Duffy was an unbelievable turkey caller using just his natural voice. In this promotional event, the Secretary of Agriculture, John Block, had dropped by and had me show him how to use a turkey call.

Sometime during this promotional event, a gentleman came up to me, and we visited about hunting. It turned out to be Wayne Bell. He asked me if I bow hunted, and I informed him I did when time permitted. He wanted to start but did not know anyone in the area who could show him a few things about the sport.

Finding out that he lived less than ten miles from us, I invited him to our house and shared my minimal knowledge about bow hunting with him. He also revealed that he had never spring gobbler hunted and asked if he might go with me some time. I found out quickly that Wayne was also a swift learner. When he got interested in an activity, he devoted his attention to learning more.

That following spring, Wayne accompanied me turkey hunting a couple of times, and he got his first gobbler. Afterward, we hunted in several other states over the years and had some fantastic hunts. Wayne was diligent in learning how to call, the kind of places to set up when to call, and what calls to use, so he was agreeable to advice or suggestions. On hunts we later made to both Kentucky and Illinois, we experienced some exciting situations.

The first morning while in Illinois, we had tried to call a gobbler for the landowner. Wayne had worked with this gentleman years before when he was stationed on the Shawnee National Forest. He was a nice guy who allowed us to hunt on his land that adjoined part of the national forest, so we all went together the first morning.

I was able to get a gobbler cranked up and found both a place to set up before sitting about 15 yards behind them. The gobbler was on the ground. At each call, the gobbler responded closer, coming up a ridge toward us. Sadly, this gentleman was hard of hearing, and I easily overheard him ask Wayne if he heard the gobbler.

The bird was close to them by this time, so I called again, and he gobbled. Then I heard him again loudly ask Wayne if he heard the gobbler. At that point, the gobbler quit responding, and we never heard him again. After some time trying to find another vocal gobbler, we went back to the house, had lunch and went bluegill fishing in his farm pond.

Later that evening, I went back to the area where we had hunted. Right at dark, I got a gobbler to answer as it went to roost. The next morning, we went to the area where I had heard the gobbler, arriving before daylight. I discussed where Wayne should hear this gobbler and left in hopes of finding another gobbling bird. It was quite foggy that morning, so I figured gobbling would be delayed but kept moving and calling in hopes of hearing a bird gobble. It seemed that the fog lifted after about 30 minutes, so I called and heard two gobblers answer. They appeared to be some distance away, and it sounded like they were together. I headed toward them, thinking they might still be on the roost, but getting closer, I realized they were on the ground.

They were on a little ridge across a steep gully with some dead trees down in it. Realizing my best chance was to get across that gully, and above these birds, I moved down into the gully. If I could reach that ridge, I figured I would see them if they continued up the ridge. About in the middle, while trying to cross the gully, I ran into some downed trees. Finally, working my way around those trees and about three-quarters way across, they gobbled very near me directly on the ridge.

I had no choice. I had to stop before being seen or heard. They continued up the ridge, and soon, I could see them just behind a dense screen of blueberry bushes. They were both in full strut, seemingly captivated with each other as they strutted back and forth behind those blueberry bushes. I called softly. They both gobbled and kept on strutting. This went on for about ten minutes. I waited anxiously for one or the other of these gobblers to come around that screen of brush as they were only about 40 yards away.

Suddenly, the dense fog rolled in. As the mist thickened and came closer to the ground, those two gobblers folded their wings and walked on up the ridge. No amount of calling could get them to respond. They disappeared quickly, so I waited about 20 minutes until the fog began to lift before calling again. But, I could not get a response.

So close, but that is a part of turkey hunting. Knowing from the sound of running water that I was above a creek some distance down the slope, I stayed on the ridge crest and paralleled the creek. I stopped and called occasionally. Finally, after about a quarter of a mile, I stopped, called, and got an answer across the creek. To hopefully avoid spooking the gobbler, I circled back some distance.

I searched for a trail to get down to the creek and a shallow place to wade across. A sharp ridge jutted out over the creek about 100 yards above me on the creek's other side. I decided to go up the backside of it and get on top before calling. It was steep, but I made my way to the top, found a place to sit, and called again. The turkey gobbled back immediately, just down in a flat below me, adjacent to the creek.

In a few minutes, he gobbled again. Occasionally, I could spot him with four hens about 90 yards up the creek. He was strutting, but the hens were ignoring him. Changing from a mouth call to my little slate, I called softly and clucked. The turkey gobbled right back. At that point, it was a waiting game, and it was doubtful that he would leave the hens. However, he soon started moving my way over to the bottom of the ridge. He gobbled again and began strutting up the slope toward me.

As he got closer, enabling me to see him better, my first reaction was what a small gobbler he seemed to be. However, he kept on coming, and when he got about 30 yards away and straightened up, I shot him. I was amazed at how light he was on picking him up, but he had a nice long beard and one and one-quarter-inch spurs. Placing my carrying strap on him, I headed back to where Wayne had started earlier that morning. When getting closer, I started crow-cawing, and Wayne came to me.

He said he had worked a gobbler until the fog rolled in and it, too, had quit gobbling. We looked my gobbler over and commented to each other how narrow his breast was and how light he was. I asked Wayne if he had heard other gobblers, but he had not. Then I asked where he had last heard the bird he had worked. He motioned down toward the creek. I hung my gobbler in a tree by the carrying strap, left my shotgun there as well, and said, "Let's go down that way and see if we might get him gobbling again."

Although by now it was after 10:00, we had to try at least. So, we started down the ridge, with me in front, which was a mistake, and Wayne behind. As the ridge began to narrow, we stopped, and I called loudly, one time on my mouth call. Immediately, from across the creek, a bird gobbled. The next thing we heard was the gobbler flying across the creek directly below us. He was so close and getting closer with every wing beat.

There was no time to waste. We dropped to the ground like a rock. The gobbler landed about 15 yards below me, over the side of the finger ridge. Wayne could not see the gobbler once he was on the ground, even though he knew he had flown down just over the side of the ridge. The gobbler did not tarry and ran back down toward the creek before Wayne could get a shot. Another close call, but no cigar.

Taking my gobbler into a check station, they weighed him at 14 1/2 pounds which is the lightest mature gobbler I have ever killed. His breast was skinny, and he had almost no breast sponge, but his wingtips were strutted off nearly square. Processing him, I could only find one spur puncture mark in his thigh that was slightly infected around the wound. His testes were swollen and bright yellow, so he was breeding even if he was not a very large bird.

Wayne and I enjoyed many other hunts over the years, and he quickly became a very effective turkey hunter and skilled bow hunter. We still communicate with each other occasionally and remain good friends.

A good friend I met while working for the U.S. Fish and Wildlife Service (FWS) in 1979 was Bob Hines, the chief artist and illustrator for FWS for many years. Many waterfowl hunters are likely familiar with the "Ducks at A Distance" booklet he illustrated. They may also know of the classic Ducks, Geese and Swans of North America book by Frank Bellrose and other books Bob did the artwork for years ago. His many illustrations depicted in different publications from books, posters, and stamps were admired by everyone who saw them. Later, after my transfer to the Department of Agriculture, we remained good friends.

Bob was interested in most of our youth educational programs, especially one we initiated called the National 4-H Adult Volunteer Leader Wildlife and Fisheries Recognition Program. This program was open to all states. We selected a panel of biologists and youth educators each year to evaluate the nominations. They then identified the six best volunteer leaders who had worked with youth on wildlife and fisheries educational programs. Those six were provided with an all-expenses-paid trip that year to the North American Wildlife and Natural Resources Conference wherever it was held.

We arranged an open reception at the conference, attended by wildlife and fisheries professionals from all over North America, and annually awarded the six winners an engraved plaque and an original piece of art. A true bonus was that Bob would create an original work of art based on their favorite species of fish or wildlife. Therefore, each year after the six winners were selected, they were requested to name their favorite wildlife or fish species. Bob then did six original pieces of art based on the winner's choice until several years after his retirement. Thus, this cooperative program with the FWS continued for over 23 years. Although the program was greatly appreciated by those volunteers who received these awards, it was also well attended by the agency administrators and provided excellent visibility for the program.

This introduction leads me to a visit that I had with Bob one day. He mentioned that although he had hunted and fished for many different species over his career, he had never killed a turkey gobbler. That was a challenge we had to remedy. Therefore, I hastily arranged with Colonel Bill Windsor at Quantico to bring Bob down for a hunt one morning that coming spring. Colonel Windsor was pleased to do so and said he would assign us to a hunt zone he knew had several gobblers.

Bob met me at our house that morning. On the drive down to Quantico, he began talking about different hawks he had seen. Thinking about hawks reminded me of a rare observation I had witnessed several years back. I shared this with Bob, explaining that it happened while working a big gobbler that was strutting to me almost in range.

That gobbler's journey, however, was interrupted by a Cooper's hawk that flew in and landed nearby. He did not sit there long, then swooped down at that gobbler. The gobbler immediately folded up and ran like the devil was after him. Now a Cooper's hawk might weigh at best one pound, whereas that gobbler probably weighed close to 20 pounds.

Yet that gobbler was terrified by and fled immediately from the little accipiter that dived at him.

We drove on down, checked in, had a brief visit between Bob and Colonel Windsor, then went to our assigned zone to try to locate a gobbler. After daylight, we got on a bird that had come up a long, narrow valley between two ridges. Bob was sitting in some Virginia pines, a place where he could see down the slope. The bird gobbled several times and was coming. I whispered to Bob to get his gun on his knee and expect the gobbler to come up the point of that ridge. I moved behind Bob and sat against a big stump. Shortly afterward, I spotted the gobbler's fan, head and wattles coming up over the ridge. He was in strut.

Bob saw him before long and pulled his cheek down on the gunstock when, amazingly, a Cooper's hawk flew into a Virginia pine between Bob and the gobbler. It hardly got settled on the limb, then dive-bombed that big gobbler. The turkey turned and ran like his tail was on fire, back toward the area he had come from. Bob turned to me and said, "I didn't doubt your earlier story about this but never thought I would witness it myself."

After moving to another area in that zone, we, fortunately, got another gobbler to answer, and Bob killed his first gobbler. That Cooper's hawk observation, however, stuck in both our memories.

Working closely with both the National Wild Turkey Federation (NWTF) and the Virginia Chapter, the board of directors requested that we find an artist who could be commissioned to do a turkey painting. From that painting, we would have prints made and sell as a fundraising opportunity. Mentioning my friendship with Bob, they asked me to check with him to see if he would be interested in doing such a painting. He said he would, so we visited a fellow who worked with artists to have prints made from an original. After some negotiations, we worked out the costs and deadlines with him.

Bob did the painting over the next couple of months, and we had prints made to sell to benefit the chapter. It was a beautiful print, and the board decided we would not sell prints #1 and #2. Instead, our thought was to present them to then-President Ronald Reagan and his Secretary of State, James A. Baker III. I knew Mr. Baker and had become friends with him after guiding him at Quantico a couple of times.

As soon as the prints were available for sale to members and the public, I purchased two prints. I gave one to my dad, and Bob asked me to bring the other one to him. So, even though it had already been matted and framed, I took it to

(left to right) Bob Carlton, Secretary of State Jim Baker, the author, and Bob Hines on the right making presentation to Jim Baker.

Cooper's hawk...

Bob. I also contacted Mr. Baker and asked if he would be interested in us presenting the first Virginia Chapter art print #2 to him at the White House and arranging an audience with the President.

We hoped to present the President the # 1 print. In a week or so, Mr. Baker called me back and said he was unsure if President Reagan would be available to receive the print, but he would. We set a date for us to visit the White House and make the presentation. We made the presentation, and I have a photo with Bob Hines, Mr. Baker, and the then President of the NWTF Virginia Chapter, Bob Carlton.

A few months later, Bob called me and asked me to come

by his house. He had retired and was doing his artwork from his home studio. I went by for a visit with him and his wife Nancy, and he presented me with my Virginia print. At the bottom right, in an artist's remark, he had drawn a big gobbler in strut, and at the bottom left, he placed a Cooper's hawk in a Virginia pine tree.

Bob was beginning to experience some health issues, so I decided to ask him if he would be interested in doing me an original piece of art. He asked me what I wanted him to paint since he had painted virtually every wildlife and sports fish species in North America during his career. I thought about it briefly and described an observation made in 1967 while working on my field research in South Florida. It was watching a Crested Cara Cara swoop down ahead of my flushing rig, then fly up into a burned-off cabbage palm tree with a diamondback rattlesnake in his talons.

Bob said he had expected me to want a turkey print, but he would do the painting for a specified amount. He said to give him about three months, and sure enough, he called and said it was ready in a few months. After discussing it with my wife, we invited him and his wife Nancy out to dinner, and he brought it with them. When it was opened, it was the exact observation we had discussed. Bob, however, had added another Crested Cara Cara flying by in the distance.

I also have a full page of U.S. Postal stamps made from Bob's pen and ink painting (sepia-colored). He had been commissioned to do that painting some time back in the 1950s. They are $0.03 stamps of a turkey gobbler flying by some pine trees on the side of a mountain. The stamp is imprinted at the top with the words Wildlife Conservation and below the gobbler, the words Wild Turkey.

CHAPTER 26

Adventures in Mexico

At one of the NWTF's Annual Meetings back in the 1990s, I bid on and purchased a turkey hunting trip in Mexico for the Gould's subspecies of turkey at the banquet auction. Unfortunately, there was not much information about this hunt or the outfitter, but I got a receipt and a phone number for later contact.

Back to my office a few days later, at a meeting in D.C. I shared with Tom Franklin that the hunt had been secured. He immediately said he would like to go with me on that hunt if possible. Therefore, I contacted the outfitter to see if he could accommodate Tom with me on this hunt. I needed to find out what his fee would be for Tom and ask him to provide some additional details.

After several attempts, I finally made contact. He said that, yes, Tom could join me for a set amount. So, we set the dates. He also told me where we should fly into and where he would pick us up. I discussed with him the idea of bringing our shotguns. He advised against that, saying they had guns and ammunition we could use. We, fortunately, took his advice.

We flew into Chihuahua and were picked up by the outfitter and his driver. He took us to his house for dinner and a night's sleep. Then the next day, after breakfast, he took us to meet several influential politicians in town for some unknown reason. We then picked up our gear and another man, whom we learned would be our cook. Our vehicle was a fancy Chevrolet Suburban. We all loaded up and began a long drive toward the Sierra Madre Mountains.

On the way, we were stopped twice at roadblocks in very isolated areas where men, young and old, were armed with

AR-15s and riot shotguns. At each roadblock, the outfitter told us to wait in the vehicle while he got out, allowed them to check the shotguns and our paperwork, then paid them some amount of money. We continued on our way, making it to the mountains well after dark.

Whatever arrangements he had made did not include clear directions to the ranch we were supposed to hunt. By the time we finally found the ranch, it was well after midnight. The outfitter was the only one who could speak any English, and neither Tom nor myself were well-versed in Spanish. He told us to stay in the vehicle while he went into the ranch house. After about 30 minutes out of the ranch house came a man, his wife carrying a baby, and a teenaged boy. They all got into a truck and left. He then had us come in with our gear and go up some stairs to an attic area.

The building itself was a log structure. The attic logs were not finished, and we could see through cracks in the logs to the outside. We had no sleeping bags. However, searching the attic managed to find some horse blankets to cover with partially. It was well below 30 degrees and a very unpleasant night. The outfitter, his driver and cook took the rancher's bed and the teenager's beds. The cabin had no electricity and only a wood heater that doubled as a stove in the cabin's main room. To say accommodations were primitive and not at all what we expected would be a gross understatement.

We arose early, not having slept much, pulled on our hunting clothes and boots and went down to the main room to find the cook busy cooking on a piece of flat iron on top of the heater. He had some coffee, and we ate whatever it was he was preparing. The outfitter got the shotguns out of the vehicle and presented them to us with six Mexican shotshells of either number four or six lead shots. One was a 12-gauge pump with a full choke barrel, and the other was a

20-gauge pump with a modified choked barrel. Both looked like they had been used to break trail. They were the two oldest Mossberg pump shotguns I have ever seen.

I suggested that Tom take the 12-gauge and I would take the 20-gauge. We loaded up in the Suburban and headed out before daylight over faint trails/roads that were terrible. The trails and roads were full of huge boulders and some very narrow ledges that dropped into a canyon. Once in that canyon, it looked like pretty good turkey habitat as it began to get light.

We tried to get the driver to stop, and the outfitter kept saying, "no, no, Senior, we drive you there." After telling him several more times to stop and let me out, he finally stopped, and when the door opened, turkeys started flying off the hillside above the vehicle. By the time they turned around and headed off with Tom, all the turkeys in the area had flown across the canyon.

I hunted the canyons hard that morning but could not stimulate a gobble, nor did I see any turkeys. Finally, I located a spring with turkey, deer, cougar, and bear tracks around it. I quickly realized that the availability, or lack thereof of surface water, was a significant factor in finding turkeys.

I met them back where they had let me out around noon, and we drove back to the cabin. Tom had seen some turkeys, but he thought most of them were hens. We visited a little about the guns, and both felt like before we hunted any more, we needed to pattern these shotguns. We would have to do so with at least one of the six shells we had been given.

When we got to the cabin, the cook had some food ready, so we ate. The rancher and the teenaged boy came by as we were going out to pattern the shotguns. The teenager wanted to go with us. After we both shot a round at some scrap cardboard, at 25 yards, it was evident that we would have to get gobblers in close before hitting them. Based on this one-shot, scattered pattern, we felt like our maximum range would have to be inside of 30 yards.

The kid questioned us, and we answered as best we could. Trying to communicate with him, we drew a crude picture of a turkey and were finally able to determine that he called turkeys "Ochohees." We were then able to get him to understand we were looking for a place that had "Ochohees." He pointed back up behind the cabin to some large steep mountains and excitedly said, "Ochohees."

While the outfitter, cook and driver slept that afternoon, we got this kid to lead us up one of the mountains he kept wanting us to go. Although Tom and I were much younger and in much better shape then, this kid was like a mountain goat. We would go as long as we could, then stop and rest. We started seeing some turkey sign around a small spring about halfway up the mountain and some scratching nearby.

We kept climbing until about 4:00 p.m. we reached the top and found a pretty flat mesa with considerable turkey sign. There was a knob to our left, and this kid kept wanting us to go there. When we got to that knob, his urging became apparent as there was a large roost site there. We looked around, and although there was a pretty sheer bluff just below the roost site, I decided to call loudly on a mouth call. Immediately, a gobbler hammered from below the bluff.

We began searching to see if we could find a trail to get below the bluff. Finding no easy way to get down there, I decided to call again. On calling, the gobbler thundered back and had already gotten halfway up the bluff. I motioned to Tom to sit down and face the direction we thought the gobbler might come and had the kid get behind me about ten yards. The boy had on no camo.

Tom sat down with a small opening in front of him just

before some thick oak brush started. After the third call, the gobbler was almost right on top of us. It ran up and stopped in the opening in front of Tom at about 20 yards. Tom took the shot. The gobbler flopped over then ran into the oak brush before he could get another shot. Immediately, the kid came flying out from behind me, ran right past us into the oak brush that seemed to be almost impenetrable.

In just a minute, we heard some flapping of wings and a long, drawn-out "arrraggghh." Looking in that direction as the kid came out of the thick oak brush carrying the gobbler by the neck, we saw it kicking and flapping. He was smiling like a jackass eating saw briars and very proud of having caught that gobbler.

We were proud as well because it is unlikely that Tom and I would ever have found that gobbler otherwise. It was an excellent Gould's gobbler, with a decent beard and busted-up spurs. We put my carrying strap on him and started back down the mountain, going back pretty much the same route we had climbed up. Before we got to the spring, I called again and thought we heard a jake gobble. Within just a couple of minutes, the jake came running up, but I chose not to shoot him.

When we got back to camp, we managed to get the kid to understand that I would like him to go with me the next morning. We processed Tom's gobbler and gave the meat to the cook. The following day, after putting a couple of water bottles in my vest, the kid and I headed about halfway back up the mountain, then proceeded westward until we ran into a small pond that had been scooped out to water livestock.

It was a very dry morning, so I gave the kid a bottle of water and drank one myself while we were waiting for it to get light. We waited there for about 15 to 20 minutes until it started to get light. I crow-cawed and heard a cascade of multiple gobbles from 200 yards above us. Quickly looking around, I saw a place where we could sit about halfway up the pond berm in a bit of cedar and oak brush. We moved there with the kid behind me.

Those birds sounded like they were still on the roost, so I waited to call again, although they gobbled often. I soon heard one gobble from the ground. I called back, then listened to the multiple gobbles again, all seeming to come from ground level. Looking up the side of that steep mountain as best possible because it sounded like they were coming downhill pretty fast, I spotted some movement.

When we could see them, most of what we saw was a mass of red wattles, shiny white skullcaps and large black objects running toward us as fast as they could. We watched them come until they slowed down, then walked out to a bit of a point that ran into the pond about 15 yards away. I counted 16 gobblers, at least ten of which were mature birds.

Afraid to shoot while their heads were up, knowing how poorly that shotgun patterned, I waited until one of the large gobblers in front reached his head down to get a drink of water, then shot. Fortunately, my shot did not hit any of the others. Gobblers went in every direction, a couple almost running over us. The kid stayed behind me this time.

Once they had all pretty much gone, we went out and picked up the gobbler. We walked back up to the dry bank around the pond, and I put the carrying strap on him. The kid kept trying to tell me something and finally got me to understand that he wanted another bottle of water.

Unfortunately, all I had left were the two empty bottles in my vest. When showing him that no more water was available, he ran back down to the pond. It was pretty much covered with green algae, and the cows had been defecating in it, but he scraped the algae back and scooped up some water and drank it. It did not seem to bother him at all, so we headed back around the mountain toward the cabin.

Not having any scales, we estimated each of the gobblers to weigh about 20 pounds. Both had nice beards but rounded off and cracked spurs only about an inch long. The Gould's subspecies have beautiful coloration similar to that of the Merriam's, with that white-tipped tail fan and rump patch. They seem, however, to have a good bit more greenish iridescence and bronze than some of the other subspecies.

After cleaning the gobbler, we gave the meat to the cook, and we ate it later fixed in a variety of dishes. This one hunt, of course, provides me with a minimal amount of experience hunting the Gould's subspecies. In my opinion, however, the limiting factor in much of their range is water availability. If you find a water source in the area where this turkey lives, it will likely have turkey sign around it. Another observation was that you need to start trying to find a place to sit if you get a bird to gobble at your call. If a response to your call is heard, they seem to respond quickly unless they have a harem of hens.

The outfitter offered to allow us to kill another gobbler for another $250 each. I am confident we could have done so, but we both declined, electing to explore the next few days before returning to Chihuahua. The ranch cowboy saddled up a couple of mules and led us on a trip into the mountains, where we found some caves.

These caves had been used at some previous time by Indians and maybe outlaws on the run. We saw the Coues subspecies of whitetail deer, numerous road runners, and various other birds, mammals, and reptiles. I do not remember how much we tipped the outfitter, but I made sure to tip the teenager well for the guiding service he provided. I do remember giving him a pocket knife I had carried along.

He seemed more appreciative of the pocket knife than the money. We both saw black bear and cougar tracks and enjoyed visiting with the rancher, a competitive rodeo cowboy.

We enjoyed some authentic Mexican food cooked on a wood heater/stove and enjoyed stopping somewhere on the way back at a museum for a short visit. Tom had made arrangements to stay a few more days and take a tour down Copper Canyon on the railroad before returning home.

My schedule required me to head on back to attend some meetings. We parted at Chihuahua, and both were glad to have the outfitter getting us through the armed guard stops on our way back. We both smuggled out our gobbler's beards hidden in our gear, although I have no idea what became of it once I was back home.

Tom Franklin with Gould's gobbler taken April 2, 2000,
in Sierra Madres Mountains, Mexico.

Author with Gould's gobbler taken April 3, 2000.

It sure was not the most pleasant or accommodating trip. The outfitter did not know much about turkey hunting. But we both enjoyed the camaraderie in camp with the cook and the outfitter. The outfitter would periodically drift off into griping and cursing about those criminal officials in Mexico City who would not issue him a permit for big horned sheep hunts.

Our biggest worry was that the driver was going to disable that Suburban before we could get back to Chihuahua. He drove, seemingly without caution over boulders and obstacles that most jacked-up 4-wheelers would avoid. By the time we got back to Chihuahua, both running boards were loose and flapping in the breeze. After thinking about it back in the states, we both agreed that we did enjoy this challenging adventure.

CHAPTER 27

The Pete and Grainger Hunt

Among my favorite mentors, friends, and former supervisors was a fine gentleman named Merrill L. " Pete" Petoskey. After his retirement in 1985, he moved back to Michigan near the little town of Lewiston. While working with Pete, we occasionally hunted for doves, squirrels and deer in Virginia and Michigan for grouse and woodcock. Pete had invited me to come up and hunt turkeys with him numerous times, which tempted me to plan on going one spring when my wife could go with me. One of Pete's best friends from their earlier days working for the Michigan Department of Natural Resources (MDNR), Dale Grainger, had come over to go with us when we arrived. My wife, Doris, and I had met Dale on previous visits, but I had never before experienced the pleasure of hunting with him.

We drove around scouting a little that afternoon and spotted a big gobbler with some hens in an area we had grouse and woodcock hunted in past years. We agreed to go there the next morning. At dinner that evening, Pete and Grainger started talking about their favorite dessert. Both finally decided it was lemon icebox pie, and Doris remembered that as she was very fond of Pete.

Both Pete and Grainger had reached their early 70s by that time, and their legs were not up to long walks. Therefore, after our first place proved unproductive, we decided to stop at a few other places. At each stop, I tried to get a gobbler going without us having to walk too far. But I had no luck. Another caveat is that all three of us were hard of hearing. Pete's hearing was the poorest, then Grainger's, and then mine. About 8:45, we arrived at an area where gas wells were scattered across the landscape, each with about an acre of openings around them. As we drove by one of these openings, we spotted a gobbler and some hens in the back corner of that opening about 200 yards away. It had a steep timbered, predominantly hardwood ridge behind it, and I needed to get above those turkeys to call to them.

So, not stopping or slowing down on spotting them, we drove over the next hill. I asked Pete and Grainger if they thought they could make it around that ridge to get above the gobbler and hens. Seemingly excited, they both felt up to it, so we got out, and they collected their gear.

We took our time and eventually made it to where we were about 200 yards above the gas well opening, where we had seen the gobbler and hens. Having no idea if they were still there, I called, and the gobbler answered. Looking around quickly, I spotted two finger ridges that dropped down toward that opening. I located Grainger a spot on the one to our left and made him a little blind. Then I spotted Pete on the one to the right and made him a little blind.

With both of them in place, I moved up above them sort of mid-way between the two, found a place to sit, and started calling. At the next call, the turkey gobbled. There was no way of knowing if he still had the hens with him, but I decided not to wait long and called again. When he gobbled again, I could tell he had begun to move up the ridge and was closer. I was confident that both Pete and Grainger had heard him gobble, but I was not close enough to communicate with either of them.

I called again, very softly. The turkey gobbled back just below the two of them, but I could not tell which of the finger ridges the gobbler was likely to come up. I did not call again because the bird was not far from the two of them when he gobbled the last time. Soon, however, he gobbled, and it sounded like he was right in front of Pete.

I sat there and waited, then heard him drumming closer. Finally, Pete shot, so I got up and started down to be sure he had killed the gobbler. I could see Grainger working his way over, so I spoke to both of them. Pete never acknowledged that he heard nor saw me. When we got closer, Pete was holding his foot on the gobbler's head. Speaking fairly loudly, I said, "That's a good bird," as he looked at Grainger and me as we approached him.

When we both got right up to Pete, I suggested that the gobbler sure must have put on a show for them, and Pete asked, "What?" Grainger said, "Yeah, I saw him come up the ridge, stopping and gobbling when you called, and I kept

Pete and Grainger with Lewiston, MI gobbler.

waiting for Pete to shoot." Then, finally, we saw Pete reach up to his hearing aids and do something, then he said, "Dang, I had my hearing aids turned off."

We both then realized Pete had not heard a thing but fortunately had spotted the gobbler and killed him. Grainger accused him of being asleep, and he may well have been, but at least Grainger got to see and hear the gobbler before Pete shot him. We took our time with Pete's gobbler, stopping to harvest a few morel mushrooms on the way back to the truck.

When we got back to Pete's place, Doris had made a lemon icebox pie and had some grouse breasts ready to cook. We took a few pictures of Pete's turkey before cleaning it for Pete and Grainger to share. Pete's gobbler had two crickets and just a few green grass leaves in his crop. We then went in, gave thanks, and enjoyed a great lunch together.

Doris and I loved the visit and also enjoyed a couple of great fishing trips for yellow perch from Pete's pontoon boat before heading south. Sadly, Pete passed away in 2019 at the ripe old age of 93. We had visited with him not too long before and enjoyed very much the time spent with Pete, one of his sons, John, and his wife.

CHAPTER 28

Female Persistence

The wife of one of my New York friends is a very fine lady named Beth Zagata. Over the years, when she could get off work a day or two while I was visiting, it was my pleasure to try to call in a gobbler for her. Unfortunately, as often happens when you want to have it all come together, all kinds of gremlins seem to interfere. This is especially difficult with some first-timers. Sorry to say, things do not always work out with every gobbler you have a chance to pursue.

Beth and I had sat down on several gobblers that she got to see and hear gobble. We also had some that did not to show themselves for her to take a shot but gobbled often and nearby. One morning we called to one that must have gobbled 100 times and walked almost entirely around where she was sitting with me 15 yards behind her. The gobbler was where I could have shot him several times. Nevertheless, she could not get a clean shot at his head and neck.

One that threw us a curve happened on a friend's property not too far from Oneonta, New York. We did not locate this bird right off the roost but got him cranked up pretty good after walking a long way and calling periodically. Finally, when responding to a hen call, he answered nearby.

We had to move quickly. I found Beth a little place within a sparse brush top, got her settled, took a couple of steps back, and laid down behind her. With every call, he would gobble. He seemed to be walking along the edge of a small hemlock swamp area about 50 yards away.

After several calls, to which he responded immediately, I spotted his fan on the edge of the hemlocks. I whispered to Beth, asking if she had seen him. But she had not yet spotted him.

Finally, he came out of the brush between us, about 45 yards away. I whispered to Beth not to move until he turned around or went behind a tree but, if he did, get her shotgun to her shoulder and be ready to shoot. The gobbler strutted around a couple of times, turning his fan to us.

Again, I encouraged Beth to get her shotgun to her shoulder. The gobbler was working his way a little closer each time he pirouetted and then turned to face us. There was a little fold on the hillside about 30 yards from us, just deep enough that you could not see him when he went down into it. She already had her shotgun pointed where we thought he would come up over the top of the fold.

We felt sure he would stick his head and neck up for her to shoot any second, and we waited for what seemed like 15 minutes. Then I spotted some movement to the left. He had worked his way up that little drain behind the fold and was about to step out 15 yards away from Beth, but almost 90 degrees to the left of where she had her shotgun pointed. At that point, even though she spotted the bird too, she knew she could not outdraw him.

So, we both sat as still as we could, hoping he would not spot us. Unfortunately, he did. Unlike most gobblers, he did not putt and run but instead started walking away up the hill to our left. He went behind some brush, and I told Beth to swing and try to shoot him as he was still less than 40 yards away. However, she could not maneuver quickly enough to feel comfortable taking the shot, so again no cigar, but a close call. Who said turkey hunting was easy anyway?

Beth had to return to her job the next day, so we planned another hunt the following spring, schedules permitting. Luckily, it worked out, and we decided to give it another try. This time we hunted the west side of a big mountain that almost always has several gobblers on it. We heard several gobblers early that morning, and we worked one of them for about 30 minutes, but his hens finally pulled him away, and he quit gobbling.

We moved to several other places and eventually found a gobbler below us. But the area was tough to find a good setup in. I located Beth a place and backed up behind her about 20 yards. Once we were settled, I called softly. The gobbler answered, and it sounded like he was more than 100 yards away but over a ridge and below us.

I used my little peg and slate call from that point on. The turkey seemed to be locked into a strutting place and did not want to come up over the ridge. We conversed back and forth for a while. Finally, I heard him muffle-gobble and knew he was coming to us. Beth looked around at me, and I pointed toward where I thought he might come over the ridge. I motioned to her to get her shotgun mounted, which she did.

Within a minute, we could see his fan coming up behind the crest of the ridge. He came on up, straightened up out of a strut, then headed toward us. He was inside 40 yards, but Beth thought he was still too far, so she waited until he had gone behind some autumn olive brush. Unsure how or why, but when she fired, she missed him at about 30 yards, and he ran and flew off. She was frustrated. But we had enjoyed a good hunt anyway. I guess that in her excitement, she had not pulled her cheek down on the stock and likely shot over him as a result.

The next morning, as it is morning hunting only there, we went to a different area on the mountainside. We heard several birds gobbling at daylight, although shortly afterward, most of them had quit. However, there was one above us that continued to respond. It was going to be a challenging climb to get into a good place from which to call. Beth is a real trooper and said she was up to it.

Cautiously, we made a reasonably large circle around the side of the mountain and slipped into an area that had a little flat ledge. We found a good place to sit, and I decided to sit with her. We quickly assembled a little blind with some fallen white pine limbs.

The gobbler had not gobbled while we were making our way up the mountain, so we were not sure whether he was still where we had heard him. On calling, however, he gobbled back. We felt like we had a good setup because the side of the mountain was very steep in places, with occasional flat ledges, and it seemed like a logical place to start calling.

When the gobbler answered, he sounded like he was less than 200 yards away. I felt good about calling him into range. By the next call, he had gotten closer. He continued to move our way, seeming to be slightly above us. On a hunch, I decided not to call again. Shortly, he gobbled very close and on the same level around the ledge that we were on. When they came into view, two mature gobblers, one strutting and the other in about a half-strut, were closing the gap.

Beth had gotten her shotgun on her knee, and as the two birds moved into range, I could see her getting a little nervous. Over her shoulder, I whispered to make her aim point on the neck right where those red wattles stopped. They stopped at about 25 yards. I clucked and, as he raised his head, she hammered him!

It was a great ending to several challenging hunts where she had not connected. I was proud of her, and she was beaming with pride over that big gobbler. It weighed over 24 pounds. Beth had earned him after following me around on several hunts, which of course, is why they call it hunting and not killing.

On our way out with her gobbler that morning, we flushed a hen turkey off a nest that contained ten eggs. I had never seen a turkey nest so exposed before as it was right at the base of a hemlock tree, with no close overhead cover.

Beth Zagata with her's and the author gobblers called up
on Fiddler's Mountain.

CHAPTER 29

Lessons They Teach

I cannot begin to describe all the hunts I have taken with youngsters over the years since I have not maintained a list. But as noted earlier, I admit to being opinionated. In my opinion, it is not fair to even consider making a youngster's first hunt one for dove, deer, turkey, waterfowl, elk or antelope.

My preference is to start a youngster hunting by first taking them squirrel hunting. Attention before the hunt, of course, needs to be provided by explaining the hunt and the quarry. This should be followed by carefully going over the basics and importance of firearms safety.

On their first hunt, I usually have them bring along a BB rifle for doing a little marksmanship practicing and allowing me to observe how safely they handle their rifle. It is also vital to help them begin to feel comfortable in the woods and understand the importance of sitting still. Then I watch how observant they are about what occurs around them.

I rarely even take a firearm myself on their first trip but make a few setups with them close by. In doing this, I point out things they might not otherwise see or know. If they have become safe handling firearms and act like they want to hunt later, my .22 rimfire rifle goes with us. I always try to position them in a good spot near a food source like hickory nuts or acorns to improve their chances of seeing a squirrel.

Once I ensure they are knowledgeable about safely handling their firearm, it is time to hunt. Hopefully, with range practice, the kids become accurate with their guns, yet I will sit near them at first. If I see a squirrel before they do, I will get them positioned to take a shot. It is okay for them to miss, as there will be other opportunities. Primarily, I want them to become comfortable with their surroundings and observe what is happening around them.

Having taught firearms safety for years, it pleased me when both our sons attended many of those sessions. That gave them a head start on what I expected of them. Next, I started them squirrel hunting and asked them what they had seen or heard after the hunt. After a few hunts, I quickly learned that once they got over the apprehension of being left alone in the woods, their observational skills began to increase.

We would stop and talk about a track or other animal sign on our way into and out of the woods. A couple of times, after they learned to sit quietly, they might see a hawk, owl, deer, opossum, raccoon, skunk, or even a snake. Both learned early on which snakes or other wildlife might pose a threat to them. They delighted me with their observations, which were more important than how many squirrels they killed. Then, when they got home, their mother and any friends who dropped by were informed of their observations. But, of course, such sightings cannot be made, setting a youngster in a pop-up blind.

Later, as our boys got older, they were introduced to dove hunting after some practice at the skeet range. After that, both became proficient wing shots. Then, when they became 11 or 12 years old, they were taken deer hunting, first with me and them without a rifle.

When a deer was killed, I observed their reactions both before and after the shot. Then I let them watch carefully as the intestines, lungs, heart, liver and other organs were removed before starting my drag back to the truck. When we got home, they observed how the animal was skinned and processed for the freezer. Both later killed deer and enjoyed venison, which they had been eating for years.

One occasion comes to mind after I had gone alone one Saturday morning and killed a nice buck. Although we lived in the city limits of Fairfax, Virginia, I had a tree in my backyard that we hung deer on for skinning and processing. My boys and a half-dozen friends came by this particular day as I processed the buck.

One of the kids named Pete, our oldest son's best friend, looked at me and asked how that deer was "caught." After telling him it was not caught but was shot, I showed him the entrance wound. Pete wondered what I was going to do with it. My response was that we were going to eat it. His retort was to make a face and say that is not where meat comes from, and he could never eat that. Because this kid spent more time at our house than his own, there is no telling how many times he had eaten dinner with us. We had venison as the meat on several occasions, but he had not asked, and we had not felt it necessary to explain.

Not saying anything more myself, our boys assured Pete that they loved it, then they took off to play football. About a week later, we were having venison steaks cooked with gravy one evening, and Pete had asked to eat dinner with us. We did not say anything until he had remarked several times how much he liked the meat. Then, I told him that was some of the deer I had processed in the backyard. After that, he never frowned when learning we had wild game for dinner. Later, after getting permission from his mom, the boys and I took Pete on his first hunt for squirrels.

The biggest mistake I likely made with our sons as they grew up was that I did not take them on camping trips as often as they would have liked. We did a good bit of camping, but for the most part, it was linked to a hunting trip or fishing trip. They enjoyed the camping part more than having to get up early for a hunting or fishing activity.

As they became teenagers, we had a solid youth group at our church in Fairfax, with over 100 boys and young men. A couple of other fathers and I decided to initiate a three-day camping trip for the guys every spring or summer. It became a principal activity. However, for various reasons, we limited it to only boys 12 years and older.

One trip in the mid-to-late 1980s was memorable for many reasons. Occasionally, we have an opportunity to visit or hear from one of those now 50-year-old men with families of their own. They still talk about what an enjoyable camping trip and adventure that retreat was for them, even though they thought they would freeze or be eaten by a bear. We had taken trips and gone on retreats before and after that, but that one was special since most of them were "city kids" at the time. Most had never experienced that kind of hands-on learning.

This story, minus a lot of detail, is related to my opinion that kids need to spend time outdoors with mentors. They also need to share such experiences in a hands-on manner with a caring adult. Being pressured to comply by setting in a pop-up blind and shooting their first game over a food plot or bait pile is not how I prefer to start youngsters hunting. These are my opinions, and I am confident others disagree.

Our grandson Brooks had been squirrel hunting with his .22 rimfire after lots of practice, with a BB gun and the .22 rifle and numerous gun handling lessons. He also had some shotgun practice before deciding he wanted to go turkey hunting when he was about 11 years old. So looking forward to this, we got up early, drove to a friend's property, and walked in the dark down across a stream and up to a ridge with a little open area on top. There was a large old white pine right on top of the knob.

After arriving there, we quickly assembled a blind for the

two of us from dead white pine limbs that enabled us to see the area well. We were comfortable leaning back against the trunk of that pine. I worked diligently to get a gobbler to answer. It was, however, one of those mornings when they did not gobble that we could hear anyway.

We sat there and observed four hen turkeys come by feeding, listened to a grouse drumming, and saw several doe deer, one with two fawns. Because we were still and quiet, many other birds singing and other animals moving around were observed and heard.

After about an hour and a half, sensing that Brooks was getting tired of sitting still, I was just about to get up and head back to the truck. I heard wings fluttering, however, and a wood thrush flew into our blind. It lit on Brooks' left shoulder for just an instant then flew away. He looked around at me and said, "Paw Paw, that was cool; what kind of bird was that?" I told him and that we would look it up in my bird books later.

We got up, stretched, and walked back down to the little stream. We found a shallow spot and crossed, getting on a deer trail that curved upward around the hill and back toward the truck. On the way up the trail looking down on the right, there was a shed deer antler. I stopped and pointed it out to Brooks.

Then, a few yards up the hill on the left side of the trail, there was the other side of that shed. Brooks picked them both up, and we discussed what had happened and why. I explained to him that the buck was likely already starting to grow another set of antlers.

We had probably walked a mile or more getting to and from our hiding spot, so I asked him if he was ready to go home and have some breakfast. He was quiet on the trip home and was asleep when we got there. On awakening him

The author with grandson, Brooks Miller, with a gobbler
he killed near Hermosa, VA.

when we arrived home, he was still holding the two sheds
in his hands. He opened the truck door and bounded toward
the house. We went in, and his grandmother started fixing
eggs, sausage, bacon, homemade biscuits and sausage gravy.

When we were through with breakfast, his grandmother
asked him what he enjoyed about that trip. He said it was
having that wood thrush light on his shoulder, finding the
sheds and our conversations about what we saw and heard
while sitting in that blind in front of the big tree. He could
have never experienced that sitting in a pop-up blind.

The following spring gobbler season, we had a near miss
on a hunt in the mountains where he got to watch a gobbler

strut below us for at least 30 minutes or more. Then, we got to watch the hens come to the gobbler and lead him away. We drove down in the next few days and had a great hunt with my friend, Chuck Bates, and Brooks got his first gobbler after several long and difficult hunts.

A hunt with a youngster in Kentucky several years back was an absolute classic. While hunting with my friend, Wayne Flowers' son, Hunter, we had an early near miss with a bunch of gobblers that paraded around me and gobbled for 20 minutes or more.

Unfortunately, where Hunter had set up, he could not see them well enough to get a shot. Having not carried a shotgun myself and sitting on a very steep slope leaning against the back of a big oak tree, moving was not an option for Hunter or me. There were three mature gobblers and two big jakes, and they strutted and gobbled on a slope above me within 35 yards for quite some time. Hunter, who also was sitting on that steep slope, was just far enough away that he could only occasionally see part of the gobblers, but not enough to risk a shot at one. Eventually, they decided to leave and quit gobbling.

After they left, we got up and discussed what happened. Hunter said he had heard a gobbler a couple of ridges away. He thought, however, that the gobbler might be on some posted land. We walked around the point of that ridge about two hundred yards, and, facing the direction Hunter pointed, I called loudly on a mouth call. A gobbler answered but sounded far away. We moved on around the ridge and down the side of it, about halfway. We found a good place for Hunter to sit and fashioned a quick blind facing down the hill. I sat down about 20 yards up the hill behind him and called again. It seemed like the gobbler answered slightly closer.

We continued this call and gobble routine for at least 15

Hunter Foster and his gobbler, his Dad, Wayne on his right and the
author on his left.

minutes, and I could tell when the bird gobbled whether he was down between the ridges or on top of one of them. Finally, I crawled quietly to Hunter's blind and whispered for him to stay right where he was. I informed him that I would quit calling as soon as it appeared that the gobbler was committed. Until then, however, I would continue to move further back up the hill and call, hoping to get him in range.

It worked like a charm. By the second move, I had probably gotten some 55 to 60 yards above Hunter. The last time the bird gobbled, he was down below Hunter. It sounded like maybe about 80 yards, so I sat quietly. Then, he gobbled again on his own, even closer, and I heard Hunter shoot.

Before moving, I shouted and asked him if he got the gobbler, and he said he did. Walking down, I found him with a beautiful gobbler that, when we weighed him, was over 23 pounds. He had a heavy beard and long spurs and was at least a four-year-old bird.

Since then, we have hunted together numerous times and have taken birds in exciting hunts, but that one sure was a good memory. There are many great rewards from hunting with youngsters aside from their excellent hearing. These rewards include their attention once they learn to focus on the hunt, enthusiasm, descriptions and re-telling the hunt.

CHAPTER 30

No Crap in Their Knees

Adult gobblers are extremely tough. Although sometimes wounded severely, they soldier on, especially if it is in the spring mating season. Over many years, I have observed quite a few injured by shot from a hunter's firearm, from fighting with other gobblers for dominance or accidental injuries. Some of these wounds are difficult to determine just how they happened and how they kept going and trying to participate in breeding hens. The following examples were enlightening observations of a few examples.

The first memory of finding something foreign in a gobbler that was somewhat a puzzle was in one of three gobblers I killed one spring on the Kinterbish WMA in Alabama. These had been gutted, crops removed and hung in a nearby deer camps cooler until heading home. Usually, I cleaned them as soon as possible after killing them, but I wanted to take these home so my two young sons could watch me process them. On arriving home, when cleaning them, with the boys watching, two were skinned and left whole, and the other was boned out.

Several weeks later, we had some friends over for dinner, so my wife decided to have wild turkey fixed two ways. She would bake one with cornbread dressing, giblet gravy and other side dishes. The other, I brined and smoked in our charcoal smoker. Our guests seemed to enjoy more of the baked turkey than they did the smoked one.

After they left and the kids were in bed, she said she would remove the rest of the meat from the smoked bird and freeze it to use later. In a few minutes, she said, "come here and look at this." One side of the breast had not yet been carved, and as she began to slice along the keel bone from that side, she hit something that, on the first appearance, looked like a bullet. Taking the knife and trimming around it, I removed it and found it had barely indented the keel bone.

In carefully examining it, I realized it was the point from a target arrow. There was no wood remaining in the point. It was just like a shell of a bullet, still partly chrome or nickel-plated. The arrow had broken on impact or broken later as the bird moved around, but it had somehow survived with no apparent debilitating issues.

Target arrow point removed from gobbler breast.

Hunting in Nebraska one spring, I called up a gobbler for a friend and colleague, Scott Hygnstrom. When we cleaned his gobbler, we found a piece of green cactus about four inches long that somehow had punctured the top of its breast and was down into the meat even with the top of the breast. Although a little discolored and purple around the entrance wound once we trimmed around it with no sign of infection, the rest of the breast appeared to be okay. Exactly how that happened is anyone's guess.

A number of gobblers over the years upon cleaning were found to have been previously shot. Clear evidence is knowing that the shot in my loads were copper-plated #7 ½ shot I used since the 1960s. What I have usually found is lead shot of number fours, fives, or sixes. Not one of these gobblers had exhibited any obvious disability from these lead shot, and most were shot in the back and legs, indicating that someone fired at them running or flying away.

Some other gobblers killed or called up for others have been beat up and wounded by other gobblers, most with deep puncture wounds in the lower breast area, the thighs and legs. A couple were so injured with deep punctures that the coloration and odor showed it significantly infected. In that situation, most or all of the meat removed from the bird was discarded. What is amazing is that these birds could still respond to a call and come in looking for a hen even though they were so wounded.

Another hunt in Nebraska later, after first hunting in Iowa for a few days, I met two friends and colleagues from Tennessee. We drove over to some property just north of the Niobrara River. We each killed a nice bird the first morning out on the private property. After learning that we had killed three birds that morning, the landowner's son asked if we would hunt elsewhere the next few days as he had some guests coming in to hunt.

We located a nearby WMA called Bobcat and decided to hunt there. The afternoon before hunting we found a place on a mesa near a windmill to park and went scouting with each of us going a different direction. It was in the Pine Hills region with large ponderosa pines and deep canyons. It had clouded up, gotten very windy and began snowing.

I had dropped off the mesa down into a steep canyon, looking around and finding a little bit of turkey sign. On my way back toward the car, before it got dark, I spotted a big gobbler. He was headed down into a steep ravine, so stopping, I watched him head downward with no hens. That evening, when we got back together, one of the guys had found a good bit of sign and knew where he wanted to go. Informing the other guy about the lone gobbler and where he had to be going to roost, he decided to go there the following day.

Fortunately, the next morning was beautiful, about 35 degrees, with little wind and the hope of a sunny day. Before we each went our way, we heard a gobbler in the black dark, followed by a pheasant crowing and a sharptailed grouse 'Kuk-kuking' nearby. We each departed. Dropping off into a long, heavily wooded canyon just at daylight, I heard a gobbler near where I had seen the bird the afternoon before. The area where I had gone into found me unable to raise a gobble. Yet, I kept moving around and finally, way up the canyon, ran into a barbed-wire fence with a "Private Land-No Trespassing" sign. Shortly I heard a muffled shotgun blast in the direction my friend had gone and was delighted for him as that limited him out. Turning to the west, I headed up the side of the canyon to see how far this inholding of private land went. Stopping periodically and calling enabled me to cover a good bit of the canyon side.

Finally, out of frustration, I gobbled on a tube call and

was answered by what sounded like two gobblers together. They were clearly on the private land but not too far away. I decided then to find a place, set up and call to those birds hoping they might move my way. After them gobbling at my every call for about 30 minutes, I decided to see if there was a high spot nearby.

Spotting a high knob from which I could look over toward where they were, a few hundred yards away, I headed there. With the aid of binoculars from that knob, I was able to look over into that private land and see what might be holding them from coming closer.

Looking in that direction, I could tell they were in a burned-over area that had greened up early. Occasionally, I could see one of the birds strutting. Not being able to hunt on that private land, I went back to my earlier setup. I waited about 30 minutes, then called, and they both hammered back seemingly right where they were before. Now getting desperate, I got my tube call out, cut real loud a couple of times on my diaphragm call, then immediately gobbled on the tube call. They both cut me off gobbling, and pretty soon, they were gobbling closer.

Watching for them when they came into view, both were almost running but would stop and strut about every ten yards. One was larger than the other, with a thicker and heavier beard. I decided to try to shoot the biggest of the two gobblers if they came under the fence. They both got to the fence, ducked their heads, squatted a little, and went under the fence not 20 yards from me. As soon as I could shoot without hitting the other bird, I took the biggest of the two gobblers.

Using my carrying sling, I carried him back to the windmill and the car. On the way there, I ran into my buddy Billy Minser, who had shot earlier, and said he would see if he could find our other friend, Jim Byford. Going on to the windmill, I hung the gobbler up and started skinning it. On skinning down one side just below the wing butt, I spotted a circle about the size of a quarter of thick yellow tissue on the side of the breast. Moving to the other side and skinning down, at about the same place at the top of the breast, there was another of these yellowish circles.

Having already removed the crop, which only had a little green grass inside and a dandelion or two, I trimmed away all the breast sponge. This enabled me to see that the yellowish tissue extended through the gobbler's upper breast, just below where the crop rested. Carefully, I cut around the hard-yellow tissue so that it was loose from the other breast meat. Then, on the other side of the breast did the same and removed about a 14-inch piece of something encased in the hard-yellow skin. I trimmed carefully around this yellow tissue on both sides and finished skinning the bird. Placing it on the frame of the windmill, I finished processing the bird.

About the time I was finishing up, here came the two other guys. Unfortunately, Jim had not killed his second bird but had a good morning working one. We visited briefly, and I mentioned that maybe the piece removed was an encased arrow. We then cut into it and found a dried splinter of ponderosa pine that had somehow penetrated the bird and broken off on each side. Around the opening on both sides of the breast, there was no apparent discoloration or infection of the breast meat. However, it had become encased over time in that hard, yellow tissue and had caused no problems for the bird. My best guess is the gobbler was flying up to roost and that dead pine limb pierced his breast, spinning him around and going all the way through him, but that is pure speculation.

My good friend and long-time hunting buddy, Thurman

Booth, and I hunted and camped together the first week of April in Arkansas for several springs. We camped on the Ouachita National Forest west of Little Rock, and turkey hunted there from a tent camp.

One year we had scouted a new area that seemed to have a good number of turkeys. In our scouting, we found an old flattened out home-site near a dim road that could not be driven in a 4-wheel vehicle. We set up camp there and prepared ourselves for a long walk up the mountain every morning. The night before the season opened, it started raining.

We both hunted every day anyway, coming back to camp to eat and dry our clothes over a fat-pine fire, and for four days, neither of us heard a gobbler. The fifth day, it tapered off raining, and he went to an area where the forest service had aerial sprayed herbicide over a large portion of the mountainside. Frustrated about where to go, I decided to go to a site where I had observed several longbeard gobblers just a few days before the season. I neither heard nor saw a turkey myself that morning, but Thurman got on three gobblers together and worked them quite a while. He thought he had a good shot at one of them at one point, took it, but missed.

For whatever reason, he had convinced himself before the season that he would shoot nothing but number two copper-plated shot that spring. We met back at camp at noon, him disgusted, and me just tired and frustrated but pleased that the rain had stopped. We ate some lunch, took a short nap, and afterward talked about where we wanted to go that evening. He said he was not going back to that sprayed area as it was extremely brushy and hard to move around in. We agreed that it might be a good place for me to try where he had heard those birds that morning, as he would hunt another area.

Climbing up and into the sprayed mountainside, moving around was indeed tricky. Although calling occasionally, I could not raise a gobble. Later, I noticed about halfway down the mountain, there were about a dozen or so big pines on a little knob that might be an excellent roosting area to watch that evening. It was getting late, and it was almost time to try to hear one go to roost.

Dropping down the mountainside, I found a good place to set up above the pines and did so. After calling a few times softly, I had just taken my call out of my mouth and put it into my shirt pocket when I heard some sound to my right. Easing my head around, I saw three big gobblers not 30 yards from me.

There was no way to move without being spotted. They headed on down and over the crest of a little ridge below me. At that point, I quickly placed my call in my mouth and clucked. Immediately I heard one of the gobblers start drumming back up the ridge toward me. When he popped up over the crest of that ridge in full strut, he was only about 20 yards away, with the other two below and to his right. Wasting no time, I shot him as he came out of strut. He went down with his neck broken.

On reaching down to pick him up by the legs, I noticed some dried blood on his thigh. Further examination showed a bright shiny number two copper-plated shot stuck under the front part of his leg under the horny red carapace. However, it had not fractured the leg bone. Carrying him back to camp, I knew my buddy would want to know that the turkey he had shot at that morning had been killed. He saw the evidence, and on further cleaning the gobbler, I determined that he had been hit by three number two-shot. One was in the lower back, one in the upper part of the thigh and one in the leg. None of these wounds had caused the gobbler any problems.

They are indeed very tough birds. A friend and colleague, Tom Franklin, hunting in Virginia, told me about shooting a gobbler and wounding him but could not find him, even though he tried to get closer for a killing shot. However, approximately two weeks later, he called in a gobbler that was gobbling in that same area. The bird was dragging a wing that had been broken for a while, and he felt sure it was the same bird.

Years back, hunting with a couple of colleagues from New Mexico State University Extension Service, a range specialist, Chris Allison, and the other a wildlife specialist, Jim Knight, we hunted a private ranch, not from Raton, New Mexico. They picked me up at the airport, and we drove over to the ranch that afternoon. We located the ranch owner, and he recommended that we camp near a spring that was fenced off from the cattle and where he had seen turkeys nearby.

My colleagues had brought a nice wall tent and other supplies, so we got everything in place just before dark, ate some food they had brought and settled in for the night. The next morning well before daylight, we agreed that we would go in different directions from camp. Most of the area was ranchland pastures intermixed with a few plateaus above us with scattered oak brush, pinyon pine, and western juniper. It also had some deep forested canyons to the north with mature Ponderosa pines.

Heading north, it took me a good while to find a way to work my way down over a bluff to the canyon bottom. Fortunately, I was able to get there by just about daylight. I heard several gobblers on up the canyon to the northwest, so I kept working my way along the little branch and heard a gobbler fairly close after about a quarter-mile. Finding a place to sit among the scattered ponderosa pines and oak brush, I made a little blind and sat down.

Once seated, I called to which he gobbled right back, looking at my watch, it was 8:10. That gobbler and I played call and gobble for almost an hour, and the sparse cover would not allow me to move. I decided to quit calling at that point as he had hung up about 75 yards upstream, and it was too open for me to try to move. After about 15 minutes, I heard him drumming upstream from me but could not yet see him.

He soon came into view and had a subdominant gobbler with him. They strutted closer to me, and when they got to about 35 yards, a clear shot was available. I shot the dominant bird. When he went down, the subdominant gobbler jumped into the air but then walked back toward the bird on the ground. When it flopped, the younger bird ran to it, and I thought he would attack it but did not. He just kept walking and circling that dead gobbler for at least five minutes.

Placing my carrying strap around his neck and legs, I started climbing back up out of the canyon to our campsite. The other guys were still hunting, so I took the gobbler down to the spring and processed him. After washing off the meat and organs, I placed the filleted portions in zip-lock bags to be put on ice back at the tent.

When the other guys arrived at camp, we shared our experiences from the morning, and they both heard gobblers but had not been able to get a shot. We ate lunch then decided to take a nap, and after about an hour, we heard the rancher's pickup drive up. We went out to visit with him, and he asked if we had gotten a bird. Having saved the beard and lower legs with spurs before disposing of the carcass, they were shown to him. He said during our conversation that although he often saw turkeys while attending to his cattle, he had never had an opportunity to see one up close.

We agreed that if one of us killed a bird the next day, I would pelt it out carefully and show him how to stretch and dry it if he wanted to hang it in his ranch house. He said he would like that. We visited a while longer, and before he left, we discussed where we would be going that afternoon. Not being able to hunt that afternoon, my plan was to scout and get a better feel for where and how I might get located on a bird the next morning.

Both decided they wanted to go back to the areas they had hunted that morning, so after they left, I walked back toward the area hunted that morning. Being curious, I decided to climb up and examine the plateaus above the brushy meadows and deep canyon to look around. Although most of the areas were pretty barren of vegetation and had no water, I did observe one gobbler track almost at the top. Working my way down toward the bluff over the canyon I had hunted earlier, more sign became evident.

As it began to get later in the day, I came to a meadow of about 60 acres with some oak brush scattered here and there. That meadow was almost directly above the canyon bottom where I had killed the gobbler earlier, and there was a good bit of turkey sign there. Still standing, I heard a whistling sound above and behind me, so I turned to see this large bird sailing from the top of the mountain. My first thought was it is a golden eagle, but I could see that it was a big gobbler as it got closer. He sailed by about 70 yards away and dropped down over the bluff.

Without question, that was a pretty keen observation and listening intently; I heard a couple of gobbles down that way just at dark. Because of the sign seen nearby, however, I decided to hunt that meadow the next morning.

Arriving at the meadow well before daylight, I listened to the night sounds and those at dawn, hearing several gobblers up and down the bluff over that canyon. I started looking for a good place to set up, realizing that those birds may take a while to work their way up into the meadow. The birds had gobbled some 15 minutes or more on the roost; then, I could tell that at least two of them were gobbling on the ground. In searching around, I had found an almost half-moon circle of scrubby oak brush about five to seven feet high and 10 to 15 feet wide that extended out into the meadow that would be a suitable blind. Most of the meadow was visible from this point, so I wiggled back into that oak brush, sat and listened.

After calling, a gobbler responded directly below and halfway up the edge of the bluff below me. Not calling back immediately, he soon gobbled almost at the top of the bluff. Hunkering down in that little patch of oak brush, I decided to wait him out. He was right at the top of the bluff the next time he gobbled, and then he strutted out into the lower edge of the meadow about 75 yards below me.

The bird stayed in that strut zone for quite a while. I decided to sit still and watch that beautiful gobbler display, occasionally stopping to gobble. After waiting about ten minutes, I called softly to him when his fan was turned toward me, thinking he is about to head up my way unless some hens appear.

Within 15 seconds after he gobbled, I heard a gobbler drumming loudly almost right behind me and realized that a silent gobbler has slipped in almost on top of me. I slowly turned my head to the right, and through the side of my face mask, I could see brilliant red wattles and neon white skull cap. He was only about ten feet away, and when he drummed, I could feel the vibration as he strutted behind me. Although not spooked, the gobbler realized something was not right.

He made a muffled putt and some undistinguishable sound as he came out of strut. He then started walking briskly back behind me and up to my right toward a little island of larger oak brush about 40 yards away.

I likely could have jumped up and shot him running or flying away, but I sure did not want to take a chance on crippling him. Besides, the other gobbler displaying below was almost in range. On a hunch, I decided to sit still watching the other gobbler. After about five minutes, out of the corner of my eye to my right, I saw a gobbler, although unsure it was the same bird.

This gobbler had appeared walking out of some oak brush to my right and stopped about 35 yards away. Having already mounted my shotgun on my knee, I quickly shot him, and he went down. Then, to my amazement, he jumped into the air and started flying straight up. Jumping up, I was about to shoot him in the air, but he began wind-milling downward, dropping behind some oak brush.

Quickly opening my shotgun, I loaded another shell, then eased around that oak brush where he had landed. He was standing on his feet with his head and neck hanging down and blood pouring out of his head and beak. I walked up to him, laid my shotgun on the ground, grabbed him by the neck with one hand and the wing butt with the other. After a little flopping and spraying me with blood, he died. Placing my carrying strap over his neck and legs, I took my time and walked back to camp.

The other guys were still hunting, so I began to cape the gobbler out before processing the meat and getting it on ice. Once finished with the caping process, I hung the cape on a corner tent pole, filleted out the meat, and put it on ice. The other guys were still not back yet, so before disposing of the carcass, I decided to examine the head and neck of the bird and skinned it out carefully. Both eyes had been shot out, the bill had been partially shot off, and the head and neck were riddled with shot holes. I started trying to count as best possible the number of those number 7½ copper-plated shot holes in the head and neck. My best count in the neck and head indicated 56 shot holes, and many of them had passed completely through.

In a bit, the rancher drove in, saw the cape, and that it was ready for him to take home, stretch and dry. I explained the best way to do it using borax to dry the skin and drying it skin side up after stretching and pinning it on a piece of cardboard. He admired that skinned-out pelt, thanked me, and asked what it had been shot with?

I pulled out one of my handloads, then showed him the skinned-out head and neck of that gobbler with all the shot holes, and told him the story of the hunt. We visited until the other guys showed up. They, too, were amazed when they examined the head and neck of that gobbler. That he could fly up and still be on his feet after such mortal wounds is evidence of their tenacity. Having shot several gobblers over the years, I never had one react that way before or afterward. They are tough birds with no crap in their knees.

CHAPTER 31

Phantoms or Apparitions?

Over the years, I have interacted with many turkey gobblers that challenged my patience, skill, and perseverance. Some seemed to be almost ghosts. Some just seemed to be lucky and extremely wary of anything new or different in their territories. A few had either adapted or learned to become known among hunters as a "camp turkey." The camp turkey was one that you put an over-confident hunter on, who felt like they could kill any turkey that gobbled.

Some examples might help explain the behavior of such gobblers. One remembered well was a gobbler up in Paint Rock Valley in north Alabama. My friend, Jim Brooks, who had a cabin there, really enjoyed spending time at the cabin, whether hunting or not, especially in the spring. He usually woke up early, grabbed a cup of coffee, and went out on the porch to listen to the world wake-up. He particularly enjoyed listening for turkeys gobbling on both sides of the valley. Some of these were harvested but most probably died of old age. I had already hunted a few days in Mississippi and Florida that spring before driving up to hunt with him.

After getting settled in, Jim described several locations where he had heard birds gobbling almost every morning. One was across the valley on a very steep ridge that jutted out over the creek and was very difficult to move around on or to set up on to call a gobbler. There was a fold in the ridge to the north and a very old dim road circumventing the ridge. If you followed that old road, it eventually opened up into a long side ridge with very open woods and very steep.

Regardless, Jim said it sounded like the gobbler would roost most nights just above the creek and when he flew down would work his way up to somewhere near the old road. Once there, he would gobble for a while, then work his way around the fold and go up the ridge to the northwest.

I was familiar with the area, having hunted there before. I had called up birds for Jim there in past years, so I felt pretty confident. I made plans to leave the cabin early the following day and try to be above where Jim said the bird usually spent time gobbling. Once in the area where I planned to hunt, I located a place to hide, setting up about 30 yards above the old road where it started curving around the fold.

Before it got good daylight, a turkey gobbled almost directly below me on the very steep face above the creek about 150 yards away. He must have gobbled 30 times or more on the roost, and I expected that when he flew down, he would have a bunch of hens with him. Some other gobblers answered a few times off in the distance.

I did not even try to call until the bird was obviously on the ground. Then I called softly, and he gobbled right back. I could tell he was working his way up the ridge, so I kept quiet. In a little while, after gobbling closer a couple of times, I spotted him coming up over the crest of the ridge about 70 yards downhill. He gobbled several times and strutted around one tiny area for quite some time. He had no hens with him but was a mature gobbler from the sound of his gobble and the length of his beard.

Although backed up in some large boulders with some dead brush in front of me, I am confident he never saw me. I anticipated that he would eventually move over to that old roadbed and come close enough for a shot. However, it was obvious that he had pinpointed where the hen call I made earlier had originated, so I stayed quiet. After several small ventures up the hill in my direction and stopping to peer toward my hide, he went back to his strutting area, started drumming and occasionally gobbled. After probably 20 minutes of his displaying and gobbling, I heard some hens around the fold. Instead of coming up to the old roadbed, the gobbler dropped down over the crest of the ridge and gobbled. I could hear the hens yelping and working their way to him, and then I called, but he never acknowledged my call. He went silent and moved away.

Admitting defeat, I finally got up and moved on up the mountain but could not stimulate any other gobbling, so I accepted what happened and went back to the cabin. I tried for two more mornings to figure out how to call that gobbler in. However, I failed each time. At that point, I decided to go and find another gobbling turkey.

Over the next couple of days, I hunted elsewhere and killed one about a half-mile north of where that gobbler hung out. Still haunting me, I thought possibly by sneaking up the mountain one afternoon, I might be able to work that bird. Coming in from the backside of the mountain the next afternoon, I got to the area, made a blind near his strutting area, sat there and called sparingly.

My thought was that if alone, he might come into a call before going to roost. My blind was very well hidden between a couple of large boulders, and I sat there until about 4:00 before even making a call. Nothing responded but feeling confident, I decided to wait him out, thinking if nothing else, maybe I could hear him fly up to roost.

After calling a few times very softly, about 4:45, looking to my right, I saw two jakes come off the ridge to my right. They headed down over the steep face, likely going to roost. A little later, about four or five hens came down and followed the path of the jakes. After they went down over the crest, I made a soft call to see if they would answer before going to roost.

Shortly after calling, I saw some movement further to the right. It was that big gobbler, and he was about 60 yards away and headed down the same direction. After he went over the crest, I made a soft hen yelp followed by a short purr. In about five minutes, I saw him stick his head up over the crest of that ridge and then peer in my direction.

He froze in place for what seemed like 15 minutes. I thought that if he stepped on up over that ridge, he would be in range. After a few seconds, he pulled down his head and disappeared. I watched for him, expecting to see him come over the ridge.

Like a ghost materializing, he suddenly stepped up over the ridge about 30 feet to the left of where I had thought he would appear. Although I do not believe he saw me, something was not right, and he knew it. Before I could take a shot at him, he ran back over the crest and flew across the valley. At that point, I gave him up for the year and decided to hunt other turkeys. I think I heard him gobble a couple of times later that week, but I accepted defeat and moved on.

A gobbler we named the camp turkey, to my knowledge, no one ever killed, was located on some timber company land in southwest Alabama. I hunted there occasionally with a good friend and colleague, Bill McKee. When meeting him at camp, he said that we have a gobbler that needs killing. That should have tipped me off that this was a camp gobbler, but I told him to tell me where to locate the gobbler, and I would give it a try. He said he would show me its territory, which he did, partially.

We agreed that I should hunt there in the morning. I drove to within a quarter-mile of where Bill had taken me the afternoon before. Parking the truck, I walked down to a small ridge running back to the southwest. Cautiously, I eased out the ridge in the dark about 400 yards, found a good place to listen and stopped. As the sky lightened up in the east, crows called like crows often do the very first thing in the morning. A turkey gobbled not more than 200 yards further out the ridge.

As it was still pretty dark, I eased as quietly as possible about another 75 yards toward his roost tree and found an old stump with vines around it. I set up there so that the top of the ridge and down the slope below me could be watched. I clucked softly and followed that with a soft tree yelp. It sounded like the bird turned around and gobbled back right at me. As it got closer to good light, the bird gobbled a few more times. I decided not to call again until he was on the ground.

As more daylight emerged, looking to my right down across a little branch, I could see an opening. It was about 150 yards away and was a very recent clearcut that had been brush cleared and burned. The turkey gobbled once more on the roost then flew out of a big beech tree to the peak of the clearcut. Once there, he proceeded to gobble and strut for quite a while. With my binoculars, I watched him until hens began to arrive around him. There was no way to get closer to that gobbler, so I went to my truck and drove back to camp.

When Bill came in, he confessed why he wanted me to kill that gobbler. I told him, however, the only way to do it would be to dig a foxhole near his strutting zone and lay down in before daylight until he came to entice the hens there. I vowed then and there not to hunt that gobbler anymore. According to Bill, he said no one to his knowledge in a later conversation killed that gobbler during the season.

Another ghost gobbler that frustrated me happened again up in north Alabama in a different season. On arriving at the cabin that spring, Jim told me about this gobbler he had heard several mornings in a row. No one had tried to hunt him because of where he had staked out his territory. My gut feeling told me to wait to hunt this bird for a while and concentrate on some other birds, which I did. In the next few days of hunting, I killed three nice gobblers in different locations.

On my last morning there, I could only hunt until about 11:00 a.m. before having to drive up to near Kentucky Lake to hunt with a Tennessee friend. I was determined, however, to at least try to get the bird Jim had talked about when I arrived. Because it was such a rough, steep area, the previous afternoon, I decided to see if I could determine the best approach. I desired to try to determine how to get to the site the next morning without sounding like a buffalo on the loose and hoping the turkey might gobble going to roost.

Looking around, I remembered an old house place where a partial chimney remained standing. There was an old dim road that passed below it and wound around the side of the mountain. Locating a good place for a setup, I made a blind out of predominantly red buckeye branches and some dead limbs near the old chimney. Listening until dark but hearing nothing, I slipped out and cautiously made my way down and across the valley to the cabin.

I headed back across the valley early the following day and worked hard at getting up the mountain and into my blind well before wake-up time. I listened first to the whippoorwills, then to numerous other birds as those first pink rays came up in the east, and shortly after, I heard a barred owl down the valley. That stimulated a gobbler that responded downhill and over a hardwood bluff farther down below the dim road.

He gobbled quite a few times, and then I could hear him on the ground below as he proceeded to the north. I called to him, and he answered right back, giving me hope that he was interested. The gobbler then came up a little drain about 80 yards to the north and headed up the mountain. He occasionally gobbled until he went out of hearing headed up the mountain.

Although I would have raced up the mountain as fast as

possible in my younger days, I knew I could not catch up with him. On a hunch, I decided to stay there and do some more calling as another bird had gobbled a couple of times earlier some distance away. After about 30 minutes of no responses to my calling, I finally decided to try something different. As loudly as possible, I called on a diaphragm call then gobbled twice behind it.

Although I thought something responded, it was so far away there was no way to be sure. After a few minutes, I repeated that sequence, and up the mountain, the way that gobbler had gone earlier, I heard a distinct gobble. He continued to come on down the mountain until he was just over a little ridge, where he gobbled several times. He was so close it did not seem necessary to call again, so I scratched in the leaves three times, and he gobbled. It was about 8:45 by then, and for the next two hours, that gobbler completely circled me, staying just out of sight. He gobbled once so close behind me I am sure he was in range, but I could not move.

If that turkey gobbled once that morning, he gobbled 150 times, but I never saw him. Once, when he was in front of me just over the crest of that little ridge, he gobbled and looking at my watch, I decided not to make a sound for 20 minutes. Sitting completely still and silent for those 20 minutes, I then clucked ever so lightly on my little slate. He gobbled right back and had not seemingly moved a step. This contest continued until 10:45, and I never saw a feather, although he was close to me for well over two hours. To my knowledge, he was completely alone the whole time. Knowing how tight the time was, I knew I had to leave soon to get to Tennessee before dark. Therefore, I crawled out as quietly as possible down the ridge away from where he had last gobbled. He gobbled once, and as I moved on down the mountain, he gobbled a couple more times.

To have worked a turkey that long and never see him is

not only frustrating but discouraging and humbling. My best guess, trying to think like a turkey, was that he was going to keep gobbling and looking until he saw a hen before showing himself. Describing a turkey like that as a ghost gobbler is an understatement, and like a bad dream, you are never sure what you should or could have done differently that would have closed the deal.

There is no way of knowing the next spring whether a gobbler would still be in the area or not, or if he had survived, but you could hope. My instincts suggested that even if he was not there, there would likely be a gobbler nearby. If not him, maybe one of his offspring. Regardless, I felt compelled to hunt that place again. The following spring, I went back to the same mountain area one afternoon and roosted two gobblers, one close and one that I could barely hear.

The first morning, I slipped back up in that area but maybe another 100 yards further up the mountainside in the dark. Locating a good hiding place on a flat shelf-like site with the steeper part of the mountainside to my back, I made a quick blind.

At just before good daylight, a barred owl hooted, and the closer bird gobbled. Then the other bird that was farther away gobbled. Choosing not to call right away, both birds gobbled back and forth a few more times. Then it sounded like the closer bird was on the ground, so I called to him, and he cut me off gobbling. Since he was below me, I thought he would soon work his way up toward me. He stayed below me and gobbled several more times, then headed east just below the crest of the ridge. Gobbling occasionally, he continued to the east, and I thought he was following hens, although I hadn't heard any calling or flying down.

I am unsure exactly what happened, but soon I could no longer hear him gobble. He either went beyond my hearing or quit gobbling, making me seriously consider getting up and trying to head east myself but staying at the same level on the mountainside. Repositioning, I turned myself a little to the east and refurbished my blind as best possible with a few limbs. Periodically I called for about another 30 minutes without hearing a gobble.

I convinced myself to sit there and try different kinds of calls hoping to get a gobbler to respond. After retrieving my glass call and striker out of my vest, I made a loud cluck to which a bird gobbled just below me but still about 80 yards to the east. I was determined not to call again and focus on watching the area where he seemed to have gobbled. After probably ten minutes, I spotted him still about 75 yards away to the east, and he had worked his way to a small open area in the timber and now popped into a strut.

Sitting quietly, I did not call back to him. Suddenly, I heard a loud crack and brush falling from straight down the ridge and watched as a huge dead oak limb fell to the ground with a big thump and sound of breaking limbs. It startled the heck out of me and the gobbler, too, because he disappeared.

What do you do after such a natural occurrence, but one that happened so close that you could almost feel the ground shake when the limb hit the ground and broke into pieces? I decided to sit quietly for about 20 minutes, and then I made a soft cluck and purr on my slate. This was answered by a gobble so close I should have seen him but could not.

In a couple of minutes, I could see him moving back into the little open area where he had strutted before the limb fell. He gobbled when he got there and started strutting in a small area about 20 to 30 feet in diameter. Staying quiet, knowing he was trying to entice that hen out where he could see her, I was afraid to move. He knew where the call came from as he would stop, go into about a half-strut, then gobble and look over my way before strutting again. Although the waiting was terrible with him so close but still out of range, there were no other realistic options.

In the next 20 minutes, that bird gobbled 35 times, not moving out of that little strutting area he had adopted. Finally, he started moving my way both below me and up the ridge a little. He would take a step or two, then stretch his neck and head upward like he was standing on his tiptoes and look directly toward me. With my shotgun on my knee, looking down the barrel toward him, he slowly progressed closer.

He never gobbled again but kept getting closer. When he was right at 40 yards and stretched his neck and head up to look, I fired and killed him. When able to move after sitting so long, I got up and walked over to him; what a beautiful gobbler that had put on a fantastic show. I looked at my watch, and it was almost noon, so I headed to the cabin for lunch and a nap. Ghost gobbler or his offspring? I am not sure, but it had been a heck of a hunt after a long morning with some unforeseen interruptions.

CHAPTER 32

Long Distance Hearing

When I was much younger and able to hear quite well, I am confident that I heard gobblers at least a half-mile away or possibly more on calm mornings in the mountains. Calling to gobblers barely heard, some appeared to come in at least that far, although you never know for sure. Sometimes, because of known or unknown physical barriers, or other reasons that prevented me from getting closer, I just had to either give up or give it a try.

Hunting in the Ouachita Mountains west of Little Rock one morning, I heard a gobbler across the Fourche La Fave River that had to be close to three-quarters of a mile from the end of the ridge I was on. Knowing how steep it was to get down to the river and that the river was likely too deep to wade across, I decided to sit and call and see what happened. I hoped another gobbler closer by might respond. But, that being the only bird I could hear, I decided to see if he possibly could hear me call.

Calling as loudly as possible, it seemed like it took 15 seconds, but he gobbled. I waited a bit and called loudly again. After the pause, he gobbled back. Continuing to call, he answered several more calls, and then I could not hear him for probably 15 minutes. When he did gobble, he was closer. If indeed it was him, he flew the river and came up that steep bluff until he got into hearing again.

Once I realized he was closing the distance and was on my side of the river, I called softer. Before I finished yelping, he gobbled, cutting me off. It sounded like he was maybe still some distance down the bluff but closer. Having set myself up about 40 yards from the crest of the bluff, the next time he gobbled, he was just down over the top of that bluff. I never called again, although he gobbled a couple of more times. In about five minutes, I saw his neon white head and red wattles come up over that bluff. He strutted into about 30 yards before he stopped, and I shot him. There is no way to prove it was the same gobbler I heard so far away, but I assume it was.

Another long-distance situation in Arkansas reminds me of a turkey I described as the "junkyard gobbler." My buddy, Thurman, and I were hunting an area north of Lake Ouachita one spring and scouting some new territory one afternoon. We were driving out ridge tops in the mountains east of the lake, occasionally stopping to look around for sign and calling loudly. At one stop, near the end of a ridge, I called loudly, and a gobbler responded, although we both could barely hear it.

We were not too sure where it was and decided to drive on and see if we could get closer to the general area. Eventually, we found a ridge that seemed to head in that direction. At that point, not hearing any other response or having any idea how to best hunt it, I decided to start from there the next morning. Thurman had another area several miles away that he planned to hunt. So we went in different trucks.

Leaving my truck very early the next morning, I walked to the west out a long ridge with a steep hollow on both sides. Stopping to owl-call and crow-caw occasionally after it got good light, I could not incite a bird to gobble. Not seeing a lot of sign, I decided to walk the area out and learn a little more about it with the hope of locating a gobbler.

Walking out that ridge approximately a mile, I finally came across a dim, grown-up road from the north that came up from a saddle and continued out that ridge. Continuing to call occasionally, about 9:15, after calling, I heard a gobbler respond. He sounded, however, like he was a long-distance away. Heading in that direction, I eventually came to another old dim road that came up to the ridge top.

I stopped to call and heard a gobbler to my right that sounded like he was down in the hollow. Moving in that direction, I came to a little opening that in previous years must have been a dumping site for locals to discard used tires, abandoned automobiles, bottles, and other assorted junk. It appeared that many years past, it might have been an old house place or peckerwood sawmill site. It encompassed maybe an acre or more that was pretty open in spots.

Looking around, I decided to sit down where the old road headed away toward the gobbler and to call. He gobbled back, still a long distance away, but this looked like as good a place as any because the vegetation was quite brushy in that direction. There were a lot of green briar and blackberry brambles below the opening.

Continuing to call, the gobbler answered and seemed to be getting closer. This went on for another 30 minutes. Each time, as I called, it sounded like the gobbler was getting closer. Looking down that old road, I spotted some movement behind a cluster of mixed briars and brambles that were about chest-high. It was the gobbler.

The ole bird seemed frustrated that he could not get through those briars because he walked from one side of it to the other. After several minutes, he walked off the side of that old road and came back into it about 45 yards from me—no need to call anymore. I watched as he strutted and slowly worked his way on up toward me. At about 30 yards, he stopped, and I opened fire.

Placing my carrying strap around his legs and neck, I decided to walk out that old grown-up road.

About three-quarters a mile from the junkyard opening, I came out to a more recently driven side road that headed back up toward the top of the ridge. Continuing upward, I eventually came to the road I had gone in on. I walked about another half a mile before spotting the truck and got back to it at about 11:15.

It had been a long morning, but I had enjoyed the success of the long-distance calling and hunting a new area. Once reaching the truck, it had warmed up considerably, and I wanted to get the turkey cooled off as soon as I could. Driving out, when arriving at a small creek, I stopped, gutted and removed the crop, which contained several acorns, a few crickets, a grub of some kind, and a few green blades of grass.

Later, looking at a county map Thurman had in his truck, we figured that gobbler must have been close to a mile from where we first heard him to the junkyard. Of course, we do not know if that was the same gobbler or not. But in any case, they will come a long distance when they want to.

Another long-distance calling session and hunt occurred in Florida one spring when I followed my long-time friend Joel Smith's suggestion and parked at an old cattle corral on opening morning. He said I should walk about a mile to a corner of a 50-year-old slash pine plantation and a large tract of hardwoods before stopping to call.

Having arrived there early enough to find where he suggested listening, I stopped and tried to listen, but the mosquitoes were terrible. After placing my face mask on, I retrieved my Thermacell, got it going and hung it from my vest.

As it began to get more light, I eased into the hardwoods and located a big cabbage palm that Joel said was a good place to listen. I found a big Magnolia nearby to sit in front of and made a sparse blind.

The songbirds had started singing, and I could hear the sandhill cranes down in the marsh beginning to call. So, I crow-cawed and heard two different gobblers answer. The closest of the two was about 150 yards away, almost back to the edge of the pine plantation. I must have walked very close to where he was roosting while walking in. The other gobbler was in the opposite direction and seemed to be maybe 200 yards away.

I turned, moving around to face where the closest gobbler had called from. They both gobbled a few more times before some hens started clucking and purring between the closest one and me. The hens soon began flying down. The turkey gobbled and soon flew down with them. Once he was on the ground, I called, and he gobbled. Soon, however, I could tell he was moving away. Then, he quit gobbling.

The other gobbler continued to answer. He seemed to be on the ground and moving closer, although he was above me, almost up at the edge of the pine plantation. It was too late to try to move without possibly spooking him, so I decided to wait him out and stayed where I was. The next time I called, he had turned. When he gobbled, he was getting further away, in the direction of the swamp. Not having heard a hen with this gobbler, I decided to go back up to the corner of the pine plantation and find a place to sit before deciding which way to go next.

A disked-up fire lane paralleled that plantation's south and west borders between it and the hardwoods. When I got to the corner and walked out each way on the fire lane, I saw gobbler tracks and nearby hen dusts around the edge. Calling loudly, the gobbler answered, but I could barely hear him. Looking around, I located a good place to sit, just inside the edge of the woods, where I could see along the fire lanes in both directions.

For about 35 minutes, I could not get a gobbler to answer or, if one did, I could not hear him. Considering moving but trying to be patient, I decided to stay and call some more. I hoped that one or the other of those gobblers might circle back my way.

I cut some palmetto fronds, made a suitable blind, and committed myself to another hour there. Calling occasionally, after about 20 minutes, I heard two gobblers respond. They were so far away, back toward the swamp, I could barely hear them. Waiting a few minutes, I called again. Both gobbled, and it sounded like they were together but still a long distance away. Thinking they might come up that fire lane, I turned, faced the western border and hoped that they would continue to come closer.

The edges of the hardwoods had many live oak saplings and briars, making it difficult to see very far into the woods. Calling yet again, I motivated those two birds to gobble back. They were getting closer. Unsure if they would come up through the woods or along the fire lane, my guess was the fire lane.

After gobbling down in the woods but not too far from the fire lane, they quit gobbling. I thought they would either come up to the fire lane or circle around me in the hardwoods. While looking down that fire lane, I soon saw two gobblers come out of the woods and stop in the fire lane, still about 100 yards away. One of them was strutting, and the other was walking along and would occasionally go into almost a half-strut, then slick back down. Both of them appeared to be headed toward me, so I stayed quiet, watching as they worked closer and closer toward me.

Although I had quit calling, it was fun watching, and each time, just before they gobbled, it sounded like one of them hiccuped. Whatever sound it was, they both immediately afterward ran their necks out and gobbled. The strutting gobbler would strut back and forth across the fire lane, then stop, come out of strut and look toward where I had called from earlier.

He definitely had pin-pointed my location and, after pausing for a bit, would pop back into a strut and, taking those little short steps with wings dragging, came ever closer. The other gobbler just followed along behind and never got to a full strut as they came closer. Although it seemed like it took 30 minutes before they got into range, it was probably more like ten. Eventually, they had closed to about 30 yards. When they were far enough apart to shoot, I clucked, the dominant strutting gobbler raised his head, I fired, and he went down.

As he fell over, the other gobbler just jumped straight up and came down close to the one I had shot. He walked around that gobbler looking down at him. I thought if the downed bird flops, he would likely get flogged by this sub-dominant gobbler. The bird I shot did not flop at all for probably three to four minutes. Regardless, this was among several gobblers I have called to until they went out of hearing, then eventually returned. You never know for sure if it is the same gobbler, but their hearing and coursing capabilities continue to amaze me.

CHAPTER 33

Gobblers in the Wind

On a southeastern Montana hunt with friend Jim Byford, after he killed his first gobbler on the second day, we continued going together as I had tagged out the first morning. We enjoyed the scouting and calling as we worked toward getting his second gobbler.

The third morning we worked a bird that gobbled all around us, but Jim could not get a shot. I found a dead mule deer buck that had a pretty nice set of antlers. Jim suggested we remove the head from the decaying body as he would like to take it back to the University of Tennessee at Martin with him. He wanted to add it to their lab displays. We decided to come back later to get it and continued hunting.

One area east of the cabin where we were staying was a scattered mix of pockets of ponderosa pine and pastures that dropped down into a vast flat canyon. That canyon had a lot of dead timber scattered through it. Late that afternoon, Jim and I heard several gobblers, all quite some distance away.

We almost got into an argument about which direction they were in because we wanted to get as close as possible to one of them in the morning. We finally decided that we would get there early and see if we could determine which one to try to go to. Before it got completely dark, we made our way back to that dead buck. By twisting and cutting, we removed the head from the carcass to take back to the cabin.

As we were walking back to camp, it was pretty dark, and a jet plane flew over as we came by a steep ridge of ponderosa pine that extended up onto a flat mesa. Jim was on my left closer to the edge of the knob, and he asked, "did you hear that gobbler?" My response was, "No, all I heard was that jet plane." About that time, the gobbler gobbled again. We both heard him that time. He sounded like he was pretty much near the top of that knob. This area was less than a half-mile from the cabin. We both slipped on toward the cabin, and after we were some distance away, Jim said, "Let's hunt that gobbler in the morning." I agreed.

We got up early the next morning, and the wind was howling outside. When we went outside, the wind was blowing somewhere between 30 to 40 miles per hour and occasionally gusting even higher. I suggested to Jim that if we went around to the right of that knob, we could climb up to the edge of the mesa without being seen.

We did and eased around it until we got pretty near where we thought we had heard the gobbler the evening before. We agreed that this was likely our best bet. I think we both had doubts that the bird would gobble at all with it so windy, much less come to a call. If we could get in pretty close, I thought we might be able to get his attention by calling loudly.

We proceeded up the ridge to the edge of the flat-topped mesa, with the wind howling and gusting, trying to stay hunkered down as we moved back toward the timbered knob to the east. When we got to the edge of the timber, we eased into it about 40 yards and saw a slight drain down the face of the steep ridge. Jim quickly located a good spot where he could see the edge of the timber and out to the top of the flat mesa. Getting behind and slightly below Jim on the slope, I found a tree to lean back against. Fortunately, we could see a part of the top across the mesa and the edge of the timber.

It was beginning to get light, and suddenly the gobbler gobbled not more than 60 yards away, very near the top of the mesa. He gobbled a few more times, still on the roost, as the wind continued to howl and gust. After a few minutes, some hens flew down on the top of the mesa, and the turkey gobbled again.

Then a jake flew down just below us. Out of the corner of my eye, I could see the jake walking right up the drain toward Jim. There was no choice but to freeze and hope the jake did not spot us. We watched as the jake walked within ten yards of Jim. If he spotted us, he didn't spook but just walked out toward the mesa crest. About that time, with turkeys all around us, the gobbler flew down just over the crest of the mesa where we could not see him. As soon as the gobbler hit the ground, he gobbled.

We had not called yet with that howling wind. I called loudly on a mouth call, to which the turkey gobbled back. Jim turned slightly in that direction. The hens and jakes started moving out along the mesa. I called again, and as the turkey gobbled, I began to see the tips of his fan.

Surprisingly, he was coming toward us. The gobbler kept trying to strut. But the wind almost blew him over when it gusted. He kept coming toward us and gobbled again. When the gobbler got to about 30 yards from us, the wind gusted, almost blowing him over. He then straightened up, came out of a strut, and Jim shot, knocking him over.

We both jumped up and ran up on the mesa. The hens and jake saw us, ran and flew. Congratulating Jim, we were amazed that this gobbler responded the way he did with the wind howling and gusting.

We picked up the gobbler and headed back to the cabin. On arriving there, we hung him up while we had some breakfast before taking some photos and Jim cleaning him. We still had that stinking mule deer buck head to clean as well. Immediately after breakfast, we started a fire down in a little gully out of that howling wind. Once the water was boiling, I put the head portion of the mule deer buck down into the bucket. It took us a few hours to get that buck head cleaned so Jim could take it back home with him in his pack. The wind was still howling as we got all our gear and frozen turkey fillets packed up and headed back to Rapid City.

CHAPTER 34

Hens and Red Maples

After moving to Fairfax, Virginia, in 1978, I could not get back to hunt the Kinterbish Management Area in southwest Alabama for several years. However, with an upcoming meeting scheduled in Birmingham, I called a friend who was familiar with the area. He said that more than half of the area had been clearcut and planted to pine. However, the uncut portions still contained turkeys.

That national meeting in Birmingham was in late March, so I decided to take a few days off following that meeting and hunt the area for a day or two. Following the meeting, I rented a pickup truck and drove down to the site. Arriving at almost midnight, I drove as near as possible to the area where I hoped to hunt, pulled off the side of the road, laid the seat back, and went to sleep.

I awoke well before daylight, having already dressed in camo before leaving Birmingham. Getting out of the truck, I stretched to get the kinks out, then took care of other needs. Next, I gathered my gear and shotgun and left the truck parked near a washed-out red sand road. I walked about a mile to the location I wanted to hunt.

On arriving, it became apparent that a large hillside above where I planned to hunt had recently been cut. I walked around the northern edge of the cutover, down toward the creek. Just entering the woods, I flushed a hen out of a tree. That prompted me to slip just a few yards farther before sitting down.

Just as it was beginning to get a little bit of light, I got settled in. Once seated, I could see something down toward the creek in a tree. What I spotted as daylight increased turned out to be seven hen turkeys roosted in a large red maple tree.

As daylight progressed, those hens started moving around in the tree, picking red maple seeds. Shortly after moving around, they were joined by two more hens that flew from nearby pine trees. Watching as all nine either walked from limb to limb or fluttered from one limb to the next, eating those red maple seeds was a real comedy.

I watched this feeding frenzy for at least 20 minutes and finally called to them. One or two answered with a murmur. Then, they all resumed feeding. During this time, I listened but never heard a gobbler. I was confident, however, that there had to be one somewhere in the vicinity.

After about 30 minutes of feeding, with likely full crops, they started looking down. Finally, one pitched down across the creek and was followed by the others. I observed them group up and head north up the creek, calling softly by purring and clucking. What a unique experience to watch! But, I was disappointed not to have heard a gobble. It would have been interesting to have examined one of those hen crops gorged with those red maple seeds.

I waited there for a good 20 minutes before calling. Then, I waited to see if they or a gobbler might answer, but getting no response, I decided to go across the creek. There were some beautiful mature trees on those rolling hills lifting away from the stream on the other side. Instead of walking directly up the hillside, I crossed the creek and decided to walk down the creek. This led me to a flat bottom area where gobblers had been killed in the past.

Easing along slowly, adjacent to the creek, I heard something. I stopped, listened carefully, and at first thought, it was a truck stuck in the mud some distance away. After a few seconds, I realized it was a gobbler drumming just across the creek. Standing pretty close to a huge yellow poplar tree, I hunched over, and as quietly as possible, crept over to it. Then I slowly stood up behind it. After a few seconds, still hearing that drumming, I peered across the creek and in a small opening, there was a gobbler strutting around.

When he turned so that his fan was in my direction, I moved my shotgun into position and clucked to him. That prompted him to come out of a strut and raise his head and neck erect, at which point I fired. I have no idea how long he had been there because he never gobbled. But curious after killing him, I walked back up the creek to my original sitting place that morning. Pacing the distance off, it was only 85 yards from the opening where he had been strutting. Why he did not gobble earlier, I have no idea. He was indeed close enough to have heard those hens and me. Apparently, he felt like his drumming alone would attract the hens to him.

CHAPTER 35

Blue Mountain Confrontation

My friend, Thurman Booth, and I had hunted Blue Mountain numerous times over the years. It is one of the highest and steepest of the Ouachita Mountains in Arkansas. In 1980, however, a prolonged drought had taken its toll on wildlife resources, especially in the mountains. Some of the locals said that it had been so dry that year that they had caught catfish with ticks on them.

I cannot vouch for that, but it had indeed caused a significant loss of mast production and a negative impact on wildlife. It was so severe that it had forced some species to move from their traditional range to locate both food and water. That following spring, I flew down to hunt with Thurman, and he suggested one afternoon, after a somewhat unproductive morning, that we go to Blue Mountain. He had seen and heard some birds there before the season.

The top of Blue Mountain had a Forest Service road that ran pretty much along the crest for several miles. Thurman let me out at a place a mile after the road got to the top of the mountain. From past hunts there, I knew that the predominant vegetation on top was scrubby. It was primarily scarlet and blackjack oaks, with some shortleaf pine, huckleberry and blueberry bushes scattered throughout.

It had been productive in the past as turkeys seemed to enjoy the normal mast production in the area, and I had killed turkeys there previously. It was about 2:30, and the temperature was in the high 80s. Therefore, I dressed lightly, with just a camo t-shirt and vest and some lightweight camo pants. I searched diligently along the top of the mountain for turkey sign under the blackjack oaks, knowing that the blackjacks usually produce some acorns even in drought years. There was no sign of any turkey scratching, nor any mast, so progressively, I began angling my way lower down the mountain, stopping to call periodically. By 4:30, I had worked my way almost to the bottom of the mountain without observing any turkey sign or hearing any response to my calling. I decided that being close, I would go to the very bottom. Once there, I soon located a small spring-fed branch that ran parallel to the base of the mountain.

Before calling, I looked around carefully for western cottonmouths that often frequent such water sources. Finding none, I took time to drink a little water from the branch. Along the branch, I began to see some scattered turkey sign. So, after quenching my thirst, I decided to walk down the branch a ways and call. These mountains have many large boulders scattered about, and there was one about 50 yards downstream that jutted out over the branch. That boulder was probably 20 by 30 feet in size. Walking toward it, I recognized that getting around would require having to cross the branch or make a circle above it.

For some reason, I decided to call. At the call, a gobbler answered. It sounded like he was maybe 150 yards or more beyond the boulder. Quickly I crossed over the branch to go around it before sitting down. However, once getting far enough around it to see, I came face to face with a big gobbler as he was running toward me.

When we spotted each other, we both just froze where we were for an instant. Fortunately for me, the gobbler hesitated just long enough for me to shoulder my shotgun and shoot him as he was turning to flee. It was only about a 30-yard shot, so I walked over to where he was flopping, sat down to catch my breath, and rested briefly. I did not tarry long because it would be a long haul up to the top of the mountain. I had to hurry to get back to the top to meet Thurman at our agreed-upon pick-up spot at dark.

After a brief rest and his flopping ended, I put my carrying strap over his head and legs and started up the mountain. He was an old bird with one and a half-inch spurs and a heavy beard. Although I had no idea how much he weighed, it quickly became clear that it was over 20 pounds. In fact, before getting to the top of that mountain, it was necessary to make several rest stops. Sweating like a tar kiln, every time that strap went back on my shoulder, it seemed like he gained ten pounds.

Before getting to the top of the mountain, it got dark. Pretty soon, I heard Thurman blowing the horn. Finally, I made it to the top and heard the truck coming. There was not a dry thread of clothes left on my body. We went to a check station to get the bird checked in, and their scales said he weighed 22 1/2 pounds. That is one of the few times I have ever observed an Eastern gobbler hesitate at all when they spotted a man, but I sure was glad he did. That was my last time to have the opportunity to hunt that mountain before the turkey population in that area began a steep decline.

CHAPTER 36

The Stand-Off

One morning, hunting alone in the Ouachita Mountains, I had gone to several of my favorite spots and could not raise a gobble. After walking several miles with no response, I decided to walk out to the point of a long ridge, sit, rest my legs, and call for a while. I made my way to the point of the ridge where it began a steep descent down toward a small branch some distance below. After getting to the point, it was possible to see down toward the branch partially. I located a good tree to sit against, got my call out, and called softly. There was no response.

After waiting about five minutes, I called again, a little louder this time. Way down the steep ridge, I spotted something black moving toward the branch, although I could not be sure it was a turkey. I soon spotted another black object moving in that general area. Calling softly again, two gobblers stepped up on the ridge.

They were still well below me, but I could see them on the slope's peak, just above the branch. Still watching the area, three more gobblers came up and crossed over that ridge. They were headed uphill toward me, approaching on my right side. When they could not see me, I carefully moved around the tree so that my shotgun could be mounted, and I waited.

I neither saw nor heard anything for about ten minutes, so I called softly on my mouth call. Shortly, I could see those gobblers coming up the ridge below me. I could tell they were headed to a small flat shelf about 30 yards away that circumvented the main ridge. I watched them approach and was just about ready to shoot one of them when the one in front spotted something. It became very alert then, leaning his head over almost in a pointing dog manner, he started putting and purring while walking around something he had spotted on the ground. The other gobblers followed him in pretty much the same way.

Five gobblers were walking, one behind the other, in a circle area that looked to be about 20 feet in size. Their purring led to some different sounds which I had never heard gobblers make. They continued to make those sounds as they walked around this circle with necks stretched out and beaks pointed down toward the ground. Occasionally, one gobbler would jump back but then fall right back in line and continue the circling. Finally, after more circling, one of them broke the circle and stepped out where he could be shot without hitting the others. He went down, and the other gobblers jumped up, then stood there for a second or two before flying off the ridge.

I walked over to where the gobbler lay, made sure he was not going anywhere then checked out the area they had been circling. I found a very angry little pygmy rattlesnake that was coiled back and ready to strike when approached. I have encountered many snakes over the years while hunting, some poisonous but mostly non-poisonous. Some encounters have made me a little nervous, but generally, I try to stay alert and leave them alone. Those five gobblers provided an observation I had not seen before, nor since. That pygmy rattler did not appear at all scared or intimidated by those gobblers' actions, but it was undoubtedly disturbed and mad.

CHAPTER 37

The Commandant

One Saturday morning, while guiding at Quantico, Colonel Windsor introduced me to the Commandant of the Marine Corps, General P.X. Kelly. Bill asked me to guide the Commandant that morning which was fine with me; it was an honor to have that opportunity. After the introduction and finding out which zone we were going to hunt, we loaded his gear into my truck and headed to the area.

It was very late in the season and sort of overcast. Although we covered a good bit of that zone trying to locate a gobbling bird, I could not seem to get a gobbler to respond. By about 9:45, feeling pretty bad about not raising a gobble, I decided to head over to a different part of that zone.

The north side was a somewhat brushy area with mixed Virginia pine and some scattered hardwoods on a ridge above a large beaver pond. I called a few times with no response, then decided to start my frantic cawing like a mob of crows after a hawk. Across the beaver pond, a bird gobbled. Looking over the landscape quickly, I had serious doubts that we could get around the long beaver pond without losing contact with that bird or spooking him.

We discussed it and located a spot where the Commandant could look down toward the beaver pond. We would see if, by chance, I might be able to entice that gobbler to fly across the pond. The Commandant agreed, so he sat down where he had a reasonably unobstructed view.

Once the Commandant was in place, I decided to back

up about ten yards behind him and called. The gobbler immediately cut me off, gobbling loudly. I hesitated a few minutes, called again, and the turkey gobbled right back. I got up and told the Commandant to sit tight. I explained that I planned to progressively move back up the hill and call to see if the gobbler might fly across that beaver pond. Moving about 15 yards back each time, the turkey continued to gobble at every call.

After several moves, it is almost 11:00. We had to quit hunting at noon, so I decided to try something new. I cut a couple of times loudly, then gobbled on a tube call. The bird gobbled, and almost immediately, we heard him fly. I could not see him myself, but I knew he had to be pretty close to the Commandant when he lit on our side of the pond.

I sat still, hoping to hear the Commandant shoot. After about five minutes with no shot, I decided to call again and did so softly with my mouth call. The turkey gobbled off to my left, almost at the same level, and shortly afterward, I saw him headed toward me. Although still holding a tag, I did not want to kill the gobbler myself. I knew, however, that the likelihood of the Commandant getting a shot, given the situation and his location, was zero. Hastily, I made a decision, and when the gobbler went behind some brush about 25 yards away, I got my shotgun up and killed him when he stepped out.

I placed the carrying strap on him and went down to where the Commandant was sitting. Embarrassed by how things had worked out, I was expecting to get an intense lecture or a good upbraiding by the Commandant when we got together. Instead, fortunately, he was delighted that I had killed the bird. He said that when the gobbler flew across the pond, it landed just below and to the left of where he sat. This required the Commandant to have to squirm around to get his shotgun to his shoulder. Before he could get a shot, the gobbler must have spotted the movement and disappeared. The Commandant said he was surprised to hear the bird gobble again just before my shot.

We admired the gobbler, and I offered to check the bird then give it to him, but he refused. He then told me what a great time he had and how exciting it was to see that gobbler flying in below him. He recognized that he should have raised his gun to his shoulder as soon as he heard the gobbler fly. I hated going back and explaining what had happened to Colonel Bill Windsor. Fortunately, the Commandant related the story of the hunt once we got back to the Natural Resources Office.

After apologizing to Bill for the way things had turned out, he said no apologies were needed. However, both of us would have preferred that the Commandant had killed the turkey rather than me. Unfortunately, I never got the opportunity to guide the Commandant again, but I sure had a lot of respect for him and his long and dedicated service in the Marines.

CHAPTER 38

Hot Gobblers In the Evening

My dad and I enjoyed many great hunts together for spring gobblers, waterfowl, and upland game birds. Most of our hunts in Arkansas included my good friend and respected colleague, Thurman Booth. One spring, hunting out of our cabin lease on the south side of Lake Greeson, all three of us killed gobblers the opening morning. The second morning Dad nor I had heard a gobble, but Thurman had heard three where he hunted. After sharing stories, we had a little lunch and took a short nap.

We planned on hunting that afternoon, although unsure of where to go. Thurman insisted that Dad and I go to where he had hunted that morning, so we listened to his directions and headed to that area. It was an area of predominantly mature hardwoods with some mixed pine. There was a recent timber harvest of approximately 80 acres on the west side.

Driving around the edge of the cutover to get Dad close to where Thurman had suggested we go, we stopped before crossing a deep branch. I suggested that he go up the branch a couple of hundred yards, make himself a blind, sit and call until dark and I would come back and pick him up. Hoping he would hear and kill a gobbler in that area or put one to roost, I turned around and drove back up near the top of that mountain. Leaving the truck, I walked down a few hundred yards into the same tract of land where I had left Dad. I wanted to be within hearing distance of where I left him. Not too far down the ridge, I looked around for a good place to both call and listen.

It was about 4:30 by the time I had gotten settled. Constructing a small blind with good vision downslope, I sat down. After occasionally calling a few times, about 5:00, I thought I heard a bird gobble way below me toward where

I had suggested Dad go. I waited a bit and called again. This time there was no question that a bird responded. Much preferring that he might call in and kill a bird rather than me, since he had to return to Alabama in a few days, I quit calling.

Before too long, I heard two gobblers down in that same direction. Then I heard what I thought were gobblers fighting. This noise continued for some time. Then things got very quiet again. After approximately 20 minutes more, I heard Dad shoot. Surprisingly at the shot, another bird gobbled below and quite close to where I was sitting. Being delighted that Dad had likely killed a gobbler, I wanted to sit a little longer and see what that nearby gobbler was going to do.

Calling softly, I heard a muffled gobble and thought maybe the gobbler was moving away. For some reason, I got up and moved about 30 yards from where I had been sitting. Finding another tree to sit down in front of, I could see down the slope a little better than my first spot.

Shortly, after just sitting down, the bird gobbled close below me. Getting my shotgun on my knee, I hardly had time to get it to my shoulder when a big gobbler came running up and stopped within ten yards of where I had sat earlier. The shot was only 35 yards, and when I shot, he collapsed and started flopping.

Because the darkness was approaching quickly, I picked the gobbler up, hustled back to my truck, and drove around to where I had left Dad. He was sitting down on a stump with the gobbler beside him. We loaded his gear and the gobbler up and headed back to the cabin. On the way, Dad related his story and observations of the afternoon. He said he had called occasionally that afternoon and thought about 5:00 he had heard a distant gobble. He waited a bit and called again. The second time he called, he heard two gobblers below and south of where he was sitting. They were closer than the one he had heard before. By this time, Dad admitted he was getting pretty excited. He watched across that little drain. When both gobblers gobbled again very close, he was focused down to full choke. He said one of the gobblers appeared at about 60 yards in a strut. Shortly after, the other gobbler showed up, and they began circling each other but were still out of range.

He said he wasn't sure what to do at that point, but then they started fighting and pushing each other around. He said they were purring loudly, with necks intertwined and wings flapping as they would jump into the air spurring at each other. Fortunately, their fighting brought them a little closer to him, and he already had his shotgun on his knee to take a shot when one presented itself. He said they fought for approximately 15 minutes before getting into range. Then, they separated briefly, and he shot, killing one of them. He said right after he fired he thought he heard another bird gobble.

Although he asked me about the bird I shot, we decided to wait until we got to the cabin. Hopefully, by comparing stories, we could figure just how and what had happened that afternoon.

After arriving at the cabin, I started processing the gobblers for the freezer before coming in for a very late dinner. With Thurman listening intently, we heard Dad's story and what a show he had observed. Then we began trying to determine just where the bird I had killed had come from.

The gobbler Dad killed was likely a four-year-old based on the length of its spurs, whereas the gobbler I had killed was a two-year-old. Dad's gobbler had fresh spur marks on its lower breast and thighs. The bird I killed showed no evidence of spur marks. We then concluded that my gobbler was not the other gobbler in the fight. He must have been somewhere in the area and had decided to stay quiet until Dad's shot had shocked him into gobbling. Yet he must have earlier coursed where I had called from. Then, when he had an opportunity, he decided to run in and hook up with a lady friend before going to roost. That was our best guess, of course, but it at least made sense to me as Thurman had heard three birds gobbling in that area that morning.

I think that was possibly the latest in the day that I can remember shooting one that came to my call. What still amazes me is their capability to course exactly where they hear a call coming from.

Hopefully, the gobbler will come in looking for the hen he thought he heard, and not for an old camo-clad hunter.

CHAPTER 39

It Happens Fast

Sometimes, it seems you cannot buy a gobble, even though you know the gobblers are there. It is more than frustrating, especially when the weather is nice, there is no wind, and the temperature is mild. My good friend and hunting buddy, Jim Brooks, told me on my arrival at the Paint Rock Valley cabin in north Alabama about a gobbler he had heard across the valley. He said that the bird gobbled his heart out every morning until about 9:30. I was excited about the possibility of hearing a good gobbling turkey. I arose early the next morning and headed across the valley to the mountain.

It was a gorgeous morning with no wind, 40°, and I fully expected to hear that bird do some gobbling. I climbed up the side of the mountain as quietly as possible and positioned myself 200 yards above where Jim said the turkeys usually roosted.

As those first pink rays in the east began to turn to gold, I watched as some black vultures roosted around the mountain a few hundred yards away sailed out over the valley. The songbirds and crows began calling before I decided to owl-call. There was no response, so I waited about five minutes and owl-called again, still was no gobble.

I decided to see if I could get those crows riled up. They responded by flying in and around the side of the mountain and cawing loudly. There still was no gobbler response. After a few more minutes, I began moving north toward the Tennessee line about a mile away. Stopping and calling occasionally, I worked my way around the side of the mountain but could not buy a gobble.

This old mountainside had been logged over some 70 plus years ago. Most of the timber was hardwood, with occasional small Virginia pine and red cedar groves scattered around.

There was an old dim relic of a road that circumvented the mountain. After getting pretty close to the Tennessee line, I turned back and headed up to locate that old road.

It had heated up pretty fast by the time I was nearing the old road and was likely 70 degrees or warmer. As I worked my way upward, I spotted a large timber rattler sunning on a flat rock near the old road. He coiled up, but I went around him and left him soaking up that sun. Finding the old roadbed, which would have been impossible to traverse even on a 4-wheel ATV, I began working my way upward and, at a very steep place, sat down to rest for a minute.

By this time, it was around 10:10, I was hungry and thinking about heading to the cabin. But instead of yelping, I decided to cluck loudly and see what might happen. That cluck was answered closely by a thunderous gobble. Not visible, but very close down over the steep side of the road below me, there was no time to pull my face mask or gloves on.

I barely got my shotgun to my shoulder. I heard him drumming just out of sight, below the old roadbed. Watching that direction, then as he strutted upward toward me, I first saw his fan not more than 20 yards below. He strutted on up, and when his head and neck could be seen clearly, I clucked again. He raised his head and neck, and I shot, killing him less than 15 yards away.

Aside from walking three or four miles up and down the mountain that morning from daylight to about 10:15, it had been a very abbreviated hunt of probably 15 seconds. But that is a part of why it is hunting. I could have disturbed him unknowingly on the roost, climbing to get above him before daylight. He could have been covered up with hens all morning, or he could have just decided to sleep in. I will never know for sure but was pleased to be lucky enough to get him anyway.

I have often had gobblers hear me walking and gobble.

Occasionally, I have killed some with them that close. Most often, however, when that close, by the time you sit down, they have either seen you or heard something they did not like and never gobble back nor come over to check it out.

Hunting in Kentucky one morning, I walked into an area where turkeys had commonly roosted. I was there early enough to work my way pretty close to the point of finger ridge before it got daylight. Locating a downed tree on the top of the ridge, I squeezed in beside it. As it began to get light, a hen softly purred and clucked nearby.

As daylight progressed, I saw a gobbler about 40 yards away when he moved to gobble from a lower limb of a giant red oak tree just to my right. Unable to move, I watched him gobble several times.

Some hens below him began calling sporadically. He began to strut out a big flat limb and gobble, and must have done that 20 times over the next 15 minutes. Some hens started to pitch down, so I called, and the gobbler turned toward me and gobbled. That made me think he was going to fly down right in front of me. But likely because some more hens left the roost and flew downslope, he turned, pitched down to them, and ceased gobbling. I stayed there for about 20 minutes more. Then, having heard another gobbler earlier that was some distance away, I headed in that direction.

I walked several miles up and down those hills and hollows over the next few hours, finally stimulating a bird to shock gobble a couple of times. I sat down and tried to work him but could not get him to respond again.

About 10:15, I began to work my way back toward the area where my first setup had been before daylight. I planned to go back near the setup and call a few times softly. I slipped in quietly to my previous setup. There was a very steep hollow directly over the ridge behind me. I positioned myself toward the finger ridge where the gobbler had strutted on the limb earlier that morning.

After getting settled in, I clucked softly. I was answered by a thunderous gobble immediately behind me, down in the steep hollow. I was unsure which side he would show up on, but I thought he would come to my right, so I did not move or call. In a couple of minutes, I could hear him drumming.

I had my shotgun on my knees, but he was directly off my left shoulder and very close when he came up out of that hollow below me. I knew that any movement with him this close would be a mistake—if I moved enough to get the shotgun butt to my right shoulder, he would likely see me. Waiting until he turned, I was barely able to get it to the top of my bicep, got my cheek down on the stock, and as he straightened up to get a better look, I shot.

He was less than 20 yards away, so I knew he was not going anywhere. But the recoil from that shot left my upper arm and shoulder hurting. They turned from blue to green to yellow over the next few days.

Following these and other similar experiences over the years, my observations are that, if by chance, you get pretty close to a gobbler without spooking him, he is very likely to respond to a soft call. This is most likely to happen later in the morning after his hens have drifted away from him. A take-home lesson is perseverance and hunting back to your camp or vehicle when possible. It doesn't work every time and is likely most effective after the gobbler's hens have deserted him to begin looking for nest sites.

CHAPTER 40

Non-Hunting Observations

Acknowledging that many people are interested in wildlife but may or may not hunt, fish or trap, I felt a need to share some observations that are, to me, at least interesting and often are available to many but are unrealized. When my wife and I were first married in 1962, as we were driving on a daylight trip, I would often sight some wildlife or related object of interest and try to point it out to her. It might be a hawk, rabbit, beaver pond, coyote, deer, turkey, or wildflowers, but rarely would she spot them.

Over time, being persistent, I continued to do this, and she became more and more observant while travelling and took some pleasure in acknowledging or even pointing something out to me. We have enjoyed countless enjoyable trips throughout most of the United States and several foreign countries, and she soon became a seasoned spotter who takes great pride in her observations. Recently on a trip through Tennessee, she spotted an albino hawk that appeared to be a red-tailed hawk but was snow white and sitting on a power pole.

Where we have lived for the past 20 years, we are blessed with an abundance of wildlife species even though we live in the city limits of Starkville, Mississippi. The only wildlife we intentionally feed is hummingbirds. However, we have established an abundance of vegetative food and nesting sources that are attractive to a diversity of wildlife species. We have also added some bluebird houses. Usually, anytime we look out, there are a variety of birds to watch. Some species like deer, crows, and raccoons require some preventative measures seasonably. If these preventive measures are not taken promptly, they quickly locate and devour our blueberries and muscadines when they begin to ripen. The buck deer annually rub some of my planted trees and blueberry bushes, and they love particular rose and hibiscus plants, which they will browse to ground level without treatment.

As an early riser, and time permitting, I enjoy sitting on our back patio and observing the flow of animal life around our place. The diversity of bird species includes mockingbirds, bluebirds, blue jays, brown thrashers, robins, a variety of peckerwoods, sparrows, doves, blackbirds, an occasional purple finch, indigo buntings, gnatcatchers, summer tanagers and goldfinches. We also have a great horned owl, Cooper's hawk, and a red-tailed hawk that nests in some woods behind our place.

The owl and hawks periodically take some prey in our yard, whether rabbits, squirrels, or smaller birds. Some leave tell-tale evidence of their predation, and some do not unless you happen to observe them in action. Although my life has been spent as much as possible in the outdoors, I recently observed some predatory actions I had never seen before or had anyone describe to me.

Between our backyard patio and our barn, some 250 yards away as I sat quietly one afternoon, two dragonflies were hovering and flitting around. Suddenly, a red-headed woodpecker in our backyard swooped down, caught one of the dragonflies in its beak, and flew up into a big pine tree nearby. I watched as it consumed that dragonfly.

I have seen on several occasions a summer tanager capture wasps in flight and occasionally a honeybee. Other observations include watching a Cooper's hawk catch and kill a Eurasian collared dove. After catching it and dropping to the ground, it proceeded to pick every feather from the carcass. After eating a portion of the breast, the little hawk labored with the remainder in its talons, getting sufficient altitude to get into the woods. Other prey evidence includes finding all the feathers from a northern flicker in the yard that I suspect became another Cooper's hawk meal. Some predatory evidence may be a real puzzle, and we had such at one of our bluebird nests that I can only guess how it happened.

This bluebird box is located directly between our house and equipment shed about 80 yards away, it has been a bluebird favorite for years, and we have a great view from both our kitchen and den. Having watched, thinking the male and female had left to forage for insects, and knowing the female had been incubating her third clutch of eggs for some time. I decided to check on the progress.

The box has a hinged front door, and when I opened it, the female was hovering with wings spread over the nest, but she was headless. Her head had been completely severed from her body, and it must have been a recent occurrence as her body was not yet rigid. There were no loose feathers in nor under the nest box. She was sitting over four eggs, and except for no head, her body was intact.

After consideration, I concluded that she must have stretched her head out of the entrance hole when some predator decapitated her. Since neither mammalian nor reptilian predators could get to her from the ground, it had to be an avian predator. It must have grabbed her head in its talons, ripping it from her body and then flew away. The bluebirds successfully nested three times this past summer with no further beheadings.

Hopefully, you too enjoy the observations and mysteries associated with God's marvelous creation. If you have not yet tried it, you need to consider rewarding yourself some time. If you are not fortunate to have such a place where you live, my suggestion is to plan an early, pre-daylight trip. It could be to a park, national refuge, forest, or just anywhere you can remove yourself from the noise of highway traffic, sirens, and the artificial lighting that seems to dominate most of the landscape. Although I know it is tempting, turn your cell phone off or leave it in your vehicle until you are ready to leave.

If you have never done this, you have deprived yourself of a great treat and a fantastic opportunity to listen to the world wake up. If you take some time in such surroundings to relax, listen, slowly observe what is happening around you, taking in the pleasures of being a participant as it becomes daylight, you will be rewarded. If you are afraid to go alone, take a family member or friend, but sit alone, soak it in without conversation until afterward, and then share your observations and thoughts.

CHAPTER 41

In Conclusion

For many years now, I have been well aware that while hunting, angling or trapping, my entire focus is devoted to the activity being pursued. I have no interest whatsoever while participating in such activities, in playing video games, reading a book, or texting someone on a cell phone unless there is some emergency. Admittedly, however, I cannot stay focused and make small talk (aside from possibly sharing with other outdoors people) at a party or social event when other things cloud my mind.

Having truly enjoyed the thrill of fair-chase hunting, calling, killing, processing and eating wild game for over 60 years, my urgency to kill more game has declined in recent years. This is partially because of physical limitations. I enjoy exposing others to the thrill of the chase and trying to mentor them in ethical hunting practices, and these efforts have replaced some of my hunting commitments. That thrill of the chase, enjoyment of being in wild places and pursuing wild things, opportunities for observations, and the excitement of calling up a gobbler for myself or others, however, remains strong.

Having been blessed with a loving, considerate, and supportive wife, I respect and acknowledge her partnership immensely. She has never questioned the significant costs associated with my hunting and angling trips, especially those involving family members, colleagues and friends. Even with the progressively rising costs of some non-resident licenses, associated travel costs, and time expended away from home, she has remained supportive. Obviously, there is no way of knowing, but I would hazard a guess that few, if any wives alive today, have cooked more gobblers, other wild game, and fish than she has. As of September 28, 2021, we have been married for 59 years, and she has been a true blessing to our family stability, financial solvency, and enjoyment. She has, however, no reluctance about jumping into my whiskers if something I did or said gets her dander up. Our mutual respect since growing up on the farm, and going to school together even before we started dating, has served us well.

Our family, neighbors, friends, house guests, and fellow brothers and sisters at church potlucks and breakfasts have enjoyed many wild game and fish gourmet meals over the years. From marinated and grilled turkey breasts, squirrel dumplings, smoked fish, deer, antelope, elk and moose venison, and upland game birds to turkey leg soup. Our two sons, grandson, and daughters-in-law always insist on roasted wild turkey with cornbread dressing, giblet gravy, and other side dishes for our Thanksgiving and Christmas meals together.

These observations and declarations are a part of what has made the spring season special to me for so many years. Yet without question, the activities, occurrences and observations described herein have been essential in strengthening that passion: These include the awakening of spring each year, with the sights and sounds of living things emerging from the cold of winter and preparing for what is ahead. The trees leaving out, flowers beginning to bloom, bull gators bellowing, eagles, cranes and songbirds beginning to sing all signal a re-awakening.

These even extend to finding a live green stink bug in a turkey's crop. Thousands of more blessings contribute to this naturalist/hunter's treasure and joy, all of which are important cogs in the wheel of intelligent thinking. Having found my way in the darkness to a mountain top or a swamp, watching those first pink rays of light appear in the east, it is an excellent opportunity to thank almighty God again while listening to and observing the world wake up.

If a haughty and majestic gobbler adds his raucous thunder to the choir, that is truly icing on the cake and, if you have not experienced it, you have been deprived of a great blessing. Regardless of my future capability to continue these activities, they are a bank of treasured gifts and memories.

Even if another gobbler is never called in for me or others, I treasure these memories. The great hunts and enjoyable times spent with family, friends, youngsters and respected colleagues will be retained and appreciated for as long as possible. For these and many other diverse and unique blessings, I remain eternally grateful. Until recently, I was blessed to serve as a deacon at churches we attended for well over 40 years.

Fortunately, most of our Christian brothers and sisters were well aware of my interest and appreciation for the marvellous creation that God provides. They may not have always understood what my choice of profession was, nor my somewhat extended absences from church during the spring, but to their credit, they tolerated me anyway.

Although my mobility was severely limited in the spring of 2021, I was able to get out hunting and killed two nice gobblers. Surprisingly, after all these years of hunting, I called up and killed a gobbler in Kentucky on April 17 that weighed slightly over 27 pounds, had 1 1/2" spurs, and an 11" beard, my biggest gobbler ever. Hopefully, it will not be my last, but if so, I ended with a bang.

I hope this book, written from a treasury of memories by an old wildlife biologist, natural resources manager and educator, has prompted you to consider where we fit in God's creation. There are so many more hunting, fishing, and trapping stories and observations that I have stored away in my memory bank that I wish I could share with those interested. These described herein, however, are especially

27 pound plus turkey taken in Kentucky on April 17, 2021.

treasured and appreciated. I feel privileged to share them and hope they are enjoyed.

As previously confessed, I recognize my opinionated, and to some, dinosaur-like perspective, yet with no apologies since I genuinely feel I gave it my best effort while enjoying the great people and work immensely. I am, however, eternally grateful to have been an active, contributing participant in some small way over the past 57 years in the most remarkable public trust wildlife restoration success in North America's history. Without a doubt, we have been blessed to have the very best wildlife and fisheries management programs in the world.

These blessings are due to the active contributions by many respected professional colleagues, leaders, and landowners/managers, past and present, whose dedication and dogged persistence made it possible. I close with a quote from Proverbs, Chapter 3, verses 13 and 14: "Happy is the man that findeth wisdom, and the man that getteth understanding. For the merchandise of it is better than the merchandise of silver, and the gain thereof of fine gold."

THANK YOU

ACKNOWLEDGMENTS

Although impossible to name them all, I am particularly indebted to the many wildlife, fisheries, and natural resource professionals whom I have interacted with across the United States Land Grant University system for so many years. I also appreciate and respect the many professionals within numerous state and federal agencies, those with non-governmental conservation organizations, and those in the private sector whom I have collaborated with and learned from. I deeply appreciate the contributions by many state wildlife agency biologists and colleagues with support from a growing National Wild Turkey Federation (NWTF) for their tireless hours capturing, moving, and restocking wild turkeys into suitable habitats across the nation. Such interactions during a 56-year professional career as a wildlife biologist, educator, and volunteer have both enlightened and encouraged me.

Many colleagues and friends have encouraged me to share some of the observations and camaraderie associated with my passion for wild places, wild things and turkey hunting and hopefully, this book will provide some insight. Their hope and mine are that the readers will enjoy and experience some of the anticipation of the thrill of the chase, the observations, and my appreciation for the love and respect of friends and colleagues. It is the authors fervent hope as well that some understanding of, and respect for, wild things and wild places, and the naturalist observations often missed by those in too great a hurry to look around at God's awesome creation are revealed.

Much of my early life was molded by my parents, my grandmother, aunts, uncles, cousins, and a slew of other kinfolks in rural north Alabama, as well as by other members of the community. Later in life as a college student, I was blessed by some of the professors who tolerated my interest in wild things and wild places, and by my interaction with friends who shared some of the same passion. I am particularly grateful for the capable guidance and mutual interests shared with my major wildlife professor, Dr. Stephen Beckwith at the University of Florida. Dr. Beckwith and I hunted bobwhite quail behind my bird dogs, doves in fields around the area, waterfowl in the sinkhole ponds and lakes, and fished in the Gulf on occasions. Without his interest and support, it is doubtful that I would have joined The Wildlife Society in 1963, or returned to graduate school when he contacted me about an assistantship in 1966.

Obviously, there are many others who contributed to my observational skills like my good friend Joel Smith who understood the landscape, and knew many people in the north central Florida area on a first name basis. Joel and I enjoyed squirrel, dove, duck, and rabbit hunting behind my beagles as we encountered numerous wild things and explored wild places. Joel's wife Polly, and their two sons Lynn and Clay became a part of our extended family and still remain cherished friends.

A great couple who contributed to our education and maturation by example, included Mr. and Mrs. Ed Sutherland who rented us a duplex apartment near their home, nurtured us as we struggled monthly to meet our obligations, and strongly encouraged me to finish my college education. Mr. Sutherland and I enjoyed fishing in the Gulf on his boat occasionally and dove hunting. Others who contributed via work opportunities was the Guy Cleveland construction company, and my wife Doris' brother-in-law, D.O Ely, via his painting contractor's business.

After graduation with my BSF degree, Mr. Sherman Whipple, my supervisor at an Auburn University Experiment

Forest near Fayette, Alabama enabled me to be innovative in both helping manage the experiment forest, and in developing its first wildlife management plan. Sherman was sorry to see us leave for me to return to graduate school, although he strongly encouraged me to take the opportunity.

Our appreciation is also extended to Mr. C. A. Vines, Director of the University of Arkansas, Cooperative Extension Service, and to Dr. Leon Holley, Associate Director for their administrative support and encouragement during the 11-year period I served as State Extension Wildlife Specialist and later as Extension Forester and Wildlife Specialist. Others in Arkansas became life-long friends and respected colleagues, and among those was Thurman W. Booth who became a trusted professional colleague, great friend and hunting buddy from whom I learned much and appreciated. We truly enjoyed both the great people we met and worked with in Arkansas, as well as the rich and diverse wildlife and fisheries resources, and both our sons were born in Little Rock.

Following a change of positions, leaving Arkansas in 1978, and moving to the Washington, D. C. area my mentors expanded even more than in the past, and over the next 23-years I had the opportunity to work with many respected wildlife, fisheries and conservation professionals. My interactions with great leaders like Dr. Laurence R. Jahn with the Wildlife Management Institute, Mr. Jack Berryman and John Gottschalk, both former U.S. Fish and Wildlife Service administrators and International Association of Fish and Wildlife Agency administrators were extremely beneficial. Even closer was the interaction I enjoyed with Mr. Merrill L. "Pete" Petoskey, a consummate professional who provided exemplary administrative and effective leadership. Pete, further supported and enabled expanded opportunities for my learning and observational opportunities. Pete and his wife Jean remained dear friends until their deaths. Others like Dale Jones with the U.S. Forest Service, V. Daniel Stiles and Bob Hines with the U.S. Fish and Wildlife Service and others too numerous to list became trusted allies. Not only were these colleague's great friends and examples, they were responsible professionals whose actions exemplified excellence.

In addition, I had the great pleasure of working with, and for, some of the finest professionals in the nation who served as Extension wildlife, fisheries and natural resources specialists within the Land Grant University System nationwide. These specialists, colleagues and friends over the next 22 years (1979-2001) served as trusted sources of exemplary expertise often called upon for developing and implementing research-based, common-sense, natural resource educational programs for landowners and managers. We established a mutual relationship that I depended on to help me be effective at doing my job, and I did my very best to support and encourage their programs, and to raise the visibility of their considerable expertise to national and international audiences.

Throughout these years my turkey hunting passion continued to grow and I acknowledge learning from others through my involvement with the NWTF, as well as from colleagues I worked and hunted with in different places across the nation. Some of these are mentioned in the book, although there are many others (not named), that I worked with, and/or guided whom I also learned from. My observational skills were further strengthened after coming to work in the Wildlife, Fisheries and Aquaculture Department at Mississippi State in 2001 and continuing to learn from interactions with respected colleagues and landowner/managers. These naturalist observation skills as one who truly cares about wildlife resources and their habitats, are strengthened by an abiding and treasured appreciation for the intricacies of God's creation.

My most deserved acknowledgement has to be for my loving wife of 59-years now, Doris who has tolerated my absences, expenditures, and passion for the thrill of the chase. I am confident that over time she may have considered some of my actions frivolous and lacking in responsibility to her and to our family, although she did not admonish or criticize me. Not only, however, has she tolerated these faults, she has often encouraged me to take a fishing or hunting trip with family, friends and colleagues any time I could. Although not a hunter herself, she appreciates and understands my passion, and that the wild game and fish I bring home are truly enjoyed by family and friends. She has likely cooked as much or more wild game than any other wife I know of, and we have enjoyed thousands of quality organic meals. I also learned from our sons, Kelly and Mike as they grew up making note of my parental mistakes as well as the many great outdoor experiences we shared.

I would be remiss not to acknowledge the able computer assistance from Dr. Ray Iglay, an Associate Professor in the Wildlife Department at Mississippi State University (MSU), Mr. John Giesemann, retired Extension Professor at MSU, and Zack Krampf, Software Engineer III for Babel Street in Starkville, each of whom have thankfully rescued me from numerous computer glitches and problems. Without their help it is unlikely I would have ever completed the drafts, proof reviews, and corrections needed.

I acknowledge the review of early drafts and helpful suggestions by Dr. Don Jackson, retired professor and author from MSU whose knowledge and experience he shared was both helpful and appreciated.

Without the guidance, extensive reviews, and recommendations by Mr. Paul Brown, exemplary wildlife photographer, author and Publisher Associate, it would likely have been impossible to complete this publication. Paul's outstanding photos added to those of the author provide illustrations to highlight some of the observations described within these pages.